T0303765

PENGUIN BOOKS
YOGI ADITYANATH

Sharat Pradhan is an independent journalist and political analyst with long experience of writing for several institutions, including *The Times of India*, Reuters, *Sunday*, *Outlook*, IANS, BBC, The Wire, Rediff.com and Daily O. He is also a popular face on several major TV news channels, YouTube and OTT platforms.

Atul Chandra is the former resident editor of *The Times of India*, Lucknow.

YOGI
ADITYANATH

Religion, Politics and Power
The Untold Story

SHARAT PRADHAN
ATUL CHANDRA

PENGUIN BOOKS

An imprint of Penguin Random House

PENGUIN BOOKS

USA | Canada | UK | Ireland | Australia
New Zealand | India | South Africa | China

Penguin Books is part of the Penguin Random House group of companies
whose addresses can be found at global.penguinrandomhouse.com

Published by Penguin Random House India Pvt. Ltd
4th Floor, Capital Tower 1, MG Road,
Gurugram 122 002, Haryana, India

Penguin
Random House
India

First published in Penguin Books by Penguin Random House India 2021

Copyright © Sharat Pradhan and Atul Chandra 2021

ISBN 9780143442431

Typeset in Adobe Garamond Pro by Manipal Technologies Limited, Manipal

www.penguin.co.in

To
Cuckoo
who flew away from us after a brave 12-year battle with cancer
Sharat Pradhan

To
the loving memory of my father
Atul Chandra

CONTENTS

1

THE KILLER PANDEMIC

On a visit to Varanasi, his parliamentary constituency, on 15 July 2021, Prime Minister Narendra Modi praised Uttar Pradesh Chief Minister Yogi Adityanath for what he termed as the 'unparalleled' and 'unprecedented' handling of the second wave of COVID-19.[1]

Modi rolled out a long list of 'gifts' worth Rs 1,500 crores in the name of 'development' for the people of his constituency. Yet, he chose to go out of his way to shower praise on the saffron-clad chief minister, who, it was widely believed, was not his first choice in 2017 when the Bharatiya Janata Party (BJP) swept the state polls.

Barely a fortnight after Modi's Varanasi visit, Union Home Minister Amit Shah flew down to Lucknow to lay the foundation stone for a forensic science institute. Later in the day, he addressed a public rally in Mirzapur, where he laid another foundation stone for the Rs 150-crore Maa Vindhyavasini temple corridor project.

Echoing Modi's sentiments, Shah too made it a point to go into hyperboles while hailing Yogi Adityanath as an exceptional and exemplary chief minister. He declared that what Yogi Adityanath has done in four-and-a-half years, his predecessors Akhilesh Yadav and Mayawati together could not do in 15 years. Praising Yogi's work in handling the pandemic, Shah said that Yogi Adityanath had done exceedingly well in controlling the second wave of novel coronavirus by ensuring large-scale sample testing and extensive vaccination.

Not many days later came BJP President J.P. Nadda, again carrying bagfuls of bouquets for the Uttar Pradesh chief minister for having done wonders with COVID-19 management.

Had such praise been showered from any other BJP quarter, it would have been construed as sycophancy for a party leader who had established himself as a brand of his own—a Hindutva icon—during his four-and-a-half year stint as chief minister. But such admiration coming from the highest levels in the BJP hierarchy could not be dismissed as superfluous.

Yet, there could be no denying that the apparent overdose of commendation did leave everyone wondering. Could it be sarcasm? After all, anyone who was familiar with the harrowing experience people had to go through during the killer second wave of COVID-19, would be compelled to take such praise after praise with a pinch of salt.

Many questions arose in the mind: Was this a bid to draw a curtain over the reality of the pandemic that literally created havoc in what is India's most populous state? Or was it aimed at changing the narrative for the next electoral battle in March 2022?

But, this was not the first time that Yogi Adityanath's COVID-19 handling had earned laurels.

On 6 January 2021, Zee News, News18 Uttar Pradesh, ABP Ganga and TV9 Bharatvarsh reported that *Time* magazine had 'praised Yogi Adityanath government's work on corona control'. They were referring to an advertorial that appeared in the Indian edition of the magazine's December 21/28 edition.[2]

Before it appeared as an advertorial in *Time*, the three-page write-up was put out as a government press release in December. Publications such as *Tehelka* subsequently ran it with minimal editing.

The *Time* ad mentioned how Adityanath's 'excellent and efficient' COVID-19 management model had allegedly seen the death rate from the disease fall to 1.3 per cent in India's most populous state. 'Being positive in a negative situation is not naive, it is leadership,' it declared. 'No other leader exemplifies this than the Uttar Pradesh Chief Minister Yogi Adityanath.'

After several Indian media outlets went to town declaring that *Time* had lavished praise on Adityanath, the magazine confirmed to Newslaundry that the feature was 'sponsored content, as indicated by the "Content From Uttar Pradesh" language that appears on the advertisement page'.[3]

Interestingly, it was Yogi Adityanath's PR team that had first described the ad on 15 December as a 'report'.

Even prior to that, praise had been showered on Yogi Adityanath by the World Health Organization (WHO) for his handling of the pandemic.

'The Uttar Pradesh government's strategic response to COVID-19 by stepping up contact tracing efforts is exemplary and can serve as a good example for other states,' Roderico Ofrin, WHO Country Representative, said in a statement issued in Lucknow by the Uttar Pradesh government.[4]

The global health body appreciated the efforts made by Chief Minister Yogi Adityanath and his government for the management of COVID-19, especially in tracking high-risk contacts, an official spokesperson of the government said.

Over 70,000 front-line health workers worked across the state to reach out to high-risk contacts of COVID-19 positive cases, he said.

After the WHO released an article titled 'Uttar Pradesh Going the Last Mile to Stop COVID-19' on 7 May 2021, several media outlets and the Uttar Pradesh government claimed that the WHO praised the state government for its door-to-door COVID-19 surveillance campaign.

In the article, the WHO merely spoke of its role in the programme. While everyone assumed that the health agency patted the state's back for carrying out the 'trace, test, track, treat' campaign, a WHO spokesperson told FactChecker that 'surveillance and monitoring are among key WHO roles' across the country.[5]

Even during the first wave of the pandemic, the WHO had cited the Uttar Pradesh chief minister's contact tracing formula as an example that should be emulated by other states and praised his Triple T (Trace, Test and Treat) strategy to control COVID-19 during the second wave of the pandemic.

As if that was not enough, the next in line to applaud the Uttar Pradesh chief minister was NITI Aayog (National Institution for Transforming India Aayog), which appreciated the strategy adopted by the state to tackle the pandemic.

Perhaps it was the din of such heaps of praise that overwhelmed the pain of the COVID-19 victims, who suffered and died in the absence of treatment or due to the non-availability of oxygen across the length and breadth of this sprawling state.

The rate of infections increased manifold in Uttar Pradesh during the second wave and touched the peak on 24 April 2021, when as many as 38,055 infections were recorded in 24 hours.

Yogi Adityanath himself got infected with the virus in April and had to be admitted to the Sanjay Gandhi Post Graduate Institute of Medical Sciences (SGPGIMS), designated as the state's number one COVID-19 centre.

Notwithstanding the official claims of the Yogi Adityanath government of 22,705 deaths on account of the deadly virus until 15 July 2021, the real picture was quite pathetic. Ruling party leader and state executive member Ram Iqbal Singh did not rule out at least 10 deaths on account of the pandemic in each of the state's nearly one lakh villages. 'At least 10 people died from every village in the state during the second wave of COVID-19 pandemic,' he alleged.[6]

Singh, who was speaking with mediapersons, rued that the state's health department had failed to learn any lesson from the first wave of COVID-19. He also demanded that Rs 10 lakh be given to the kin of those who succumbed to the deadly virus. He lamented that after 75 years of freedom, his home district (Ballia), with a population of 34 lakh, had 'no doctors or medicines'.

On being reminded that during his visit to Ballia, Chief Minister Yogi Adityanath had expressed satisfaction with the arrangements made by the Health Department, Singh said the officials had misled the chief minister, and that the truth was not shown to him.

Earlier in May, Rakesh Rathore, BJP's member of the legislative assembly (MLA) from Sitapur, had joined the list of ruling party lawmakers in Uttar Pradesh expressing resentment over the alleged COVID-19 mismanagement in the state. He went to the extent of saying that he feared sedition charges to be brought against him for speaking out. 'What standing do MLAs have? If we speak too much, treason and sedition charges will be slapped on us as well,' Rakesh Rathore had told reporters.[7]

On 9 May, Union Labour minister Santosh Gangwar had complained to the chief minister about the situation in his parliamentary constituency, Bareilly, saying that officials were not taking calls and government health centres were sending back patients for 'referrals' from the district hospital. In a letter to Yogi Adityanath, he had also complained about the 'huge shortage' of oxygen cylinders and difficulty in procurement of medical equipment in Bareilly.

A day later, Ramgopal Lodhi, the BJP MLA from Jasrana in Firozabad, claimed that his COVID-19 positive wife was not admitted to an Agra hospital for over three hours, with officials saying that beds were not available.[8]

The second wave hit hard at the time that the Yogi Adityanath government was still revelling in the success of having 'overcome' the onslaught of the first wave of COVID-19, which, in fact, had receded on its own. The government was heaving a sigh of relief that the damage suffered by the state during the first wave was far less than what had been feared at the outset. It was around this time in March 2021 when there was a sudden return of the virus in a much deadlier form.

Come April and it began to rain COVID-19. By the 10th of the month, the number of fresh cases began to shoot up. In the first nine days of April, the number of cases surpassed the total reported between January and March 2021 put together. 'At least 47,165 cases have been reported in the first nine days of April while the cumulative cases between January and March this year were 31,292', said a report in the *Times of India*.[9] As many as 4,059 new cases were detected on 10 April in the state capital Lucknow alone, while the state reported 17,000 cases, according to the daily press release issued by the state health department.

The spiralling trend sent alarm bells ringing in the corridors of power, propelling the administration to devise ways and means to bring down the numbers. On the night of 11 April, a decision was taken to once again shut down private laboratories in Lucknow for two days. The story goes that the administration was unhappy with the private labs because the percentage of COVID-19 positive cases reported by these labs was much higher than the government labs. Sure enough, the shutting of private labs on one pretext or the other did help to bring down the number of fresh cases.

What further added to the decline in the number of cases was the sudden slowdown in the COVID-19 testing process in all government-run labs. No wonder, the most reliable of all tests, RT-PCR, which used to take 12–48 hours until 10 April, began to take 2–6 days. This systematic slowdown instantly helped to depict a convenient fall in the daily figures.

The Uttar Pradesh government was still savouring the 'appreciation' it had received in the *Time* magazine for its handling of COVID-19 when someone no less than Uttar Pradesh's Law Minister Brijesh Pathak gave them a wake-up call. It was like telling the chief minister to come to grips with the ground reality rather than continuing to pat his own back, while relying on illusory data fed by mandarins, who were apparently out to make their own brownie points. Brijesh Pathak, who represents the Lucknow assembly constituency, shot off a letter to the state's top health authorities, lambasting them for extremely poor COVID-19 management in the state capital. The 'highly confidential' letter addressed to Additional Chief Secretary (Health) and Principal Secretary (Medical Education) found its way to the social media and went viral.[10]

The letter reflected the minister's disgust with various aspects of the state's COVID-19 handling, including non-availability of ambulances and acute difficulty in admitting patients to hospitals that were facing a deluge of COVID-19 positive cases and for whom the number of beds were grossly inadequate.

The minister went to the extent of blaming the state machinery for the death of renowned historian and Padmashree awardee Yogesh Praveen, who waited for hours to get an ambulance before succumbing to the virus. 'Despite my personal intervention and my direct talk with the chief medical officer and other officials concerned, neither an ambulance could be provided to Dr Yogesh Praveen nor could he be provided any treatment following which he passed away unattended,' lamented Pathak, whose letter is in the public domain. A copy is available with the authors too.

The minister also raised serious issues like the sudden and repeated bans on COVID-19 testing by private labs and a systematic slowdown in the testing process in all government labs. He wondered why the state government was not able to ensure adequate supply of testing kits, while urging the authorities to increase the number of beds in all hospitals to meet the increasing rush of COVID-19 patients.

Meanwhile, the pandemic extended its tentacles to the portals of the chief minister's personal secretariat. Through a tweet, Yogi Adityanath announced his own isolation with immediate effect after his principal secretary-cum-additional chief secretary, S.P. Goel, secretary, Amit Singh, and officer on special duty, Abhishek Kaushik, tested COVID-19 positive.

The focus of the minister was essentially on Lucknow. And the city alone accounted for 25 per cent of the state's total COVID-19 cases. The addition of three more districts—Kanpur, Varanasi and Prayagraj (Allahabad)—took the tally to 50 per cent of the state's overall COVID-19 cases. The state has 75 districts.

The bulk of the remaining districts showed extremely low occurrence of the disease, which raises suspicions of the fudging of figures. It was evident that the number of tests done in these places was abysmally low. Even some of the heavily populated districts of both eastern and western Uttar Pradesh showed the daily tally of fresh COVID-19 cases only in double digits even during the worst times in April 2021. It was alleged that the priority of the administration lay in keeping the numbers as low as possible, irrespective of the ground reality.

Strangely, the focus of the authorities was on drawing a curtain over the harsh ground reality of the number of deaths rising alarmingly due to the pandemic. Pictures of mass cremations—that looked more like a wild forest fire—going viral did cause the government much embarrassment. Instead of facilitating easy cremations, the district administration got down to erecting a tin-sheet wall around the cremation area to block the view of the cremations from the outside. A board was affixed at the entrance, banning the entry of people (read media) inside the COVID-19 cremation ground. 'Unauthorized entry into the area' was declared as a punishable offence.

About the official statistics on the number of deaths, the less said the better. To cite an example, the official press release issued on 13 April 2021 (copy with the authors), stated that there were only 18 COVID-19 deaths in the state capital when ground reports suggested much higher fatalities. The city's main electric crematorium at Bhainsakund and the two conventional cremation grounds recorded as many as 59 bodies, of which 48 were stated to be of COVID-19 patients. In addition, the burial of 23 COVID-19 bodies was reported from the city's main graveyards, which took the toll on that date to 71 in Lucknow alone. The official press release, however, put the statewide COVID-19 deaths at just 85. Significantly, such was the story almost every single day—there was a wide disparity between the official declarations and the actual count at the cremation grounds and graveyards. In fact, this disparity grew as days went by and casualties rose.

State Law Minister Brijesh Pathak, who had already created a sensation by lambasting the administration for serious lapses in COVID-19 management, was once again in the news for telling the Lucknow district magistrate (DM) to pull up his socks. Close on the heels of his letter to the additional chief secretary (health), Pathak shot off a letter to the DM, urging him to take measures in the larger interest of COVID-19-affected people. He also announced his decision to donate Rs 1 crore out of his constituency fund towards improving COVID-19 arrangements in the state capital.[11]

Undeniably, admission in any COVID-19 hospital seemed impossible as there were no vacant beds. The government's decision to dedicate all 3,500 beds of King George's Medical College (KGMU) to COVID-19 clearly showed the poor perspective of the bureaucracy, which did not seem to take into account the plight of thousands of non-COVID-19 medical emergencies. Earlier, only 500 of KGMU's beds were allocated for COVID-19.

Meanwhile, the availability of oxygen cylinders became a serious problem about which the administration appeared to be blissfully silent. While black marketing in cylinders became the order of the day in many private hospitals, no action was taken by the government to put a cap on its price. Reports said that an oxygen cylinder that used to cost less than Rs 3,000 before COVID-19 struck, began to be sold at up to Rs 10,000–12,000.

21 April 2021 proved to be another major turning point when as many as 33,214 new cases cropped up across the state in just 24 hours. The number of active cases shot up to 2.42 lakhs while the official death toll stood at 10,346.[12]

The alleged official tendency to keep the actual number of casualties under wraps continued unabated. That was once again demonstrated in the official death toll of the state, which was stated to be only 187, when cremations and burials recorded in Lucknow alone were close to 100.

Alleged fudging of the number of deceased is thought to have continued. Thus, as against an official declaration of just 21 deaths in Lucknow on 21 April, the number of cremations of COVID-19 bodies at Lucknow's main cremation ground Bhainsakund stood at 103. Yet, the overall death toll of the entire state was officially stated to be only 195.

Lucknow continued to remain a COVID-19 hotspot with nearly 6,000 new cases. Varanasi was at second place with 2,564 new cases, followed by Prayagraj (1,828 cases) and Kanpur (1,811 cases). While 1,273 new positive cases were reported from Meerut, the remaining 70 districts of the sprawling state reported combined new cases only in three digits.

There was no end to reports of patients dying in the absence of oxygen cylinders or due to the failure of securing a bed in any hospital. The acute shortage of ventilators too became the cause of many deaths. But what made the people's plight worse was that in the event of death it was not easy to carry out the last rites without waiting in long queues outside cremation grounds and graveyards.

On 22 April, two Lucknow-based leading private hospitals, Mayo Medical Centre and Makewell Hospital, put up notices declaring acute shortage of oxygen. They also urged the relatives of patients to take their kin to some other hospital. The *Indian Express* reported,

> A majority of the 160 COVID-19 patients in Mayo Medical Centre, and Makewell Hospital and Trauma Centre are on oxygen support. But due to the lack of oxygen supplies, the facilities put up notices asking patients' relatives to take them to other hospitals. This caused chaos, with families confronting the hospital administration.[13]

In a grim situation like this, the chief minister's announcement to stop supply of oxygen cylinders to individuals added to the people's plight.[14] That left hundreds of COVID-19 patients undergoing treatment in their homes at God's mercy. How such persons would survive in the absence of the now-officially-denied oxygen did not seem to concern anybody. A sobbing 35-year old Rajul Jaiswal told the authors,

> My mother, who has tested Corona positive four days ago, could not get a bed in any hospital, so I managed to somehow procure an oxygen cylinder and get her treated at home only. Since yesterday, I have been running for a refill but could not get one, with the result that I finally lost my mother today.

Another unilateral policy of the government to route hospital admissions only through the district chief medical officer had created many problems for the common people, who had to literally run from pillar to post before they could get their kin a bed in any hospital. It was only following intervention of the State Human Rights Commission (SHRC) that this lopsided policy was done away with, bringing the much-needed respite to people.

The availability of oxygen—which is believed to be the lone effective weapon in the fight against the COVID-19 onslaught—continued to remain a distant dream, in government as well as private hospitals in most parts of the state. But the situation was at its lowest ebb in the state capital, where countless people were stated to have died gasping for the life-saving gas. For several days, black marketing in oxygen cylinders continued unabated in most parts of the state, even as the chief minister repeated his oral threats of deterrent punishment for those responsible for it. Why the state government could not create regulated outlets for the sale of oxygen cylinders, no one knows.

Most private hospitals in the state capital complained of acute oxygen shortage, while many began to refuse admission to patients because of non-availability of the life-saver.

Even Medanta, the city's top corporate hospital, openly admitted to the depletion of its oxygen back-up. 'Our existing stock will not last more than 24 hours', Medanta director Dr Rakesh Kapoor told the authors on 15 April.

For those who had the misfortune of experiencing the infamous Bhopal gas tragedy, the situation of patients gasping for oxygen was a chilling reminder of the 1984 ordeal. 'The only difference was that in Bhopal people were being choked by the leaking of a poisonous gas and here people are getting suffocated to death in the absence of their lifeline, oxygen,' recalled Mukesh Hajela, a former journalist who happened to be in Bhopal on the fateful day of 2 December 1984.

Undue efforts of some mandarins to falsely project low counts of COVID-19 fatalities failed, as crematoriums, cremation grounds and graveyards went on overflowing with bodies of those who were unable to arm themselves to battle it out with the deadly virus.

The official machinations did not help to contain the rising count of fresh cases, which shot up to an all-time high of 37,238 on 23 April, taking the total number of active cases to 2,73,653. The official death toll stood at 10,737.

Far from rising to the occasion well in advance, it was evident that the state machinery was least prepared for a situation like this. It would be an understatement to say that the state was caught napping when the onslaught of the second wave of COVID-19 came like a tsunami, taking the number of fresh cases well beyond 3,00,000 over the next two days.

As the saying goes that offence often comes in handy as the best form of defence, Yogi Adityanath made it a point to adopt an aggressive stance to cover up his government's glaring unpreparedness in dealing with the devastating second wave of the pandemic. Not to speak of the crisis of hospital beds, acute shortage of ventilators and even basic medicines and injections, what killed many was the non-availability of oxygen, a fact which was widely acknowledged but saying it in public was made an offence punishable by the feared National Security Act.[15] The apparent denial mode that the chief minister adopted was a stark reminder of his refusal to accept that shortage of oxygen had snuffed out the lives of some of the 70 children at the Baba Raghav Das Medical College in Gorakhpur, his hometown, a few months after he assumed the chief ministership in 2017.

Instead of taking appropriate steps to augment the oxygen supply, the chief minister preferred to order drastic measures against all those who dared to draw attention to the dark truth of oxygen shortage. Yogi Adityanath was yet again out to prove that no one died of non-availability of oxygen anywhere in the state. 'If anyone spreads rumours about deficiency of oxygen, book them under the National Security Act (NSA) and seize their property,' was Yogi's firman, which seemed like a warning to scribes who had been reporting on the plight of COVID-19 sufferers gasping for oxygen in not only government and private hospitals but also in the confines of their homes.

'There was no shortage of oxygen in any hospital—government or private; the actual problem was black marketing of oxygen cylinders', Yogi Adiyanath said in his monologue with select editors and senior journalists over an online 'interaction'.[16] Going a step further, he even talked about 'wastage' of oxygen and emphasized the need to curb such 'wastage'. His cabinet member Suresh Khanna, who holds the portfolio of Medical Education and thus handles the state's 52 medical colleges, went a step further by adding, 'There is surplus oxygen in the state.'[17]

As if taking a cue from the chief minister, Uttar Pradesh's additional director general of police (law and order) went on to issue a statement raising concerns on 'black marketing in oxygen cylinders, medicines and other essentials'. And alleging that there was an obvious attempt 'to tarnish the image of the government', he declared that FIRs be registered against 'rumour-mongers'.[18]

It was, therefore, no surprise when Amethi district police booked a young man who sought an oxygen cylinder for his ailing grandfather through a tweet.

The Uttar Pradesh Police filed a criminal case against 26-year-old Shashank Yadav for allegedly 'circulating a rumour with the intent to cause fear' about oxygen supply.[19] In his tweet, the young man had not mentioned whether his grandfather had COVID-19 or not.

Shortage of oxygen was rampant, but the government remained in denial. Desperate relatives of ailing patients took to twitter and social media seeking help in finding oxygen cylinders. Shashank Yadav was one of them. Instead of helping him, the administration chose to target him.

Shashank sent an SOS on Monday evening and tagged actor Sonu Sood, who had become known for his philanthropy during the pandemic. Yadav's friend, Ankit, shared the message and sought help from journalist Arfa Khanum Sherwani of The Wire. A few hours later, Arfa posted a tweet, seeking help for Shashank's grandfather. Arfa also tagged Union minister and member of Parliament (MP) from Amethi Smriti Irani, who promptly responded. The Amethi MP stated that having called Yadav multiple times without getting any response she had asked the district magistrate and the Amethi police to follow up. Eventually, Shashank's grandfather passed away and the death certificate stated 'cardiac arrest' as the cause of death.

In another case, a girl in Lucknow, traumatized after her father's death due to COVID-19, posted a video daring the chief minister to arrest her for saying that her father died due to the shortage of oxygen.[20]

It was only after the Supreme Court warned that no coercive action should be taken against those appealing for help or putting out their grievances on social media during the pandemic that the government could be leashed. In an unambiguous order a Bench headed by Justice D.Y. Chandrachud said, 'We want to make it very clear that if citizens communicate their grievances on social media and internet then it cannot be said it's wrong information. We don't want any clampdown of information.

We will treat it as a contempt of court if such grievances are considered for action.'[21]

Interestingly, even as the state government was busy making tall claims about the abundant availability of oxygen, a press release was issued on behalf of the chief minister on 25 April, stating that a decision had been taken to set up oxygen plants in all government-run hospitals with more than 100 beds. The same press release said that a decision has been taken to establish oxygen plants in each of the state's 855 community health centres at semi-urban locations. A special allocation of Rs 488 crores for this purpose was also made out of State Disaster Relief Fund.[22]

The most interesting part of the press release was the loud claim that 39 oxygen plants were already being installed. 'It is not that the decision has been taken now, it was decided by the chief minister long back and was only being implemented now,' the press release emphasized. It also added that unlike other states, the Uttar Pradesh government made it a point to prepare well in advance to meet the challenge of the pandemic. Ironically, by the time installation process began, the second wave had already dealt a knockout punch.

The first respite came in the form of Oxygen Express—a special train, all the way from Bokaro. The train arrived in Lucknow on 25 April with 30,000 litres of oxygen. It took nearly a whole day to transfer the oxygen into storage tanks at the state capital's key hospitals, where many patients were in dire need of it. A part of the train moved on to Varanasi for a similar exercise in that region, where the need for oxygen was equally acute.

The next good thing to happen was the setting up of a 500-bed makeshift hospital by the Defence Research Development

Organisation (DRDO), thanks to Defence Minister Rajnath Singh, who had initiated the move following appeals made to him by people from his constituency, Lucknow, including a request from a Uttar Pradesh minister. Even though these steps came somewhat late in the day, there could be no denying that it was better late than never. The hospital was laid out inside the three giant halls at Avadh Shilpgram—a 'Dilli Haat' kind of structure created during the preceding Akhilesh Yadav regime. And sure enough, the DRDO succeeded in setting up what became the second largest COVID-19 Level 3 facility in record time. With 500 oxygen-equipped beds, including 150 ventilators, this became the biggest COVID-19 facility after the King George's Medical University. Even Sanjay Gandhi PGI did not have 150 ICU beds dedicated to COVID-19 patients. The DRDO hospital had piped oxygen supply for every bed and the supply was maintained from a huge oxygen tanker that was duly installed in the premises. The medical and para-medical staff were drawn from the Army Medical Corps, which has its national headquarters in Lucknow. Sources close to the defence minister said that but for the delayed response by the Uttar Pradesh government, the hospital could have been readied much earlier.

The Yogi government was moving heaven and earth to prove anyone and everyone wrong who sought to draw its attention towards the grossly inadequate health infrastructure and official preparedness to meet the challenge thrown by the second wave of the pandemic. However, what came as a huge embarrassment to the government were the remarks and observations of the Allahabad High Court, which took serious note of the state of affairs in government hospitals, dispensaries and primary health centres at various levels.

On 19 April the Allahabad High Court suddenly ordered a week-long lockdown in the five worst-affected cities of the state.[23] The High Court castigated the state administration for its failure in providing the adequate number of sample testing facilities, hospitals beds, and the required amount of oxygen.

That the state government found the intervention of the High Court unwelcome became evident when it lost no time in filing an appeal against the order in the Supreme Court, which promptly stayed the High Court's order. The Supreme Court took cognizance of the arguments made on behalf of the Uttar Pradesh government by Solicitor General Tushar Mehta.[24]

However, the High Court's scathing observations could not be overlooked or ignored. The High Court Bench comprising Justice Siddharth Verma and Justice Ajit Kumar, which had taken suo motu cognizance of the serious pandemic situation, said that it was taking up the issue even though it was a matter relating to the policy of the state government. The Bench said:

> Before it further spirals to engulf in it the entire population of these badly hit districts, it is necessary to take some harsh steps in larger public interest. We know that putting a lockdown to public activities is a matter purely in the nature of policy decision by the concerned government and it was in keeping with this principle that we in our last order dated 13.04.2021, had directed the government to think about restricting public movement to break the chain of COVID-19 infection.[25]

In its opening remarks, the court said,

> The recent surge of pandemic COVID-19 has virtually incapacitated all our medical infrastructure in the State of

U.P. and specially in cities like Prayagraj, Lucknow, Varanasi, Kanpur and Gorakhpur. It appears that the pandemic is teasing the system in a situation where patients have outnumbered the hospital beds and people are just running from pillar to post and in this process attendants of patients are not only getting infected but others in public are also getting infected and a complete chain has got formed.

The Bench regretted that the state government had failed to come up with any new measure in the latest affidavit filed by the state.

Without referring to the government's much-hyped self-praise amplified through its advertisements, the court felt,

> In any civilised society if public health system is not able to meet the challenges and people die for want of proper medication, it means there has been no proper development. Health and education go side-by side. Those at the helm of affairs of governance are to be blamed for the present chaotic health problems and more so when there is a democracy which means a government of the people, by the people and for the people.

The court also did not hesitate to criticize the government for holding panchayat elections and, therefore, compelling teachers and policemen to perform various duties in the elections, where all COVID-19 norms and protocols were being blatantly flouted. 'The police was virtually shifted to polling places giving priority to election above public health', the Bench lamented. Castigating the government, the Bench added, 'It is a shame that while the Government knew of the magnitude of the second wave it never planned things in advance.'

The Bench felt that the government was still far from coming to grips with the worsening pandemic situation in Uttar Pradesh. Despite issuing routine statements with tall claims of 'improvement' in the daily situation, the fact remained that people were dying helplessly in the absence of treatment and their kin were compelled to stand in long queues to perform the last rites.

> If people die of pandemic in a large number due to paucity of sufficient medical aid it would be the governments to blame which failed to counter the pandemic even after one long year of experience and learning. One would only laugh at us that we have enough to spend on elections and very little to spend on public health.

Expressing deep concern over what is commonly called the 'VIP culture', the Bench observed,

> We find from the scenario that emerges from the Government Hospitals that admission of patients to ICUs are largely being done on the recommendation of VIPs. Even supply of life saving anti viral drug namely Remdesivire is being provided only on the recommendation of VIPs.

It lamented, 'VIPs and VVIPs are getting their RT-PCR report within 12 hours, whereas, ordinary citizen is kept waiting for such reports for two to three days and thus, spreading further infection to other members of his/her family [sic].'

The judges further made it a point to clarify why they were compelled to order action. They were of the view that if the popular government failed to check public mobility on account of its own political compulsions, the court was duty-bound to step in. 'We can't shirk away from our constitutional duty to save innocent people from the pandemic which is spreading due to the negligence of a few. Thus in the larger public interest, we are called upon to pass orders to break the chain of the pandemic COVID-19,' they declared.

The remarks and observations of the bench spoke volumes of the prevailing plight of people on account of the pandemic. Also, it doubtlessly showed the wide gap between the oft-repeated and loudly echoed claims of the government and the ground reality. That the apex court's stay against the High Court order was largely on technical grounds and not on issues of merit was also clearly evident. The Uttar Pradesh government stated that the order by the Allahabad High Court was likely to cause administrative impediments. It was further argued that clamping lockdown through a judicial order did not go well with the established conventions and practice. Senior advocate Sanjay Bhasin felt, 'Apparently, the Supreme Court chose to stay the High Court's order essentially because it was a question of the government's routine policy in which the High Court is usually not expected to intervene.' The comments made by the High Court Bench about the prevailing conditions across the state were not questioned by the apex court. Thus, there was no way that the state government could absolve itself of its responsibility—even though it may have done its best to do so by going into complete denial.

THE DRAMA BEFORE YOGI'S
RISE TO THE HOT SEAT

'Gorakhpur me rehna hai, toh Yogi-Yogi kehna hai!'[1] (Chant Yogi Yogi, if you wish to live in Gorakhpur!) That was the slogan popularized by Yogi Adityanath's war team at the time of the 2017 Assembly election. And no sooner than he rode on to don the mantle of the chief minister of India's most populous northern state of Uttar Pradesh, the slogan was tweaked to read: 'Uttar Pradesh mein rehna hai toh Yogi-Yogi kehna hai.'[2] Some dreaded the thought, others drew strength from it.

On 18 March 2017, the BJP office in Lucknow was abuzz with speculation about who would helm the state as chief minister. There were many names doing the rounds after the party's historic mandate in the Assembly elections. The landslide verdict saw the BJP win three-fourths majority with 325 of the 403 seats—belying fears that the party may not do well as it had not named a chief minister candidate before the polls.

Many vied for the post of chief minister. Topping the list was the high-profile Union Home Minister Rajnath Singh, followed by IITian Manoj Sinha (the Union Minister of State for Railways and Communication). Others in the race were Keshav Prasad Maurya (the then BJP state president of Uttar Pradesh), Lucknow Mayor Dinesh Sharma and Union Tourism Minister Mahesh Sharma.

Suspense was building up in the jam-packed party headquarters. Maurya's supporters expectantly raised slogans in his favour. In fact, Maurya had played his cards quite openly. He made no bones about staking claim to the top job. And his plea was plain and simple—he had worked single-handedly towards wooing the backward castes towards the BJP. He also contended that the massive mandate for the party was essentially due to the turn of the Other Backward Class (OBC) vote, largely attributable to him. What he sought to obviously ignore was the Modi factor around which the whole election had hinged. Apart from the Modi magic, what he also seemed to overlook was the fact that Modi's OBC lineage would also bound to have gone a long way to ensure the turn of the backward vote in BJP's favour. Yet, Maurya was busy, quite blatantly, hogging all the credit. Having addressed nearly 200 meetings during the run-up to the poll, he had managed to build sufficient clout in the party rank and file, who converged in and around the BJP office to cheer him and raise the pitch for his nomination as chief minister.

With Rajnath Singh having already declined the offer for the position he had held twice earlier, Manoj Sinha continued to be seen as the key contender from Delhi. He was perceived as Prime Minister Narendra Modi's first choice for the simple reason that other than Rajnath Singh, he was the only man with the desired experience and political acumen that was being sought to run a complex and gigantic state like Uttar Pradesh.

Some kind of reassurance perhaps prompted Sinha to go to Varanasi on 17 March to carry out an auspicious puja (rudra-abhishek) meant to boost his prospects. He was all set to drive down from Varanasi to Lucknow the next morning, when a new development dashed all his hopes. The party bigwigs in Delhi sent a chartered plane to fetch Yogi Adityanath from Gorakhpur. And that became a clear indication as to who was going to be coronated in Lucknow. Sure enough, it provoked Sinha to pack his bags in Varanasi. Instead of Lucknow, he was headed for New Delhi. He refused to have any word with the media.

Meanwhile, scores of Hindu Yuva Vahini (HYV) activists rushed from Gorakhpur to Lucknow, raising chants of 'Yogi-Yogi'—the latter until then known only as the vociferous saffron-clad Hindu rabble-rouser, who headed the Gorakdham temple in Gorakhpur. The BJP state headquarters—diametrically opposite the state's seat of power in the Vidhan Bhavan—began reverberating with two loud slogans: one asserting Yogi's claim to the coveted chair, and the other seeking Keshav Prasad Maurya's elevation.

Even as it had become evident in Delhi's corridors of power that the crown of Uttar Pradesh chief ministership was likely to be handed over to Yogi, in Lucknow speculation was still rife over the choice. Maurya was not ready to accept that his claim could be set aside, and there were many in the party rank and file who were still ready to bet on him.

On 18 March, while the newly elected legislators were collecting in Lok Bhawan—the new, opulent 600-crore-rupee chief minister's office building (erected by Akhilesh Yadav) at a stone's throw from the BJP office—the supporters of Yogi and Maurya continued to loudly raise slogans for their respective leaders at the party office, next door. Short of coming to fisticuffs, the frenzy was visible on both sides.

The suspense was over as soon as Yogi Adityanath stepped into the hall where only the newly elected members were seated. Yogi's presence at the venue was unwarranted as he was a Lok Sabha member and had not contested the Assembly election. His arrival, therefore, was a clear-cut indication of the course of events likely to follow.

Amit Shah's point man and BJP state organizing secretary Sunil Bansal, apparently, quietly slipped a small chit into the hands of the party's senior-most MLA, Suresh Khanna. And just as he opened the slip, the astonishment on his face was starkly visible—it bore the name of 44-year-old Yogi Adityanath.

Minutes later, Khanna dutifully proposed Yogi's name for the position of chief minister. There was stunned silence for several moments, followed by gasping and humming of whispers. After a brief pause, which made it seem like an afterthought, a few MLAs rose to second the proposal. Thereafter came the loud applause and a reverberation of badhais (congratulations).

There were several theories about how Adityanath managed to bulldoze his way to become chief minister and how the other contenders—Maurya and Sinha—got sidelined at the last minute. Informed insiders, who didn't want to be named, said that Maurya, apparently, was initially encouraged by a senior party functionary who promised him the moon. He fuelled Maurya's ambition to such an extent that the latter let loose a host of his followers to raise loud slogans in his favour. Taking serious note of this 'indiscipline', BJP's national general secretary Om Mathur, who had been given the charge of Uttar Pradesh, allegedly managed to get Maurya out of the ring. He felt that allowing the latter's supporters to resort to such loud lobbying was a reflection of insolence and indiscipline, that was not acceptable in a cadre-based party like the BJP.

On the other hand, Mathur chose to ignore similar loud tactics adopted by Adityanath's HYV, better known as his 'private army'.[3] And senior Rashtriya Swayamsevak Sangh (RSS) leader Krishna Gopal, who was already averse to the name of Manoj Sinha for the chief minister's post, took the opportunity to put a spanner in his works. With two key contenders out of the race, Krishna Gopal himself called for considering a third name. And pat sprung the name of Yogi Adityanath, who had been pressing his own case through the HYV. He also enjoyed the blessings of RSS chief Mohan Bhagwat for being a strong and vocal proponent of Hindutva.

RSS supremo Bhagwat also managed to convince Prime Minister Narendra Modi that the saffron-clad mahant (chief temple priest) from Gorakhpur would be a better political bet than an IIT graduate turned Union minister, Manoj Sinha, who was the PM's choice for Uttar Pradesh's top job.[4] This clearly set the party's agenda in Uttar Pradesh—Hindutva getting precedence over good governance. And Adityanath fully demonstrated this through most of his actions during his very first year in office.

By zeroing in on Yogi, Prime Minister Narendra Modi and BJP National President Amit Shah had chosen not merely a saffron-donning head priest of Gorakhnath temple with no previous experience in administration other than running the temple trust, and being a member of the Lok Sabha (albeit for five consecutive terms). They had picked someone who carried a sack full of controversies on his priestly shoulders to head the country's most populous and, therefore, politically most crucial state.

Apprehension, awe and jubilation marked Adityanath's arrival on the centre stage of Uttar Pradesh politics. His elevation 'erased the line demarcating religion and politics'. It was like a pontiff being appointed the Prime Minister of England.

For some, there was reason to be apprehensive of this monk (who also wears the hat of a politician), going by what he told a journalist in February 2009. 'I will not stop till I turn Uttar Pradesh and India into a Hindu Rashtra,' was his candid remark to Rohini Mohan of *Tehelka Magazine*.[5] Yogi has his own 'clear code of right and wrong'. According to this code, 'being Muslim is right' but being 'Muslim in India is wrong'.[6]

Such dogmatic views gave a large section of Hindus, who look at the Gorakhpur-based Kshatriya priest with pride, reason to rejoice.

Questions were asked if Modi and Shah were sincere about the development of Uttar Pradesh or their objective was to implement the RSS-driven Hindutva agenda of Hindu Rashtra, Uniform Civil Code, doing away with Article 370 of the Indian Constitution, and paving the way for building the much-debated Ram temple in Ayodhya. As an aggressive Hindutva would be antithetical to an inclusive growth, the question was: how did Prime Minister Narendra Modi and Amit Shah zero in on Adityanath as most suited for the chief minister's post?

The choice of candidate was especially surprising because although Adityanath had been with the BJP for long years, he had always been a domineering satrap in a part of eastern Uttar Pradesh. There were times when ties between the five-time MP from Gorakhpur and his party's leadership came under severe strain, to say the least.

The differences between the party and Adityanath, the stormy petrel of politics, cropped up mostly over Hindutva. Yogi turned critical of the party whenever he felt that the Hindutva agenda was being diluted. He raised an army of his own under the banner of HYV, not only to further strengthen his own power base in eastern Uttar Pradesh, but also to be able to dictate terms to the party.[7] In 2002 he revolted against the BJP and fielded Dr Radha Mohan Agarwal on a Hindu Mahasabha ticket. Agarwal defeated BJP's Shiv Pratap Shukla by a big margin.

As the founder of the HYV, Yogi Adityanath was known more as a Hindu rabble-rouser and for his anti-Muslim rhetoric. In 2005, he led a drive to convert Christians back to Hinduism in collaboration with another equally rabid saffron-clad Hindutva aggressor Sakshi Maharaj (the BJP MP from Unnao). As part of that drive, 1,800 Christians were reportedly converted to Hinduism in Etah.[8]

Instances of Yogi Adityanath's blatant anti-Muslim stance abound. After being elected to the Lok Sabha, Adityanath changed the name of Miyan Bazar in Gorakhpur to Maya Bazar, that of Urdu Bazar to Hindi Bazar, and Ali Nagar was renamed Arya Nagar. At a show hosted by a private TV channel in Lucknow on 17 February 2017, Adityanath aggressively defended his acts of changing Muslim names of localities in Gorakhpur. An uncompromising Adityanath asserted, 'Miyan Bazar and Ali Nagar are not the only places whose names I changed. Humayunpur was changed to Hanumanpur and Islampur was made Ishwarpur and there is nothing wrong in it and we will continue doing this.'[9]

His argument has been straightforward—actions of invaders in any time period needed to be undone. For Adityanath, giving Muslim localities a Hindu name is about fighting for the country's cultural freedom to which he has been, and will continue to be, committed.

As it appeared from his public life, whether rightly or wrongly, Adityanath's mindset is simple and straight—whatever is required in the interest of the country has to be done, and done with commitment. The bitter pill, if required, has to be administered without any sugar coating. A clear pointer of things to come as majoritarian politics gained currency in the state.

The February 2017 television interview also made clear that Adityanath does not view Mughal monuments as part of India's virasat (heritage); even renaming Taj Mahal as Tejo Mahalay is not beyond him, though he says he would like the issue to be debated.

Speaking at Vishwa Hindu Parishad's (VHP's) Virat Hindu Sammelan on 25 February 2015 in Rohtak, Adityanath said, 'Conversions spoil communal amity in the country. [They] should be banned. If conversions continue, I feel Ghar Vapasi programme will continue.'[10]

He also alleged that 'anti-national activities breed' in 'Muslim areas' and that 'secularists' should answer his questions. 'India's problem is not malnutrition or poverty. India's problem is vote bank politics fuelled by jehadi fervour. In Hindu society everyone feels safe, every mother and sister feels safe. There is guarantee of safety of each and every religious sect here.'[11]

For those expecting him to further bare his fangs, Adityanath swiftly went on to assert that more Muslims partake of food served at the Gorakhnath temple compared to Hindus, and more Muslims come for treatment at the temple-run hospital.

Prior to being anointed as chief minister, Adityanath faced three criminal cases. While two of these were filed in January 2007 for allegedly inciting violence and making communal speeches, the third one was filed way back in 1999, accusing him of 'murder, criminal intimidation, trespassing on burial spaces, destroying/defiling any place of worship'. However, he got relief in each one of them, after he was installed as chief minister.[12]

In 2007, Adityanath was arrested for violating prohibitory orders following communal tension over the killing of a Hindu.[13] He was put behind bars for 11 days by the Mulayam Singh Yadav government, describing his ordeal in the Lok Sabha with tears flowing down his cheeks. According to him, there was a political conspiracy behind his arrest. He told the Lower House that he had never treated politics as a profession and that he had left his family as a sanyasi.

Ironically, from being a full-time ascetic, in March 2017 he left the Gorakhdham *math* to reside at 5 Kalidas Marg, Lucknow (the official residence of the chief minister) after elaborate shuddhikaran (religious cleansing ritual), which naturally entailed becoming a full-time politician.

According to Sudha Pai (National Fellow of the Indian Council of Social Sciences) and Sajjan Kumar (PhD scholar at Jawaharlal Nehru University):

> There is much speculation that despite some murmurs in the party, the RSS 'persuaded' Modi and Amit Shah, who were keen to appoint a leader with a developmental image, to accept Adityanath as the chief minister. There are a number of reasons why the BJP–RSS selected him to head the state. First, the 2000s have witnessed the attempt by the BJP to create a strong 'non-Brahmin Hindutva', not only in Uttar Pradesh but in many states in the country. While in the 1980s and early 1990s the BJP was viewed as largely an 'upper'-caste Hindu party, since at least the mid-1990s in Uttar Pradesh there has been an attempt to consciously mobilise and bring

into the ambit of the party non-Yadav OBCs and non-Jatav Dalits, who constitute the large majority, in order to meet the challenge posed by the SP and the Bahujan Samaj Party.[14]

Adityanath, with his HYV, contributed greatly to the mobilization of OBCs and Dalits, who owe allegiance to the Gorakhnath *peeth*, an ancient non-Brahmin Hindu institution. Its mahants have been Thakurs. Pai and Kumar have created Adityanath by bringing into being 'a subaltern Hindutva which is pro– "lower" caste and at the same time anti–"upper" caste and anti-Muslim'.

Pai and Kumar add in the same article,

The goal of the BJP–RSS is not only to win elections but to make India more Hindu. The idea is not to have large-scale riots, but slowly to make Hindutva acceptable in the eyes of the common man and render the Muslim as the 'other', in which the yogi has been very successful through long-term mobilisation, patronage and work among the people. The RSS found him very successful in this venture and making him chief minister sends a message to the people and the party workers about the goals of the BJP.

Yogi Adityanath was known for his love–hate relationship with the BJP leadership. He established himself as an independent power centre with a distinct form of Hindutva. His strong communal statements and tall demands for his HYV during the election campaign did give anxious moments to the BJP leadership. Yet, the BJP and RSS leadership hoped to 'contain and control' Adityanath by appointing him to the most sought-after political office of Uttar Pradesh, while simultaneously using him to consolidate their Hindutva hold over the rising, upwardly mobile, non-Brahmin elite. Ever since he became chief minister, Yogi Adityanath has been busy trying to give the impression that 'communal' charges were falsely slapped on him, when he actually never indulged in any kind of hate speech.

In an exclusive interview given to the authors at the chief minister's official residence in Lucknow in October 2017, Yogi Adityanath sought to make the media his punching bag. Asked to comment on his widely perceived 'communal' agenda and the tendency to give everything a Hindu–Muslim colour, he did not mince words in pointedly accusing the media of painting him black. 'The media has its own bias and mindset against me and therefore it tends to always depict me in negative light', was his charge. As a counter-question, he asked: 'I would like to know what you understand of secularism? Can there be a more secular nation than India, where people of all castes, creed or faith have lived together for centuries?'

He was, however, caught on the wrong foot when his attention was drawn to his speech on Nepal, where he expressed his displeasure about the new Nepali dispensation favouring secular and democratic values. He said, 'my views were twisted in the media.' He added, 'Please view what I said in the context in which I spoke. What the media does is to skip the context and give out half-truths in order to project me in poor light. If you make it a point to view my remarks in a particular context, you will never find me wrong.'

That secularism is not his cup of tea has been expressed quite explicitly by Adityanath in his article penned under the headline, 'Antar-raashtreey saazishon ke jaal me phansta Himalayee Rashtra Nepal' (Nepal getting caught in international conspiracies), which is part of the dissertation 'Hindu Rashtra Nepal: Ateet aur Vartman' (Hindu Rashtra Nepal: Past and

Present).[15] Describing 18 May 2006 as a 'Black Day', when the country's kangaroo parliament passed an 'unfortunate and unexpected' resolution declaring Nepal a secular state, Adityanath squarely blames Maoists, Islamic militants and Christians for the 'unconstitutional' decision.[16]

He expressed the same sentiment when he was asked whether he had altered the course of the philosophy of Gorakhnath who did not believe in hardcore sanatan dharma[17]—a practice now being aggressively advocated by Adityanath.

> You have again got it wrong. I cannot imagine that an educated man like you would not know what sanatan dharma is. If Gorakhnath did not believe in 'sanatan dharma', then tell me, what did he believe in? What he practised and preached was sanatan dharma only and that is a Hindu practice which has been going on for ages. Where is the conflict and where is the question of any deviation from Baba Gorakhnath's philosophy? I am only carrying on his spiritual legacy. Here again, you need to look at his teachings in the wider perspective then you will understand that whatever he did and preached was no different from sanatan dharma. After all, it began with the worship of 'shakti'—something that Lord Shiva too believed in. There is absolutely no difference.[18]

While asserting that he had not deviated from the line laid down by Gorakhnath, whose philosophy was deeply rooted in secularism, he sought to know:

> Where has the secular fabric of this organization been violated? Many jogis were traditionally used to moving from place to place. They did not necessarily make the Gorakhnath temple

their home. Therefore, it was natural for them to be shifting base with the passage of time. They used to sing bhajans also. And no one is denying them entry to the temple even now. You are making a false allegation if you seem to think that I have driven them away. Why should I?[19]

Adityanath went on to add:

Haven't you seen how so many Muslims come to my janata durbar at the Gorakhnath temple every day, whether I am there or not? And you can check for yourself that there is no discrimination of any kind with them. Their problems are dealt with just the same attention and commitment as that of any Hindu. The trouble with the media is that they are always looking at me with their own coloured vision.[20]

Instantly, he reverted to his familiar territory of minority bashing, accusing them of being responsible for India—a 'Sanatanee' Hindu state since time immemorial—not becoming a Hindu Rashtra. 'But for the "scheming" Muslims and Christians, India would have become a Hindu state,' was his prognosis.

Fact remains that several commercial establishments within the premises of the Gorakhnath temple are being run by Muslims and a few of the temple employees also belong to the minority community. And that is surprising to many.

At the end of the day, there could be no denying this sadhu-turned-politician has made it big, not by dint of any merit but by using religion and playing the politics of hardcore polarization. Having created his own political space at the highest level in the state, Adityanath is now aspiring for a bigger role in national politics—using the same tools.

3

EARLY LIFE, FAMILY AND EDUCATION

In his affidavit filed for the 2014 Lok Sabha elections, Yogi Adityanath gave the name of his spiritual guru, Mahant Avaidyanath, in the column for father's name. The Lok Sabha page also shows Mahant Avaidyanath as his father.[1] Nothing unusual in that in some traditions after renunciation, the spiritual guru's name figuratively replaces that of the biological father. Like guru bhai (brother, disciples of the same guru), one has the term 'guru pita' where the guru is looked upon as a father figure. Even Mahant Avaidyanath described his guru, Mahant Digvijaynath, as being a 'father' to him, in the Lok Sabha's Who's Who, 1991.[2]

Yogi Adityanath was born Ajay Mohan Singh Bisht on 5 June 1972 to Savitri Devi (a homemaker) and Anand Singh Bisht, at Masalgaon—a nondescript village in the Uttarkashi district of Uttarakhand—where his father was posted as a forest range officer.

Ajay's college friend Sandeep Bisht described the family as prosperous. 'I stayed at Ajay's house for five–six days when we were in college. His family owns large tracts of land and jungle. You can categorise them as thogdars [zamindars],' he told the authors in an interview at Kotdwar in October 2017. Ajay's youngest brother denied they were thogdars and owned forest land; he told the authors that the family does have some landed property.

Ajay is the fifth born in a brood of seven. His three sisters—Pushpa Devi, Kaushalya Devi, Shashi Devi—and brother Manendra are elder to him. Shailendra and Mahendra are younger, the latter being almost eight years his junior.

By the time Mahendra was 15 years of age, Ajay had renounced his family bonds to become a yogi of the Nath sect, whose followers trace their lineage to Lord Shiva, the Adi Yogi. 'I was studying in Class IX when he became mahant in 1994,' Mahendra, the youngest of the siblings, told the authors in an interview on 7 October 2017. Mahendra works as a journalist for the Hindi newspaper *Amar Ujala* and writes about the problems facing his village Panchur and the Yamkeshwar block (of which the village is a part) in Pauri Garhwal district of Uttarakhand.

Ajay's biological father Anand Bisht, sister Shashi, youngest brother Mahendra and his classmates from BSc provide a glimpse into his youth, but share little about his childhood.

In *Yogi Adityanath: The Rise of A Saffron Socialist*, author Pravin Kumar has this to say about Ajay Bisht's childhood:

> After the first six months of his life in Masalgaon, Ajay spent the next fourteen years in his village. His first two sisters, Pushpa and Kaushalya, nineteen and sixteen years his senior, were the first to initiate him into the world of letters. A bright student by the time he turned five, Ajay was ready to go to the primary school at the nearby Thangar village, about a

kilometre away, where his third sister Shashi and elder
brother Manendra were already studying . . . He had very
few friends and instead of playing with boys of his age group,
he would spend time with books and tend to pet cows when
he was a little older.[3]

Shashi fondly remembers accompanying Ajay, five years younger
than her, to the Government Primary School at Thangar, about
a kilometre away from their home in Panchur where the family
decided to build a home. Here he studied till Class VIII. Ajay
then joined the government school at Chamakot for one year.
After passing Class IX from Chamakot, Ajay did his Class X
from a school at Gaja in Tehri and was ready to move to college.

As a child he was 'precocious and focused on his studies',
Shashi told a journalist.[4] She does not remember 'when Ajay
became Adityanath'. 'All I remember is my brother telling our
father as a child, "You remained within the four walls of your
house but I want to serve society,"'[5] she told her interviewer
with a touch of pride.

Although her brother is the chief minister of a neighbouring
state, Shashi and her husband toil for a living without any
complaints. On a visit to Kuthar village (30 km from Panchur),
in October 2017, this writer found that the couple owns two
shops near the Neelkanth Mahadev (Lord Shiva) temple and
also have an outlet near a temple of Goddess Parvati. Located
near Rishikesh, both the temples are in close vicinity of one
another and not far from their house.

With too many shops around the two temples, competition
is tough. Business is brisk during the tourist season but in the
off season the flow of pilgrims turns into a trickle and earnings
dip. The numerous shops sell flowers, tea, snacks and food to

pilgrims. Shashi, like all other traditional women in the hills, helps out her husband in the shop at Goddess Parvati's temple, selling flowers and other puja material.

Being a sanyasi, Yogi Adityanath is not expected to maintain any ties with his sister or worry if she is happy or sad. However, Shashi is not a sanyasin and, therefore, remains emotionally attached to her brother. She misses Adityanath the most on Raksha Bandhan, she told a TV journalist.[6] Her only regret was that for the last 26 years she has been unable to tie a rakhi on her brother's wrist. Nonetheless, every year she sends a rakhi by post to her brother. In the absence of any acknowledgment from Adityanath, she told the TV journalist, 'I don't know if it even reaches him.' She prays that her brother remains out of harm's way and is successful as chief minister.

Shashi's husband has also been the gram pradhan of his village, Kuthar, situated about 30 km from his sasural (in-laws' place) at Panchur. Shashi and her husband do not expect Adityanath to help them. Being content with their lives, neither has approached him for any assistance. Nor have the two sought any special benefits from the BJP government of Uttarakhand on the basis of their ties with the Uttar Pradesh chief minister.[7]

With journalists chasing her for interviews, Shashi had stopped sitting at the shop. When the authors visited Neelkanth Mahadev temple in October 2017, instead of Shashi, her son Abhishek—who has done a course in hotel management from Dehradun—was looking after the eatery at Neelkanth, because of her 'adverse portrayal in the electronic media', he told the authors. Shashi's younger son is now in charge of the other outlet. Apparently, instructions were sent from Lucknow for Adityanath's kin to desist from talking to the media.

Cutting grass from the forests for cows is a normal chore for women in the hills but the media projected it differently, said Shashi's elder son in defence of his mother. Wary of talking about his maternal uncle, Abhishek refused to say anything about his interactions with him.

Shashi, from her accounts on electronic media, is content with her life and has no complaints about her VVIP brother.

Ajay's brother Mahendra, besides being a journalist is also the administrative officer at the family-run Mahayogi Guru Gorakhnath Mahavidyalaya. He described his brother to NDTV as an 'elusive figure' because he hardly got a chance to see him.[8]

In a brief chat with the authors at the Mahayogi Guru Gorakhnath Mahavidyalaya, Mahendra had this to say about his elder brother: 'When he came home from Rishikesh or Kotdwar we used to avoid him for fear of being asked to do sums or answer questions related to studies.' Mahendra has very carefully kept his brother's books and notes, proudly claiming that Ajay was very meticulous in his work. According to him, Ajay was particular about always instructing his siblings to focus on their studies. 'At a later stage, I did miss his guidance while studying mathematics,' Mahendra told this writer.

Ajay's father Anand Singh Bisht, who passed away in April 2020, was very energetic even in his eighties, and was appreciative of Ajay's seriousness towards his studies.

'Whenever I made a surprise check while he was at Rishikesh I found him studying,' Anand Singh told this writer on telephone. Ajay did his Intermediate (Class XI and XII) from Shri Bharat Mandir Inter College, Rishikesh, with physics, chemistry and mathematics as his subjects.

Bharat Mandir was also the alma mater of Ajay's guru Mahant Avaidyanath, but thus far he had not caught the senior mahant's attention.

Ajay and his elder brother Manendra (who was then pursuing a bachelor's degree) stayed together in Rishikesh. Anand Bisht said that during his surprise visits, he often did not find Manendra in the room but Ajay was always there, poring over his books.

'Other students would come to him for tuition,' said Anand Bisht, adding with a sense of pride that Ajay passed with a first division in Class X and XII, as well as in BSc. However, he could not recall the exact marks/percentage scored by his son.

College Life

After clearing his Intermediate, Ajay appeared for the entrance test conducted by Garhwal University for admissions to BSc in 1989. He was among 74 students who qualified for admission in the science stream in the Dr Pitambar Datt Barthwal Rajkeey Mahavidyalay at Kotdwar. The number of those who opted for the physics, chemistry and mathematics (PCM) group was smaller than those in other groups.

Two years later, in 1991, he graduated.

With him were Sandeep Bisht, Arvind Bansal, Digambar Singh Rawat, Babita Rana, Raj Bhushan Singh Rawat (Raja Bhai to friends) and a few others. Raj Bhushan Singh Rawat *is* now Officer on Special Duty at Lucknow in the Uttar Pradesh chief minister's office, and is the link between Adityanath and his college friends. Sandeep Bisht teaches physics in an intermediate college at Kotdwar, Digambar Rawat was in the air force, Arvind Bansal is into business, while Babita Rana is a teacher.

Digambar Rawat often met Ajay Bisht in Delhi when the latter was an MP. He and a couple of others would occasionally descend on Ajay's residence for a meal, according to Arvind Bansal whom the authors met in Kotdwar.

'Raja Bhai' is instrumental in organizing reunions of the BSc group every year. Ajay has not been able to attend any of them so far but 'has promised to be there at the next reunion,' said Arvind Bansal.

Bansal recalls Ajay scoring 64–65 per cent. He was among the top five, he said. Other class-fellows like Sandeep Bisht and Digambar Singh Rawat, whom the authors also met, were not sure of his BSc percentage but insisted that he was a first divisioner.

For all the class-fellows, Ajay—now 'maharaj'—has acquired an exalted, 'godlike status', and they touch his feet whenever they get a chance to meet him. 'Now I am Sudama and he is my Krishna,' said Arvind Bansal for whom, and others too, Ajay was once 'Ajju Bhai' who spoke of rashtravadita (nationalism) with a passion 'uncommon among youth our age'.

Full of praise, Ajay Bisht's friends described him as being moralistic and religious even during his college days. 'He would never participate in any frivolous conversation about girls, which is a natural thing to do as a teenager. He would disapprove of "affairs" in college as it was a place for study and not romance,' Bansal said.

His other friends recalled how they would all run from Kotdwar's Jhanda Chowk to the Siddhbali Hanuman temple, a distance of little over 3 km at five in the morning. 'It was a routine we hardly ever missed. While we would stay back to play badminton after the run, Ajay would return to his room for his daily puja and studies,' said Bansal, with Sandeep Bisht nodding in agreement.

According to them, Ajay was an early riser even as a student, getting up at 4.00 a.m. for the morning run and returning to his place of stay latest by 6.00 a.m.—emphasizing that nobody could change his daily bathing, puja and study schedules.

Not ready to accept that Ajay is a hardliner, Bansal said, 'Kattarvaad kee baat main nahee maantaa' (I don't accept that he is a hardliner). His classmates mentioned 'two Muslim friends' from college and recalled the name of one, Hashim Ali, towards whom Ajay had 'no dislike or hatred'.

What did they think of his anti-Muslim speeches? 'He is not anti-Muslim but Muslims too should not be anti-national,' asserted all three of them almost in unison.

The friends recalled Ajay Bisht's participation as a student in a few agitations to underscore their point that from the very beginning, RSS and religious and social issues engaged his mind. In 1989–90 he took part in the anti-reservation agitation and burnt the effigy of Prime Minister V.P. Singh. When the police resorted to lathicharge, he saved his college's student union president from blows by blocking them with both his hands.

Once, Ajay had to be hospitalized to be treated for jaundice at the government hospital in Kotdwar. When he found that proper care was not being given to him and other patients, he asked his friends to talk to the doctors about the other patients' neglect, which they did. Thereafter, doctors attended to patients, including Ajay, more seriously, the friends recalled.

But the most talked about incident of his college life was his defeat in the student union election which he contested as an independent candidate in 1991 after the Akhil Bharatiya Vidyarthi Parishad (ABVP) refused to field him. As there was another student wanting to contest for the post of secretary, the ABVP decided not to field either of them and gave the ticket to a third student. Ajay decided to rebel. He campaigned along with his friends and devised a strategy which, Sandeep Bisht said, did not work. 'In college elections there is no need for a candidate to visit every fellow student's house seeking votes but Ajay insisted that this is what he was going to do and he did.'

His opponents confined their campaign to college. Ajay ended runner-up, with one Arun Tiwari emerging victorious. The official ABVP nominee came third.

Sandeep Bisht gives another reason, the science–arts divide, for Ajay's defeat: 'The science group had 74 students but was outnumbered by those in the arts stream. He got fewer votes from arts students.'

Babita Rana, one of the three girl students in the class, came to know of her classmate's transition from Ajay Bisht to Yogi Adityanath only in 2013. 'During our BSc batch's reunion somebody showed me his photograph and asked me if I could recognize him. When I could not the person said it was Ajay Bisht. I was surprised to see him in that attire,' she told the authors over telephone.

The quality of Ajay Bisht which stands out in her memory is that of an angry young man. 'Shuroo se hee unko gussa bahut aataa thha (He was short-tempered from the beginning)', Babita said, recalling an incident when he stood in front of a roadways bus and forced it to a halt so that she and some other students could board it. 'It was done out of anger to help the girls reach home safely and in time', she explained. In those days roadways buses did not stop midway for students because they preferred free rides to buying tickets.

While some of his friends said he belonged to 'garam dal', Mahendra, his brother, substantiates the point. 'Compared to earlier days I will put him in "naram dal" now. He has mellowed from what he was before becoming the chief minister,' he said.

As a student, Babita said, Ajay respected girls. That is why, she said, she was surprised to read about his strong opposition to the Women's Reservation Bill in the Lok Sabha in 2010. She refused to comment any further saying that she does not follow politics.

From the description of his friends, Ajay has 'a mind of his own, is righteous, resolute and a spiritual person' and so for many of them seeing him join the Nath order was no surprise.

Given his interest in studies and having always stood first, it was only natural for Ajay to go in for post-graduation. Mathematics was his choice of subject for MSc. He chose to once again move to Kotdwar where, in 1992, he got admission to the Pandit Lalit Mohan Sharma Government PG College.

His friends are unsure whether Ajay joined MSc Part I in mathematics, but his brother Mahendra insisted that he did complete his first year of the master's programme.

According to Sandeep Bisht, in a theft at Ajay's room in Kotdwar all his belongings were stolen. These included his high school and intermediate certificates and marksheets. 'Ajay had gone to attend an RSS programme and decided to stay there for the night when thieves broke into his house,' said Sandeep. He was very upset with the loss of his certificates and chucked everything to join the math at Gorakhpur.

Mahendra differed with Sandeep. Mahendra asserted,

It is true that his marksheets and certificates were stolen. In fact, the thieves took away everything, including my father's clothes that were kept there. But he was able to procure the documents from the UP Board, enrolled for his post-graduation in Pandit Lalit Mohan Sharma Government PG College, Rishikesh and finally completed his MSc Part I in mathematics.

It was at Kotdwar that he came in frequent contact with Mahant Avaidyanath, who was born Kripal Bisht at Kandi village (a few kilometres away from Panchur), also in Pauri Garhwal. There are a lot of stories, mostly unsubstantiated, about Kripal Bisht being a blood relative of Ajay Bisht, a factor which drew him to the Nath sect.

Pratul Sharma wrote in *The Week*:

> A little known fact is that Yogi and Mahant Avaidyanath are blood relatives. The mahant is the son of Yogi's grandfather's sister. Avaidyanath, born as Kirpal Bisht, left home after his parents died when he was young. No one to look after him, he joined Mahant Digvijaynath at Gorakhpur. Little was known of him, among his relatives or villagers, after he became an ascetic. It was only after he was elected MLA from Maniram that people from his area came to know that he was from Kandi village. Some of them went to him and got Rs 40,000 to start water supply in the area. That was a princely sum 40 years ago.[9]

Mahendra dismissed all talk of kinship between the guru and shishya: 'My taijee (wife of his father's elder brother) was from Kandi village so people put two and two together to conclude that Mahant Avaidyanath was related to us but he was not.' Nobody in Panchur village had heard of Mahant Avaidyanath until 'my brother decided to join him,' said Mahendra.

Strongly reacting to a pointed query from the authors in this regard, Adityanath angrily shot back, 'The last time a journalist asked me this question, he had to apologize to me. And you can confirm this with that Gorakhpur based correspondent of a national English daily.' He went on to emphasize, 'there is no relationship other than that of "guru" and "shishya".'

Once, on being asked what was so special about him that Mahant Avaidyanath handpicked him as successor to the powerful spiritual lineage of Gorakhnath, the obviously displeased chief minister retorted, 'ye aap unse poochhte (you should have asked him)'.

Muslim Principal's Views

Among the Muslims who remained unperturbed by Adityanath's appointment as chief minister was Dr Aaftab Ahmed, principal of the Mahayogi Guru Gorakhnath Mahavidyalay in the Yamkeshwar block of Pauri Garhwal, a family-run college offering Bachelor of Arts degrees.

Funded by the Gorakhnath temple, the college was expected to formally become a government-aided degree college sometime in October 2017 with prospects of a better salary structure.

With over 200 students, the college stands out for having a Muslim as its principal. A doctorate in economics from Kashi Vidyapeeth, Dr Ahmed did his master's in economics from Banaras Hindu University and held several senior faculty positions before the social worker in him brought him to his present location in the remote Yamkeshwar block.

Dr Ahmed stays alone in the Bithyani village near the college and has no other Muslim for company. He was appointed principal two-and-a-half years ago by a panel of three experts

and the college manager, who in this case was Anand Singh
Bisht—father of Yogi Adityanath.

The soft-spoken professor told the authors when they met
him at the college,

> Some of the locals tried to dissuade me from taking up this
> job. They spoke ill about Yogi Adityanath in a bid to poison
> my mind and make me run away. I ignored them all and
> kept to myself. Gradually the whisperings stopped and I have
> had a trouble-free stint in the college and a peaceful stay at
> my village.

Whatever anti-Muslim perception there might be about
Adityanath, Dr Ahmed remains unaffected. 'I have not met
Yogi Adityanath till now and if he was such a diehard Muslim
hater he could have had me thrown out of the college long time
ago,' Ahmed said, indicating that the Gorakhpur Mahant did
not interfere in the running of the college.

With Anand Bisht as manager, Mahendra, who is an
administrative officer, also worked until recently as a part-time
political science teacher. Elder brother Manendra works as a
computer operator completing the family's hold on the college
which has two buses to ferry students from distant places.

Dr Ahmed is not alone in contradicting the popular
perception about Yogi Adityanath being anti-Muslim, an image
which the head priest of Gorakhnath temple has so assiduously
created through his speeches.

Muslim clerics reacted cautiously to his becoming the chief
minister. Shia cleric Maulana Kalbe Jawwad told the authors,
'Modiji was also seen in a similar manner but things changed
(after he became PM). A leader belongs to the party before

becoming the chief minister, but he belongs to the state after being sworn-in.'

Maulana Salman Nadvi of Darul Uloom Nadwatul Ulema, Lucknow, said, 'The controversial statements made by Adityanath in the past cannot be called appropriate . . . But now, he should show that he believes in the slogan "sabka saath, sabka vikas" [everyone's support, everyone's development] . . .'[10]

'He can change . . . he needs to change in order to govern. There is no fear in the Muslim community as such, but communal talks do create an atmosphere of fear and wrong notions,' he was quoted as saying.

Maulana Khalid Rasheed Firangimahali rejected any idea of fear among Muslims arising out of Adityanath's appointment as chief minister. 'Muslims only fear Allah, and not any government or individual,' he said while talking to the authors. Maulana Rasheed, who is a member of the All-India Muslim Personal Law Board, went on to add that it is the responsibility of the government and its head to remove any misconception in the minds of minorities. He was disappointed with the government for not doing anything for the benefit of the minority community, not even preparing a road map for its welfare. Closure of slaughterhouses and impediments in selling of meat, and goods and services tax (GST) on chikan and zardozi has rendered hundreds of people unemployed, but the government has not done anything for them, Khalid Rasheed said.

Only the Shahi Imam of Delhi's Jama Masjid, Syed Ahmed Bukhari, claimed in a letter to Prime Minister Narendra Modi that Muslims of Uttar Pradesh are in a 'dire state of fear and dread'. *India Today Magazine* (29 March 2017) quoted him as saying: 'No government should be dreaded by the people. Instead, an environment of confidence and trust should prevail.'

He also hoped that the Adityanath government would follow the principle of 'sabka saath, sabka vikas' as laid down by the Prime Minister.

An *India Today* report (26 March 2017) by Ilma Hasan said that there was 'palpable unease' on the Aligarh Muslim University (AMU) campus over Adityanath's appointment. The magazine quoted a professor as saying, 'I'd rather not say anything, because if I do I know the RSS will lash out at me. Anyway, we all know what kind of man he is. What is the point of voicing an opinion anyway?'

Professor Ali Nadeem Naqvi of the university reportedly said, 'Choosing a man who is so divisive, should make us think about what is happening in our country.'[11] Professor Shafey Kidwai of the mass communication department told the magazine, 'Culturally it could have an impact because AMU is cosmopolitan. It could have a demoralising effect on our students who feel deprived because they don't have enough representation in the government.'

Even though it may turn out to be a rare case of a tiger changing its stripe, the 'palpable unease' can be felt in the state, beyond the AMU campus.

Renunciation

As a student Ajay took part in the Ram Janmbhoomi movement and activities of the RSS. His brother Mahendra told the authors that Ajay first met Avaidyanath in 1989–90. The latter was travelling across the country to mobilize public opinion for the Ram Janmbhoomi movement.

His friends and sibling are unsure of how long Ajay was in touch with Avaidyanath before joining the Gorakhpur-based math. Some of his friends said that after a couple of meetings Ajay was convinced about joining Mahant Avaidyanath at the Gorakhnath math as a disciple, as 'his heart was more in the Ram Janmbhoomi movement than studies'.

The year 1993 proved to be a life-changing period for Ajay. 'In early 1993, during the peak of the Ram Mandir Movement, he went to Gorakhpur to visit the Gorakhnath temple and also got the chance to meet Mahant Avaidyanath' who told Ajay that he 'was a born yogi'.[12]

According to these friends, the year 1993 proved to be a life-changing period for Ajay. Shortly after the demolition of the Babri Masjid in Ayodhya, during the peak of the Ram Mandir movement, Ajay Singh Bisht visited the Gorakhnath temple in Gorakhpur, where he managed to get an audience with Mahant Avaidyanath,[13] who offered him a place in the Math. Even though Ajay could not immediately make up his mind, he did give it serious thought while returning home.

Later the same year, when Mahant Avaidyanath was hospitalized in New Delhi, Ajay made it a point to not only pay him a visit but also stayed over for some time to look after him in the hospital. Impressed by Ajay's dedication and sincerity, Mahant Avaidyanath once again offered him a permanent disciple's position in the Gorakhnath Math.[14]

This version removes the perception that Ajay was declared the senior mahant's successor within a few years of his induction into the Gorakhdhampeeth as the two were blood relations. He was given deeksha in 1994, made Avaidyanath's election campaign manager in 1996, and was declared his heir apparent in 1998 after being named candidate for the Lok Sabha in 1998, in place of his guru. The rest, as the cliché goes, is history.

The senior mahant's persistence had its effect on a mind that was already inclined towards Hindutva and the Nath order. 'One fine day in 1993 he left his studies and was gone. His mother thought he has gone looking for some job,' reminisced Anand Bisht in a telephonic conversation in 2017. The senior Bisht said he wanted him to study further.

The reticent Ajay apparently discussed his plan to visit Gorakhpur with his eldest sister Pushpa Devi before leaving his family and friends to take up the life of a yogi. Mahendra said that his father went to Delhi looking for Ajay, where his sister Pushpa Devi told him that Ajay was talking of going to Gorakhpur.

Anand Singh then went to Gorakhpur 'three–four months after' Ajay had left his family and friends. 'I found him in an ascetic's attire.' Mahendra describes the moment father and son met at the Gorakhpur math: 'My father was climbing the stairs when he saw him coming down.'

Anand Singh said his first reaction was that of shock.

'Were your parents unhappy with Ajay's decision?' the authors asked Mahendra.

'Would you be happy if your child joins a spiritual order?' he shot back.[15]

It was an emotional moment for the Bisht household when Ajay returned home for the first time as a renunciate. 'It was in 1999 when he came home and stayed overnight. As is the practice among yogis, he asked for bhiksha (alms) from his mother and was given foodgrains with which he cooked his own "saatvik" meal,' recalled Mahendra. Mahendra said he had not visited 'Gorakhpur or any other place in Eastern Uttar Pradesh even once'.

Since then, Adityanath visited Panchur twice again, in 2004 and 2017, and stayed back for the night, according to Mahendra. In 1991 he campaigned for B.C. Khanduri, former chief minister of Uttarakhand, in Yamkeshwar block. Khanduri won the poll by 5,000 votes. Adityanath's visit to Yamkeshwar and Panchur in 2017 was as the BJP's star campaigner, but this time he was there to seek votes for Khanduri's daughter Ritu Khanduri.

Anand Bisht who was initially disappointed with Ajay had come to terms with the situation. 'Once children become adults they take their own decisions', he told the authors.

While he was at the Gorakhnath temple, Anand Bisht recalled, Mahant Avaidyanath asked him to let go of one son. 'You have four boys, give one to me,' the Mahant said to Anand. The latter replied, 'My son is already yours.' Seeing his son's resolve, Anand Bisht did not resist Ajay joining Avaidyanath.

It has been over 25 years that Ajay took the life-changing decision. As time passed, Anand Bisht reconciled with his son's choice of metier. He said he sometimes went to Delhi and stayed with Ajay, whom he now addresses as mahant ji.

For Savitri Devi, the sight of her son in a monk's cowl was distressing. She was in tears when he returned home as a monk and, as per the sanyasi tradition, begged her for food.

When Adityanath was chosen by the BJP to head the Uttar Pradesh government in 2017, the aged parents were proud of their son's rise as the chief minister of Uttar Pradesh even though he chose not to invite them to his swearing-in ceremony.

Yogi's father has not visited the Gorakhpur math since 1994, when he went there with his wife to meet his son after he joined the Nath order. Adityanath's parents and some of the siblings have sometimes met him at his Delhi residence. 'Every time we go, we take two kilograms of barfi and some dal,' said Anand Bisht. 'Sometimes he calls me pitaji; I feel happy. I call him Mahant ji,' said the father, who passed away in April 2020.

4

THE SEER WHO
BECAME CHIEF MINISTER

The appointment of Yogi Adityanath as chief minister of Uttar Pradesh came as a huge surprise to all and sundry. Considering that Prime Minister Narendra Modi had concentrated heavily on the development agenda during his entire campaign across the country's most populous state in early 2017, it was logical to expect a development-oriented, balanced BJP leader to be given the reins of the new government. It was only towards the final days of the campaign that Modi changed his narrative and began giving it a subtle communal turn.

It was not a sheer coincidence that Hindutva found resonance particularly at poll time. Once the 2017 Assembly election bells started ringing in Uttar Pradesh, the saffron brigade began to find ways and means to bring it back to the fore in one form or the other.

It was, therefore, no surprise to find echoing references by different BJP leaders to the much-debated Ram temple in Ayodhya. Having tried and tested various other ways to whip up Hindutva passions, BJP star campaigners reverted to their ultimate Hindutva card—the Ayodhya temple.

Why they continued to see it as a 'trump card' one fails to understand. Anyone who has been following the temple movement would easily understand how the temple issue had lost its vote-catching potential for quite some time.

Until the Babri Masjid stood there, the Ram temple could be used quite effectively to boil the political cauldron in Uttar Pradesh. But once the sixteenth-century mosque was razed on 6 December 1992, its political utility remained on the wane.

It could be recalled how 6 December became Shaurya Diwas (victory day) for the entire saffron brigade. Every year, this day would draw senior and prominent BJP leaders to Ayodhya to hail their 'accomplishment' of 1992 (it was another matter that they always pleaded 'innocent' when it came to their prosecution before courts). However, barely six years after the demolition, when BJP stalwart Lal Krishna Advani descended on the Ayodhya soil to celebrate shaurya diwas, he could not draw an audience of more than 500 to 600 people. There were many more cops than those who could raise only feeble cries of Jai Shree Ram. A visibly chagrined Advani chose to cut short his much-publicized visit and flew back shortly after carrying out the ritual in the name of shaurya diwas.

What clearly disgusted him was the failure of the organizers to mobilize a few thousand people to fill up the small venue in Ayodhya—where a couple of thousand saffron-clad sadhus can be seen strolling along the lanes and by-lanes anytime.

More than a quarter of a century after the demolition of the mosque and the setting up of a makeshift temple in its place, it must be naive on the part of the BJP to hope that it would be able to garner votes by reiterating for the umpteenth time its promise to build a grand Ram temple there.

It was, therefore, surprising to find an astute politician like Prime Minister Modi raking up the temple call at his Dussehra rally in Lucknow in 2016. He was, however, quite discreet in raising cries of 'Jai Shree Ram' that were justified by his supporters, who wondered, 'What was wrong in saying Jai Shree Ram on a Vijay Dashmi evening that marks the elimination of the demon king Ravana by the god of gods, Lord Ram?'[1]

Those who had followed Modi during his 2014 Lok Sabha campaign would remember how he skillfully avoided even a remote reference to the Ram temple or to any other connotation of Hindutva. No wonder he could easily endear himself to even those multitudes who may not have subscribed to the BJP–RSS line and, therefore, did not form part of BJP's captive vote bank. And sure enough, it was they who made all the difference to give Modi an unprecedented surge.

No one would dispute making a salutation to Lord Ram, particularly on a day like Dussehra. What the ardent BJP activists did not seem to understand was the subtle distinction between salutation and a battle cry. 'Jai Shree Ram' is a battle cry, that got popularized with the Ayodhya temple movement. 'Siyapati Ramchandra ki Jai' was the traditional salutation to Lord Ram, but that was not what happened on the evening of Dussehra in 2016 at the historic Aishbagh Ramlila Maidan in Lucknow.[2]

Thus, when the prime minister raised that battle cry of 'Jai Shree Ram'—not once, not twice, but a good five times until the crowds joined him to get the Ramlila Maidan reverberate with that cry—it seemed Modi was giving some kind of a green signal to his party's cadres to go ahead with their aggressive Hindutva agenda in the run up to 2017 state elections in whatever form they wished. On the face of it, however, he would probably still harp on his 'development' agenda, while his official propaganda machinery would go on to dismiss statements issued by the rabble-rousers as 'not the party line'.

In a clear-cut departure from the past practice of prime ministers attending Dussehra celebrations in the national capital, Modi's preference for Lucknow in 2016 could not have been without political motivations. After all, the 2017 Uttar Pradesh state Assembly election was seen as some kind of a semi-final to Modi's larger battle for a second term in 2019, which he won hands down.

The March 2017 Uttar Pradesh Assembly poll was spread across seven phases over a long 40-day span. Such a long process could have had its advantages in terms of logistics by what one saw in Uttar Pradesh, but sometimes the stretching of the poll can also have its pitfalls.

Nothing could have demonstrated that better than the changing narrative of different political parties with every passing phase of the Assembly election in Uttar Pradesh.

What began as a healthy democratic exercise on 4 February 2017, largely focused on 'development' as the key poll plank, seems to have rapidly turned into a murky war. The 'development' card played by Akhilesh Yadav, who had lots to showcase, was instantly picked up not only by his key political adversary Prime Minister Narendra Modi, but also by Bahujan Samaj Party (BSP) supremo Mayawati, who's so-called 'development' agenda could never rise beyond statues and monuments dedicated to some Dalit icons (herself included).

Akhilesh was busy showcasing his achievements—the 301 km Lucknow–Agra Expressway, the Lucknow Metro Rail, the world-class international cricket stadium, four-lane connectivity between districts, free ambulance service and a host of social security schemes, freebies including laptops, and so on.

At some point during the election campaign, the BJP leadership suddenly decided to change tack from 'development' to 'Hindu–Muslim'. What surprised many was Prime Minister Modi switching his language to that of an Amit Shah, or a Yogi Adityanath.

Modi, who never talked in communal terms all through his historic campaign in 2014 (when he romped home with 73 of Uttar Pradesh's 80 Lok Sabha seats), suddenly began speaking in terms of 'kabristan' and 'shamshan', Eid and Diwali. The message was loud and clear that BJP was out to polarize the votes on religious lines. It left everyone wondering why the prime minister should take recourse to this old RSS tactic when he had systematically avoided it in 2014—and yet, that brought rich dividends.

The writing on the wall became clear when Modi made the first reference to 'kabristan' and 'shamshan'. Modi told a huge crowd during one of his poll rallies that he had heard that Akhilesh was building 'walls around kabristaans' (graveyards). So, he wished to know 'why not around shamshaans'.[3]

Evidently, he took advantage of Akhilesh Yadav's budgetary provision for raising boundary walls around Muslim and Christian graveyards. Akhilesh claimed that he had to do so because of numerous complaints of increasing encroachments in and around graveyards. But all said and done, the policy was ill-conceived, prompting right-wing nationalists to take advantage of the situation and use it to give the election campaign a communal twist. And eventually, Akhilesh had to pay dearly for this kind of a crude attempt to garner Muslim votes. It helped

BJP to impress upon the electorate that the Samajwadi Party (SP) government was actually pursuing a policy of minority appeasement.

Amidst apprehensions that such statements may trigger communal clashes, fortunately things did not turn into another Muzaffarnagar-like situation on the eve of the 2014 Lok Sabha election, when more than 65 persons were killed and thousands rendered homeless.

Some felt that the idea behind Modi's changed strategy was to provoke Akhilesh Yadav. Well, to that extent, it served their purpose as the then Uttar Pradesh chief minister was quick to hit back with his infamous 'Gujarat ke gadhe' (donkeys of Gujarat) remark,[4] which was in reference to Amitabh Bachchan's much-publicized Gujarat Tourism advertisement campaign, promoting wild asses of the state. Akhilesh, who had maintained his cool all along, finally joined the slanging match.

What followed was an unprecedented twist to the poll campaign, with Modi also bringing in Pakistan-sponsored terrorism. He not only blamed the two rail accidents in Kanpur in November and December 2016 on the Inter-Services Intelligence (ISI) of Pakistan, but even went to the extent of terming the Akhilesh government as some kind of 'sympathizers' of the Pakistani espionage agency.[5]

Even as there was no evidence so far either with the National Investigation Agency (NIA) or with the state police to even remotely suggest sabotage, the prime minister openly described the mishaps as acts of terror.

Addressing a rally in Gonda during the March 2017 Assembly poll campaign, Modi said,

Gonda humara seemavarti zilla hai, Nepal se sata hua hai.
Aap ne dekha hoga abhi Kanpur me rail hadsa hua, usme
kuch log pakde gaye hain, sainkaron log maare gaye the . . .
Woh akasmaat se nahin, ek shadayantra ke tahat hua tha.
Aur shadayantra karne wale kahan baithe huye the? Seema
ke us paar.[6]

(Gonda is a district bordering Nepal. There was a rail
accident in Kanpur, hundreds of people were killed. Some
persons have been arrested . . . This was not an accident; it
was a planned conspiracy. And where were the conspirators
sitting? Across the border).

He went on to ask:

Agar seema paar ke dushman apna karobaar, seema ke us
paar se chalana chahte hain, toh Gonda me zyada suraksha
ki zarurat hai ki nahin? Agar wo log chun ke aayenge jo aise
logon ki madad karenge, toh Gonda surakshit hoga kya?
Gonda surakshit nahin hoga, toh desh surakshit nahin hoga.
Gonda me toh aise logon ko chun ke bithana hai jo desh
bhakti se bhare huye hain.[7]

[If the enemy wants to mastermind its conspiracies from
across the border, isn't there a need for better security in
Gonda? If you were to elect such people who patronize them,
will Gonda be safe? If Gonda is not safe, the country will not
be safe. You should choose patriotic people in Gonda.]

Even as he made such insinuations, what Modi skillfully avoided
mentioning was the fact that each of the three persons arrested
in Nepal and interrogated in Bihar were Hindus.

Meanwhile, as if to add insult to injury, Amit Shah took to coining an acronym of Kasab—'Congress, Akhilesh, Samajwadi Party and Bahujan Samaj Party'.[8]

Thus, just as the fifth round of polling came to an end on 27 February 2017, all the initial talk about development took a backseat, while the politics of polarization clearly gained precedence over everything else, including fundamental issues like unemployment, economic upliftment of the poor and downtrodden, or the well-being of farmers.

What was also noticeable was that the passage of time had led to increasing exchanges of personal attacks not only between Modi and the Akhilesh–Rahul duo but also with BSP supremo Mayawati. Perhaps, it was after Modi realized that Akhilesh had much more to showcase in the name of development that he chose to change his own narrative from development to polarization.

Meanwhile, as if to compound his folly, Akhilesh Yadav sought to introduce yet another policy—of awarding all Muslim girls passing Class XII with a special scholarship of Rs 30,000. Perhaps, it would have been fine if the scholarship was given only to poor Muslim girls or meritorious ones. When this author sought to point this out to him, Akhilesh insisted that his decision was 'politically right'. Predictably, this decision came as an easy handle for the BJP to polarize Hindus.

It was rather late in the day that Akhilesh realized his blunder so he altered the policy by extending the scholarship to all girls. However, that was apparently a little late in the day. Surprisingly, Akhilesh's decision received instant approval from his peers in the SP who were far more mature leaders who could have foreseen that any policy like this would blatantly reflect its appeasement bid, and could prove to be counterproductive.

Even a naive politician was expected to have the sense to understand how BJP was actively pursuing its policy of Hindu–Muslim divide. Therefore, it was grossly inept of Akhilesh to provide the BJP additional fuel on a platter.

Finally, the BJP succeeded in getting its political mileage, and the party did earn dividends when the outcome of the election unfolded itself, taking the BJP tally to an unprecedented 324 seats in a 403-member Legislative Assembly. Sure enough, it was way ahead of all estimates—not only of psephologists but even that of insider BJP analysts. It was only the poll estimates of *India Today's* Chanakya that came right, even as everyone initially felt that they had gone overboard in making their calculations. And while everyone was wondering how the entire opposition could get virtually wiped out, something was cooking in the backyards of Yogi Adityanath's bastion—the Gorakhnath temple. Yogi was planning how to muscle his way to grabbing the ultimate seat of power in Lucknow.

He was busy doing a rough headcount of committed supporters among the newly elected MLAs, who were ready to swear by his name and would be ready to stand behind him under all circumstances. A few from the neighbourhood of Gorakhpur were clearly the ardent followers of the Gorakhnath temple, so their loyalty could not be questioned. The idea was to identify a support base that could help to raise his bargaining power for the top job.

At a juncture when the party had romped home with a record mandate, Narendra Modi—widely perceived as the architect of the historic victory—was surely not in a position to afford even a whiff of dissent.

Knowing Yogi Adityanath and his assertive ways, a vocal insolence could not be ruled out. After all, Yogi was known to have gone to the extent of fielding parallel candidates against the BJP nominees in at least two Vidhan Sabha elections in Uttar Pradesh in the past.

Adityanath's rise in politics is solely attributable to his communal utterances, which have given him space in national politics too. In fact, that was what gave the party a huge edge in western Uttar Pradesh in 2017, where he succeeded in forging a sharp communal divide and polarizing Hindus—more particularly the OBCs in that region.

Yogi Adityanath was appointed mahant on 14 September 2014, after the death of his guru Mahant Avaidyanath who had already laid down a political path for the math. However, it was Yogi who, over the past two decades, got down to expand this political base by converting the large poverty-ridden expanse of 'poorvanchal' (eastern Uttar Pradesh) into what is often described as his 'Hindutva laboratory'.

There is much speculation that despite murmurs in the party, the RSS 'persuaded' Modi and Amit Shah, who were keen to appoint a leader with a 'good governance' image, to accept Yogi as the chief minister. Several reasons were given for Yogi getting precedence over other names that were in the reckoning for the top job in Uttar Pradesh. Insiders claim that it was after a prolonged debate that the BJP–RSS leadership zeroed in on his name for a variety of reasons.

The move was aimed at impressing upon the electorate that BJP was not a Brahmin-centric party anymore. And since Yogi (a Rajput) was known to have brought into his Gorakhnath temple fold many OBCs and Dalits, his elevation to the top job in the state was expected to send a positive message to them as well. Sure enough, a large chunk of the non-Yadav OBCs as well as non-Jatav Dalits did switch loyalties to the

BJP in the 2017 Assembly election, leaving the SP and BSP gasping for breath.

Yogi was also seeking recognition for having contributed heavily in the polarization of the Hindu vote by letting loose the otherwise eastern Uttar Pradesh-centric HYV right across the state, particularly in the communally charged western Uttar Pradesh districts. Adityanath's strategy was largely limited to building a neo-Hindutva that encompassed the lower castes, while maintaining a somewhat anti-Brahmin and a staunchly anti-Muslim stance.

The love–hate relationship between Yogi and the BJP stretched back to 2002 when he supported Dr Radha Mohan Das Agarwal as a candidate of the Akhil Bharat Hindu Mahasabha (ABHM) against Shiv Pratap Shukla, who was a cabinet minister in the then Kalyan Singh government. Agarwal won the elections but later joined the BJP.

Adityanath's popularity as a firebrand Hindutva leader in eastern Uttar Pradesh forced the BJP to keep him in good humour, even as it tried in vain not to let him gain an upper hand.

Before the 2007 Assembly elections, the monk politician again flexed his muscles and threatened to field 70 candidates in eastern Uttar Pradesh under the banner of ABHM. Yogi Adityanath was even alleged to have silently worked against the BJP candidates in the 2009 parliamentary elections, leading to the party's defeat.

According to Sudha Pai and Sajjan Kumar:

Adityanath has propagated a form of grassroots communalism which has struck a chord in eastern UP, giving him a Robin Hood image. Today, he holds *janta durbars* to resolve people's problems and is viewed as the protector of the 'middle' and 'lower' castes, including the business community. Even Muslims make requests at his durbar, which points to his complete control, particularly in north Poorvanchal in the stretch from Gorakhpur to Bahraich, though in recent years he has extended his sway over the entire eastern region. The goal of the BJP–RSS is not only to win elections but to make India more Hindu. The idea is not to have large riots, but slowly to make Hindutva acceptable in the eyes of the common man and render the Muslim as the 'other', in which the yogi has been very successful through long-term mobilisation, patronage and work among the people. The RSS has found him very successful in this venture and making him chief minister sends a message to the people and the party workers about the goals of the BJP.[9]

What goes to his credit is that he has never allowed his HYV to become subservient to the BJP. Rather, every time there was a conflict of interest between the two organizations, Yogi managed to have his way with the BJP leadership. Write Pai and Kumar,

By making him the chief minister, the BJP and RSS hope to 'contain and control' the yogi, yet use him to consolidate its hold over the rising, upwardly mobile, non-Brahmin elite which is visible today in UP and within the party. The yogi is useful to the party at this political juncture and there has perhaps been a negotiated settlement that he will follow the path laid out by the leadership; it remains to be seen whether he will keep to this understanding.

They hold the view that Yogi rose to prominence in the late 1990s, 'by replacing the earlier "upper"-caste mafia of the 1980s such as Harishankar Tiwari (a Brahmin) and Virendra Pratap Shahi (a Rajput) who dominated the politics of the region. This mafia had control over government tenders, vast patronage and connections with political parties, but no communal linkages.'

According to them,

> The decline of this mafia provided space to the yogi, leading to a shift from caste-centric mafiadom to religious criminalization. This was possible as Yogi had two advantages: he was a Rajput during a period when "upper"-caste dominance was being challenged and he has successfully forged an alliance with the 'lower' castes – the OBCs and Dalits – to maintain his dominance.

Eventually, when Yogi Adityanath was fielded as a 26-year-old, saffron-clad lieutenant of the head of Gorakhnathpeeth in 1998, he won hands down. Besides being seen as inheritor of the religious legacy of his 'guru' Mahant Avaidyanath, who had enjoyed undisputed mass following in the region, Yogi not only succeeded in decimating the erstwhile mafia but also rose as a dominant political force, which came in handy to communalize the politics of the entire region.

According to Pai and Kumar, 'In March 2011, a documentary film *Saffron War—Radicalization of Hinduism* accused Yogi Adityanath of promoting communal disharmony through a "Virat Hindustan" rally in rural Uttar Pradesh.'

However, in an obvious bid to strike a caste balance, BJP chief Amit Shah and Prime Minister Narendra Modi had two deputy chief ministers of their choice appointed—to fulfill both caste as well as the 'development' agenda. Word was systematically spread that it was the chief minister himself who sought two deputies—though they had actually been aspirants for the top job. While deputy chief minister Keshav Prasad Maurya represented the OBCs, Dinesh Sharma was brought in to balance the aspirations of Brahmins, who at the end of the day could not be ignored. As for Rajputs, Yogi was there himself, even though his lineage was from the hills (now Uttarakhand).

A completely raw hand with no past experience at all, Maurya got the prized slot of deputy chief minister solely because of his OBC background, as well as his proximity to Amit Shah. Merit of any kind was surely not a consideration. Having never held any position in the party hierarchy, he manoeuvred his way to directly don the mantle of BJP state president just before Uttar Pradesh went to poll. His only credential was that of being a one-time protege of the VHP supremo, the late Ashok Singhal. And his claim to fame was essentially because he ran an anti–cow slaughter organization, that did little to earn any credibility. Rather, there were allegations that his organization was often, ironically, involved in baling out rogues engaged in cow smuggling.

Dinesh Sharma, the other deputy chief minister, was in sharp contrast to Maurya. He came to the post with a proven track record—both as the party's Brahmin face, as also two stints as Lucknow city mayor, a position he was bestowed upon after years of professorship in the commerce faculty of Lucknow University. Sharma has not only established himself as a loyal party worker with deep roots in the RSS for two generations, but also as a man of integrity and as someone who had Atal Behari Vajpayee's blessings.

Those who advocated for Yogi Adityanath argued that the Yogi was a 'no nonsense' man with a corruption-free track record. He was, therefore, expected to provide clean governance and would be able to maintain good control over the state's inefficient, caste-ridden and corrupt bureaucracy.

Yogi vehemently opposed the BJP's move to induct former BSP minister Babu Singh Kushwaha, an accused in the Rs 8,000 crore National Rural Health Mission (NRHM) scam during the Mayawati-led BSP regime.[10] 10 He claimed that the NRHM scam had hurt the interest of eastern Uttar Pradesh the most, as several children had died in the region due to lack of proper medication. The other reason why he opposed Kushwaha's entry into the party was that the latter was under investigation for large-scale corruption.

'We raised the issue of corruption inside and outside Parliament. Entry of corrupt leaders from SP and BSP would have dented our fight against corruption,' said Yogi defending his stand against Kushwaha.[11] Significantly, it was only when Adityanath threatened that he won't campaign for the BJP candidates that the party dropped Kushwaha like a hot potato.

But the manner in which some BJP leaders were trying to run the state through remote control shortly after Yogi became the chief minister was becoming increasingly visible. BJP's organization secretary Sunil Bansal, who was brought in from Rajasthan, was a glaring example of that remote control, and there was precious little that the chief minister was able to do to keep the powerful man's undue influence at bay.

Evidently, Modi and Shah played a big gamble, specially since the crucial 2019 Lok Sabha elections were not far away. Perhaps their urge to blend the twin agenda of development and Hindu consolidation prompted them to go ahead. The way things were, it seemed that the promise of bringing development to the state would continue to remain a distant dream, since the inherent passion for Hindu polarization had propped up intermittently. After all, who is not aware that the mandate the party received, both in the 2014 Lok Sabha as well as in 2017 Uttar Pradesh Assembly elections was substantially attributable to the polarization?

According to Sudha Pai, 'The victory of the BJP in the 2017 assembly elections has put India on the path of a majoritarian democracy, in which a strong and developed Hindu nation is to be created.'[12]

Yogi Adityanath always blamed Muslims for communal violence. Spelling out his accusations, he said at an election rally:

> [T]rend in riots in different parts of the country shows that there is less communal tension in places where Muslim population is 10–20 per cent. Wherever their population is between 20–40 per cent, the communal tension is grave. And places, where Muslim population is more than 40 per cent, non-Muslims have no place there. They (non-Muslims) are forced to migrate from there, else they are wiped out. We have to accept the truth about what happened in the Kashmir Valley. If we don't we are misleading people . . .[13]

'The way Hindu girls are insulted, I don't think a civilised society would accept it. One community is allowed to spread anarchy. If the government is not doing anything, then the Hindus will have to take matters into their own hands,' Yogi said.[14]

Significantly, it was against such a backdrop that the BJP decided to nominate him as among the party's star campaigners for the March 2017 Assembly elections in Uttar Pradesh.

Soon after he was sworn in as chief minister, while he was in hectic consultation with the BJP bigwigs in New Delhi to finalize the portfolios of his newly appointed ministers, Yogi Adityanath's 84-year-old father Anand Singh Bisht had an important piece of advice for him. 'He will need to take everyone along. Women in burqa have also voted for him. He needs to respect all religions, win their hearts,' *The Times of India* quoted Bisht, as saying.[15]

Bisht, a former forest ranger, asserted that his chief minister son had a huge responsibility towards those who voted in favour of the BJP in support of party's stand on the issue of triple talaq. 'People from all faiths believe BJP and Adityanath can take them on the path of progress. That has to be kept in mind,' he said.

Perhaps the father's words of wisdom had some positive effect on Yogi, which was reflected in his parting speech in the Lok Sabha, in which he vowed to work for development of all sections by creating a 'new structure' of progress.

However, the unexpected appointment of Adityanath as chief minister was met with outrage and disappointment in most quarters, other than the staunch right-wing groups, that hailed the move no end.

In his analysis of the Uttar Pradesh poll results and the choice of Adityanath as chief minister, renowned right-wing journalist and BJP Rajya Sabha member Swapan Dasgupta wrote in the *Hindustan Times*:

The past few days have witnessed an explosion of stupefied bewilderment in India. The Uttar Pradesh election result, followed by the election of Yogi Adityanath as the chief minister, created a wave of disorientation among those deemed opinion makers . . . the BJP followed its 'disruptive' mass outreach with the anointment of Adityanath as the chief minister. This decision has proved too much for the forces of intellectual enlightenment to stomach. The prevailing image of the Mahant of the Gorakhnath temple as one of India's foremost 'communal' monsters, one who went a hundred steps beyond dog whistle polarisation, produced unequivocal outrage. Along with charging Modi and BJP President Amit Shah with hubris, the very fundamentals of democracy were questioned. It has been suggested that the selection of such a controversial saffron-robed sadhu implied, first, an end to the politics of development and, second, the advent of a nasty Hindu rashtra where the safety valves of democracy will be shut . . . For those engaged in the rough and tumble of electoral politics where victory and defeat are occupational hazards, Adityanath will be judged on the strength of his performance rather than in terms of abstruse theory.[16]

In an article on Rediff.com, Editor of the RSS organ *Panchjanya* and former BJP Rajya Sabha member Tarun Vijay wrote, 'The 2017 electoral results in Uttar Pradesh are the result of Hindu liberalism and a free mindset that has refused to come under the bigots for centuries.'[17]

He further wrote:

Yogi Adityanath was kind to invite me last year as the chief guest on the birth anniversary of Mahant Avaidyanath*ji*, his guru.

What I saw at his Gorakhpur Dham was incredible. He runs several degree and polytechnic colleges, the best hospital catering to the poor and a Sanskrit college with free boarding facilities.

The grand temple in his ashram sees maximum number of shops run by Muslims and Muslims have a good presence in his schools and colleges.

There has never been a single incident against any Muslim in his area of influence.

He lamented, 'Pity that journalists shield mullahs in Assam who threaten a young singer, but spend all their abilities trying to create a false perception about a person who happens to be a Hindu monk and someone who commands great popularity.'

Vijay added:

Yogi's UP will be as development oriented as the best Indian states . . . I believe Yogi Adityanath will prove to be the most popular and effective chief minister, overseeing a regime of peace and justice, harsh on wrongdoers and rabble rousers, encouraging those who work for India.

Senior editor of Rediff.com Syed Firdaus Ashraf wrote:

[W]hen Yogi Adityanath was sworn in as Uttar Pradesh chief minister, many secularists and Muslims in my circle exclaimed, 'This is it, this is the end of secular India!'

Some Muslim friends called it the end of the Ganga-Jamuni *tehzeeb* (composite culture) they were brought up in.

Another friend commented that the Muslim vote has become irrelevant in India if you are voting against the Bharatiya Janata Party or Prime Minister Narendra Modi. Social media was abuzz with videos of Adityanath's speech in which he said if a Muslim marries one Hindu woman and converts her, Hindu men will marry 100 Muslim women and convert them . . .[18]

Given this long list of 'accomplishments,' a secular friend asked if it was right to appoint such a man to a high Constitutional position.

'It is the will of the people of UP that they want a BJP government to lead them,' I replied. 'And it is the BJP that decided that Yogi must lead them. So there is no option for Muslims and secularists but to accept him as chief minister.'

'Oh, so you have sold your soul to Yogi,' my friend taunted me.

I didn't know how to respond to my friend's taunt.

International Media Reaction

According to a *New York Times* (*NYT*) report

The choice of Yogi Adityanath—who has been repeatedly accused of stirring anti-Muslim sentiments—to lead Uttar Pradesh, came as a shock to many political observers here, who have become accustomed to the carefully moderated public positions of Prime Minister Narendra Modi in line with his projected image as a pro-development leader and global statesman.[19]

In an editorial dated 23 March 2017, the *NYT* said,

Emboldened by a landslide victory in recent elections in India's largest state, Uttar Pradesh, his party named a firebrand Hindu cleric, Yogi Adityanath, as the state's leader. The move is a shocking rebuke to religious minorities, and a sign that cold political calculations ahead of national elections in 2019 have led Mr Modi's Bharatiya Janata Party to believe that nothing stands in the way of realizing its long dream of transforming a secular republic into a Hindu state.[20]

It added that 'Mr. Adityanath has made a political career of demonizing Muslims.'

The *NYT*'s editorial invited a sharp reaction from the Indian government which 'questioned' the paper's wisdom to write such a piece. 'All editorials or opinions are subjective. This case is particularly so. The wisdom in doubting the verdicts of genuine democratic exercises, at home or abroad, is questionable,' Gopal Baglay, the External Affairs Ministry spokesman said.[21]

An Al Jazeera report while calling him a firebrand in the headline, highlighted his alleged anti-Muslim stand. It also mentioned the time when Yogi Adityanath lauded US President Donald Trump's decision to impose a travel ban on some Muslim-majority countries. 'He has also supported strong laws for cow protection, and said minority groups that oppose yoga should either leave the country or drown themselves in the sea,' stated the report.[22]

The BBC news report focused on the criticism surrounding Yogi's appointment. It mentioned that the opposition leaders had criticized the decision but BJP MPs defended it. The report also quoted Congress leader Manish Tewari. It added, 'Mr Adityanath is widely regarded as a polarising figure because of his well-publicised anti-Muslim comments. The BJP leaders probably believe that their election formula of consolidating the votes of the Hindu majority will help them to sail through the next general elections.'[23]

In his dispatch of 19 March, Douglas Busvine of Reuters wrote:

A saffron-robed Hindu holy man was sworn in on Sunday to lead India's most populous state, sealing what appears to be a shift in course by PM Modi that could redefine the world's largest democracy as a Hindu nation. The choice as Uttar Pradesh CM of Yogi Adityanath, a firebrand Hindu ascetic with a history of agitation against minority Muslims, stunned observers who said it marked a departure from the platform of development for all on which Modi rose to national power in 2014.[24]

According to *The Economist*:

> The unusual choice has raised alarms, not least among Uttar Pradesh's 40-million strong Muslim minority; the BJP won 312 of 403 seats in the state legislature without fielding a single Muslim candidate. Mr Adityanath, who has a long record of bigoted and inflammatory rhetoric, has named just one Muslim to his 43-person cabinet. Some analysts say Mr Modi chose a controversial sectarian as reward for his most ideological followers' crucial grassroots help in the voting. Others say that with his prospects of re-election in 2019 strengthened by winning a state with 220 m people, Mr Modi has less fear of revealing a darker Hindu-nationalist tint.[25]

David Frawley, Padma Bhushan awardee and founder of American Institute of Vedic Studies, backed Adityanath in an article in Daily O. 'Yogi Adityanath's statements have caused some concern with India's media and certainly his views should be carefully studied. Yet many of his comments have been distorted. So it is important to let him clarify his views, and not to go back to old allegations.'[26]

Later in his article Frawley said,

Let us see what Yogi Adityanath and the new BJP rule in UP actually does before casting aspersions. The records of the defeated SP in terms of human rights and law and order issues in UP were abysmal, with many communal clashes. UP under SP was at the bottom of most development indexes as well.

In his column in *The Indian Express*, renowned columnist Pratap Bhanu Mehta of Centre for Policy Research and then vice chancellor of Ashoka University, scathingly described Yogi's appointment 'an odious and ominous development'.[27]

He elaborated thus:

It is odious choice because the BJP has picked someone who is widely regarded as the single most divisive, abusive, polarising figure in UP politics. He is a politician who has, for most of his political career, been the mascot of militant Hindu sectarianism, reactionary ideas, routinised conflict and thuggery in political discourse, and an eco-system where the vilest legitimations of violence are not far away.

It is an ominous development because it sends as clear a signal as possible to send at this time; the already accomplished political fact of the marginalisation of minorities in UP and elsewhere will now be translated into a programme of their cultural, social and symbolic subordination . . .

A stronger disapproval followed, 'This is now not a statement just about Uttar Pradesh: It is a statement about the prime minister's inclinations and judgement. In the moment of his political triumph, he has chosen to defeat India.'

Four days after Yogi Adityanath's destiny moved him from his priestly duties to manage the affairs of the state, veteran journalist Chaitanya Kalbag asked in *The Economic Times* (of 23 March), 'Can you imagine Pope Francis being named the President of Brazil, which has the world's largest Roman Catholic population (and the same number of people as in Uttar Pradesh)?'[28] Answering the question himself, Kalbag said, 'That is not going to happen, because the Western way of thinking says there ought to be a separation of the temporal and the spiritual, the Church and the State.'

This is what R. Jagannathan, Editor of *Swarajya* magazine had to say in defence of Adityanath and his elevation as chief minister:

> The election of Yogi Adityanath as the Bharatiya Janata Party's (BJP) choice to head Uttar Pradesh may be a risky one, given his firebrand Hindutva credentials, but he ticks all the right boxes when it comes to delivering on Narendra Modi's 2019 agenda and the development expectations of the state's electorate . . . As a Hindutva icon, Adityanath has the advantage of having his right flanks covered. He does not have to look over his shoulder to see whether his decisions have the approval of the Rashtriya Swayamsewak Sangh.[29]

The response of most political parties was predictable with regard to Yogi Adityanath's selection as the chief minister.

Senior Congress leader Veerappa Moily said, 'It is a big assault on secularism in the country. Maybe, the BJP or RSS would like to endorse their cause of Hinduism. India is not Hinduism. Hinduism is not India.'[30] The party's chief spokesperson Randeep Surjewala said, 'Excessive delay in arriving at a decision as also the compulsion to create two posts of Deputy chief ministers reflects a bitter conflict to share spoils of power despite overwhelming majority of over 300 MLAs.'[31]

CPM leader Brinda Karat said, 'It is clearly the RSS agenda and Uttar Pradesh is the new experimental field for it. Since it is the victory of RSS (in Uttar Pradesh elections), it has chosen the chief minister.'[32]

The Biju Janata Dal (BJD), which is ruling in Odisha, also questioned the BJP's decision to appoint Yogi Adityanath as Uttar Pradesh chief minister. BJD leader Bhartrahari Mahtab said, 'He never held any administrative post. This is an opportunity for him to prove his mettle. I hope he lives up to the expectations of all the people in Uttar Pradesh.'[33]

Trinamool Congress, which is ruling West Bengal and has no presence in Uttar Pradesh, was also wary of the BJP's decision. TMC leader Saugata Roy said, 'The BJP is in majority and it is their prerogative as to whom they name as the Chief Minister.

But it is evident that the BJP wants to pursue a strong Hindutva line in Uttar Pradesh.'[34]

Shiv Sena, BJP's ally at the Centre (and adversary in some states), too, had a piece of advice for Yogi Adityanath. Shiv Sena leader Sanjay Raut said, 'The controversial remarks won't work now as he is chief minister of the Uttar Pradesh, India's largest state. If he continues to make such remarks, it will create chaos in the state. Now he should talk about development.'[35]

Senior BJP leader Subramaniam Swamy tweeted: 'Yogi Adityanath as CM is the best answer to Uttar Pradesh people's prayer for a bright future.'[36]

To top it all, Yogi Adityanath himself asserted, 'In Uttar Pradesh, the new model of development will be based on "Sabka Saath, Sabka Vikas".' He emphasizes, 'My government will be for everyone, not specifically for any caste or community . . . We will work for development of all sections and castes and create a new structure of progress.' And made it a point to add, 'My government will create a new model of development under the guidance of Prime Minister Narendra Modi.'[37]

5

HINDU YUVA VAHINI

Within two months of Yogi's ascension, red flags began to be raised over the 'outsider' HYV's growing clout in the state. The issue was first raised at the state executive meeting in May 2017 by Deputy Chief Minister Keshav Prasad Maurya, who was then state BJP president. Without naming the Vahini, he said that 'outsiders' were getting preferential treatment in the government while the party cadre was being ignored. This, he warned, was 'unacceptable' and described the Vahini as a threat to the BJP.[1]

The trigger, apparently, was a scuffle between the Vahini and BJP workers over putting up of flags in Basti town, where a meeting to review the state's law and order was scheduled. Although the BJP workers managed to remove the HYV flags, Yogi warned them not to take law into their hands.

The increasing complaints against ochre scarf–wearing Vahini men harassing people in the name of Hindutva and cow vigilantism also prompted Yogi to claim that they were 'imposters' in Vahini disguise. He warned that he would expose those who were using saffron to malign his government.

Earlier, soon after taking over as chief minister, Yogi Adityanath had instructed his party's legislators, MPs and fringe elements not to take law into their hands. The BJP and RSS interpreted the warning as being directed against them and meant to project them as troublemakers.

With Yogi and Maurya striking discordant notes over the flexing of muscles by the Vahini, a coordination meeting became necessary. Maurya, who has been a functionary of the VHP, found support from the all-powerful RSS. The RSS's reservation was conveyed at a coordination meeting in Lucknow on 14 May 2017. The meeting was attended by the Sangh's Krishnagopal, Chief Minister Yogi Adityanath, BJP's national general secretary (organization) Ramlal, and Deputy Chief Ministers Keshav Maurya and Dinesh Sharma, besides the all-powerful Sunil Bansal, who while holding a low-key office of state BJP organization general secretary, is known as the eyes and ears of Amit Shah.

Another coordination meeting was held in October 2017 and the issue of outsiders getting preferential treatment flagged. A national daily reported:

Sources have told *The Indian Express* that the RSS top brass is believed to have conveyed to Yogi their reservations regarding an organisation (read HYV), on the ground, that runs 'parallel' to both the RSS and the BJP. More so, when several complaints have come from across the state against aggressive HYV workers flexing their political—and, in some cases, physical—muscles in several 'communal' incidents over the past two months . . . Sources said that a prant pracharak in the meeting complained that leaders of parties and organisations other than RSS offshoots and BJP were given space in government committees in corporations and boards. Sources said that CM was asked to 'adjust' eligible and dedicated workers of RSS offshoots and from the BJP.[2]

This was the second coordination meeting between Yogi, RSS and the BJP in a month, the first having been held in April. The Sangh's prant pracharak was especially upset that leaders of the party, its allies and frontal organizations other than 'the RSS affiliates and BJP were being given space in government committees and public undertakings'. The party cadre and workers, it was emphasized, needed to be given 'priority'.

The BJP and the RSS also expressed concern that muscle-flexing by the HYV would adversely impact the government's image and consequently the party's prospects before the 2019 Lok Sabha elections. The Sangh feared that if allowed to grow unchecked, the Vahini could become a strong parallel Hindu force like the Shiv Sena in Maharashtra and, therefore, an unwelcome challenger.[3]

In April 2017, Yogi reportedly held separate meetings with Vahini and RSS workers, and urged Vahini members to maintain 'decency', not use saffron as the party's colour, monitor government work, flag any discrepancies to their BJP colleagues, and not misbehave with any government official.[4]

The ties between BJP and HYV had worsened during the 2012 elections to the Uttar Pradesh Assembly when the BJP denied tickets to those recommended by Yogi. In retaliation, the HYV fielded candidates against the BJP on several seats. Yogi had then dismissed as 'mischievous' allegations of fielding Hindu Vahini candidates against BJP nominees.

Even in 2017, the Vahini rattled the BJP by fielding six candidates for the Assembly poll before Adityanath intervened.

The Vahini's State President Sunil Singh told the media, 'We have fielded candidates on six seats spread over three districts in the eastern region of the state.' Three of the seats were in Kushinagar district (Padrauna, Kasya, Khadya), two in Maharajganj district (Pharenda and Siswa) and Paniyara in Gorakhpur district. Alleging that their leader had been 'insulted' by the BJP, HYV claimed to have identified 64 seats in the region to field its candidates.[5]

The HYV was demanding that Yogi be declared chief ministerial candidate and resented that only two out of the ten names recommended by the monk-politician were given tickets by the BJP. Yogi himself kept a distance from HYV's announcements. 'It is a social organization and there are no plans before it to join politics,' Yogi said.[6] He also warned HYV members that action would be taken against all those venturing into politics 'as this is illegal and against the ideals and policies of the HYV'.

Days after this warning, the head priest of Gorakhnath temple sacked Sunil Singh, the HYV president and his once-close lieutenant, from his post. With its patron Yogi now holding the reins of power, it was natural for the Vahini to go on a membership drive. It began to attract new members in large numbers, which seemed to have unnerved the BJP. The sharpest increase in enrolment for Vahini membership was witnessed in western Uttar Pradesh. In Meerut alone, Vahini's membership jumped from a few hundred to thousands in just a week.

'At this rate we would have enlisted 4000 members by the end of this month (March, 2017) from just Meerut alone,' Sachin Mittal, district president of the outfit was quoted as saying. The HYV's state office in-charge told the *Indian Express*, 'In the past only around 500 to 1000 people used to contact

HYV for membership in a month. But after 19 March, since Mahantji (Yogi Adityanath) was sworn in as chief minister, we are receiving membership requests, including over phone, from more than 5000 people every day.'[7]

The increase in violence in the name of love jihad and cow protection, forced the HYV to stop its membership drive for one year. The HYV's state general secretary P.K. Mall stated that his organization would not accept any new membership for the next six months. There was an 'exponential' growth in HYV's membership after Yogi became chief minister, Mall claimed.

However, the Vahini website said that online membership was open, but it was to be given only after a thorough scrutiny of the applicant. 'Online registration is open but membership will be allowed after proper verification which may take six months,'[8] Mal said in a statement.

With hundreds of membership applications reaching the Vahini office daily, its office-bearers said that they found it difficult to sift the genuine from the fake, and hence decided on a year-long freeze on new recruitment. The freeze was said to be a consequence of Keshav Prasad Maurya's outburst against 'outsiders' in the presence of the then BJP National President Amit Shah on the concluding day of the executive committee meeting.

Yogi's April 2017 advice to his 'sena' went unheeded when Vahini members purportedly lynched a 60-year-old Muslim man in Bulandshahr in May 2017, for allegedly helping his relative elope with a Hindu woman.[9] Following a statewide uproar, the police arrested Vahini suspects involved in the incident.

Yogi defended the HYV and denied its hand in the incident. 'There is no remedy if someone makes up his mind that he has to blame a particular outfit,' he said.[10]

Coming out in defence of his outfit, Mal said that those arrested were 'framed'. A cautious Mal painted a savvy image of his outfit. 'We are now in the process of visiting districts and holding meetings to check infiltration in the ranks. Yogi ji's message is clear: the Vahini needs to be an instrument of delivery mechanism of government schemes and not a self-appointed custodian. Such acts will not be tolerated,' he said.[11] This became necessary as, according to Mal, goons from non-BJP parties were carrying out violent acts to tarnish its image.

Rakesh Rai, who was appointed executive president of the HYV after his predecessor Sunil Singh was sacked from the post, told News 18 in an interview that Chief Minister Yogi Adityanath convened a meeting of Vahini's leaders at his residence on 6 August 2019. Rai said that Yogi asked them not to heed the rumours about them and work to end differences between various sections of society and take the government's achievements to the 'last person' of the state. The chief minister is also said to have given them a target of planting 10,000 saplings in every village.[12]

Despite Yogi giving it a clean chit, the Vahini image will be hard to refurbish because of the infamy it has acquired over the years.

Hindu Yuva Vahini Is Formed

Yogi's narrow victory margin in the 1999 parliamentary elections must have left him a worried man. The ascetic had won his debut election from the Gorakhpur constituency in 1998 by a margin of 26,206 votes. A year later, in 1999, when the then Atal Behari Vajpayee government fell and the nation went to poll again, his winning margin was reduced to a paltry 6,279 votes, putting a question mark on the young Yogi's appeal.

The narrow victory margin was also worrisome because Gorakhpur was the constituency nurtured by Yogi Adityanath's guru Mahant Avaidyanath, who represented the seat in Lok Sabha in 1970, 1989, 1991 and 1996. The Gorakhnath temple followers and the hardline Hindutva approach provided Adityanath with a captive voter population to cash on.

After his first electoral victory, Yogi created a Gau Raksha Manch. Though it was meant for the protection and care of cows, it was perceived by some as a tool to drive a wedge between communities to consolidate his position. The electoral jolt in 1999 made Yogi realize that cows were not effective in arousing religious sentiments and he needed 'to develop a wider base among Hindus'[13] to mobilize voters in his favour.

However holy a cow may be, it is still a symbol of docility if one goes by the oft-used simile in rural areas—woh toh gau kee tarah hai (he/she is docile like a cow). The ascetic, on the other hand, needed a macho image that would be in keeping with the image of the order to which Yogi belonged.

So, on a cold February morning in 1999, Yogi along with members of Gau Raksha Manch allegedly reached a Muslim-dominated Panchrukhia village in the neighbouring Maharajganj district in a fleet of cars, where they incited Hindus and dug up graves. When the Mahant's fleet was obstructed by a group of SP workers who had gathered to court arrest in protest of the BJP government of the state, the protesters were beaten up and fired at, injuring one of them.[14]

On 10 February 1999, Maharajganj police registered a case against Yogi and others for murder, trespassing a Muslim graveyard, defiling a place of worship, rioting, promoting enmity between two religious groups and carrying deadly weapons. That day, a militant Hindu monk was born. The attack on the minority village did not, however, bring electoral gains. Three years later, BJP lost power in the state to the SP.

Even as Yogi mulled over the options to boost his electoral prospects, his moment came in February 2002 when Sabarmati Express coaches were set afire by a mob at the Godhra railway station, killing 59 pilgrims returning from Ayodhya after a religious ceremony. Carnage followed in Gujarat. Over 2,000 people, mostly Muslims, were massacred. As the divide between Hindus and Muslims became disconcertingly wide, Yogi gave the slogan, 'UP bhi Gujarat banega, Padrauna shuruaat karega' (Uttar Pradesh will now also become Gujarat, the process will start from Padrauna, a small district in eastern Uttar Pradesh).[15]

The first thing which Yogi did was to change the name of Gau Raksha Manch to Hindu Yuva Vahini, whose mandate now went beyond cows to protecting Hindus and responding to any act which they perceived as a threat to Hindu religion.

Capitalizing on the 'nationwide split between Hindus and Muslims after the riots in Gujarat', Yogi hit the ground anew. He expanded its jurisdiction beyond cows to anything and everything that could project minorities as the enemies of Hindus.'[16]

Adityanath's organization of 'social and cultural workers' came into existence in April 2002, a couple of months after the pogrom in Gujarat. The auspicious day of Lord Ram's birth, Ram Navami, was chosen to launch the force that would take on Muslims using violent means to protect Hindu culture. According to Dhirendra Jha, the HYV was formally launched in 2002 on Ram Navami day 'in a public meeting in Kushinagar'.

According to Sunil Singh, former HYV president, 'In the beginning, there was a debate on the name. The first suggestion was to call the new organization Hindu Sena . . . Finally it was decided that it would be Hindu Yuva Vahini.'[17]

Although the HYV was founded as a social and cultural organization dedicated to Hindutva and nationalism, little, however, is known about its social work, barring 'sahbhoj' (common feast) by HYV members with Scheduled Caste and Scheduled Tribe families; unless its vigilantism to protect Hindu culture is counted as one. The Vahini came to be feared in eastern and western Uttar Pradesh for the violent methods it used in the name of cow protection, love jihad and ghar wapsi (reconversion of Muslims and Christians to Hinduism).

According to the Vahini's new website, 'It is a fierce social and cultural organization dedicated to Hindutva and nationalism.'[18] Under 'Declaration', the site says, 'We pledge to join hands and work together to: 1. The integration of and mutual good faith within the massive Hindu society, through the complete abolition of the differentiation between touchable and untouchable and high-low, promote the harmonious development of society. 2. To protect cows by opening gaushalas all over India.'

Before it was sanitized, the organization's constitution as given on its website said, 'Hindu implies Vedic, Buddhists, Jains, Sikhs, Nagas and others, subscribing to the Hindu culture. He/she must believe in and have respect for "Aum", oppose cow slaughter, believe in rebirth and have full faith in Hindu religious texts.'[19]

To qualify for the Vahini's code of conduct, its constitution enjoined upon a Hindu to pave the way for an honourable

return of all those 'brethren' who have left Hinduism on their
own, out of fear, due to allurements or ignorance, or were forced
to leave due to ill-treatment by other Hindus. It is this provision
which prompted many Vahini activists to start 'ghar wapsi'
programme, mainly targeting the Christians, though Muslims
also were in their Hindutva cross hairs.

At one of the meetings in Siddharthnagar, Uttar Pradesh,
a Vahini leader told his audience that according to his vision
of Hindu Rashtra, Muslims will be reduced to second-rate
citizens which would eventually lead to their voting rights being
forfeited.

Mau Riots

In 2005, communal clashes broke out during Dussehra festival
in Mau, a town of weavers who are largely Muslims. As it also
happened to be the month of Ramzan, the district administration
in the communally-sensitive district was on the alert. As Mau
was the territory of mafia-turned-politician Mukhtar Ansari and
the HYV, too, had a significant presence there, the ingredients
made for a volatile situation.

The immediate trigger was playing of songs on loudspeakers
during a Ramlila function which clashed with the time of prayers
being offered by Muslims. After objections from Muslims, some
Hindus agreed to stop the loudspeakers, but the next day a
group of Vahini activists led by its prominent leaders broke the
truce. In the melee that followed the snatching of the equipment
by Muslims, one Vahini leader opened fire. Five Muslims were
injured. The situation turned ugly thereafter, and the communal
frenzy left 18 dead. Officially, 8 people died and 37 were injured
in the clashes.

Cases were registered against Mukhtar Ansari, the Qaumi
Ekta Dal leader and BJP MLC Ramji Singh, implying that
Adityanath had no role in the riots.

An investigation by a civil society group claimed that
HYV, and its leader Yogi Adityanath, had allegedly incited
violence. However, BJP leaders, as it was apparent, seemed to
have supported the HYV. Its National Vice-President Kalyan
Singh, State President Keshari Nath Tripathi, and leader of
Opposition in the state legislature, Lalji Tandon, claimed that
the government's appeasement of Muslims was responsible
for the violence and blamed Muslim strongman and SP MLA
Mukhtar Ansari for provoking it.[20]

Hindu–Muslim Clashes in Gorakhpur

In January 2007 clashes broke out between Hindus and Muslims
during a Muharram procession in Gorakhpur. Sensing that the
situation was delicate, the district magistrate (DM) advised
Adityanath, who was then an MP, not to visit the area for fear
of aggravating tension.[21]

Adityanath initially heeded the DM's advice but
subsequently defied the order and reached the site, where he
announced a dharna along with some of his followers. Although
the sit-in was supposed to be non-violent, provocative speeches
inflamed passions and some of the men set a mazaar (tomb)
on fire. Curfew had to be imposed to control the worsening
situation. Adityanath defied the curfew order and was arrested.

His brief imprisonment only added fuel to fire. Vahini
activists allegedly burnt some coaches of the Mumbai–Gorakhpur
Godan Express in retaliation. Riots broke out in Gorakhpur.
Ten persons were killed. Several mosques, houses and vehicles

were razed. 'This was by no means the first riot in which the
HYV was clearly involved. In fact communal riots became
unusually frequent in Gorakhpur and its neighbourhood after
the formation of HYV . . .' writes Dhirendra Jha.[22]

The HYV's guiding mantra is Adityanath's 2005 speech,
as recorded in an hour-long documentary, *Saffron War—
Radicalisation of Hinduism,* by Rajiv Yadav, Shahnawaz Alam
and Lakshman Prashad. In it, he can be heard threatening to
avenge the killing of even one Hindu.[23] In his inflammatory
speech Adityanath declared that he won't allow tazia processions
in the entire Gorakhpur district. While exhorting his followers
to get cracking, he roared, 'We will use them to burn Holi in
celebration'.

The game plan, it is said, was to follow the Gujarat template.
To facilitate identification of minority community, he is alleged
to have asked Hindus to fly saffron flags atop their houses.

HYV: Yogi's Unique Creation

The HYV is not an offshoot of the VHP nor is it an affiliate of
the RSS. It was raised by Yogi to wield his authority in eastern
Uttar Pradesh as a powerful Hindu chieftain.

The idea of an army which would be only at his command
may have taken root in his mind after the 1999 election results
but it took some time to actualize. Existing Hindu outfits like
the Bajrang Dal, Dharm Jagran Samanvay Samiti and the Hindu
Mahasabha were aggressive but were directly or indirectly linked
with the BJP, the RSS or the VHP.

Yogi did not want his band of Hindu sena to be beholden to
anyone other than him. He wanted his Hindu force to not only
make him invincible in Gorakhpur but to also implement his

ideas, forcefully if needed. In short, it was created to give him a more distinct muscular identity.

In pursuance of that objective, Vahini was kept outside the purview of the Sangh Parivar and the BJP, a permanent irritant to both, despite its leader representing the saffron party in the Lok Sabha and subsequently as chief minister of Uttar Pradesh.

With Hindu Mahasabha, Bajrang Dal and other fringe groups also indulging in violent activities there seemed to be a dangerous race between them and the Vahini to grab headlines and TV footage. Somewhere along the way, Vahini lost track of the harmonious development of society visualized in its constitution, as ghar wapsi and love jihad began to dominate its agenda.

The Yuva Vahini, as per its constitution which was available on its earlier website, consists of four categories of members. It has Yogi as the chief patron, lifetime members, active members and special invitees. The well-structured organization has a 25-member executive committee with a chairman at the top and a media in-charge at the lowest rung. The HYV's constitution specifies their rights and duties. One of the tasks assigned to the chairman is to acquire movable and immovable property for the organization and also maintain it.

The Vahini has a state-level working committee, a district-level working committee, a block working committee and a working committee each at the nyaya panchayat and village panchayat level. Sunil Singh told the authors in a telephonic conversation that the old Vahini 'having been wound up, its website also has been removed'.

He claimed it was done after Amit Shah told Adityanath that 'sangathan mein sangathan anushasanheenta hogee' (an organization within an organization will amount to indiscipline). He also claimed that Varun Gandhi and Keshav Prasad Maurya (one of the two deputy chief ministers) were also told to fold up their outfits formed outside the purview of the BJP.

Quoting Adityanath, Rohini Mohan wrote in *Tehelka News* on 14 February 2009: 'When I speak thousands listen . . . when I ask them to rise and protect our Hindu culture, they obey. If I ask for blood, they will give me blood.' According to Mohan, 'to channelise these energies he founded the Hindu Yuva Vahini, a radical and violent group consisting mainly of unemployed youth and small time criminals who pledge to serve "Yogiji" and destroy his enemies, the non-Hindus'.[24]

Not very long ago, in 2002, when he founded the Vahini, Yogi could not have imagined that barely a decade and a half later, his own brainchild would become a cause of worry for him.

No sooner than he became the chief minister of Uttar Pradesh in 2017, the Vahini went into an overdrive. Largely formed of young men, this 'private saffron army' began to be seen on the forefront of all that was going wrong in the state.

What began with the Vahini's self-styled cow vigilante aggression, that manifested itself in the gruesome lynching of Akhlaq Ahmed in Dadri (in September 2015) on a wild accusation of storing beef in his fridge, continued in other forms: the 'anti-Romeo' squads, the moral policing in the name of combating love jihad and a tirade against suspected religious conversions.

Yogi's Vahini activists soon became notorious for taking law into their hands with impunity. Things turned worse with Vahini's blatant attacks on the police. The most glaring incident was the ransacking of the residence of Saharanpur senior superintendent of police. Vahini activists left no stone unturned to announce to the whole world who they were. And sure enough, the police turned a blind eye to everything until the issue was publicized in the media.

Some restraint became imminent and finally the 45-year-old chief minister is believed to have sent word to his lieutenants to be disciplined. Apparently, that failed to have any impact on them. There was a lull for some time after the two Saharanpur incidents (Hindu–Muslim clash followed by a Thakur–Dalit violence) in May. But by 27 June, a group of Vahini activists chose to flex their muscles once again—this time at a police station in Bareilly, where a case of alleged gang rape was registered against a Vahini volunteer. Two Vahini leaders stormed the Subhash Nagar police station in the town demanding withdrawal of case against their supporter.

A senior police officer is said to have approached his superiors in Lucknow who, in turn, reported the matter to the chief minister. Realizing how his failure to come to grips with the deteriorating law and order in the state was tarnishing the image of his three-month-old government, the chief minister ordered the arrest of both Vahini leaders—Jitendra Sharma and Pankaj Pathak. Evidently, the idea was to send out a message to his youth brigade that 'enough was enough'.

Earlier, Vahini's Meerut district members had gone to the extent of storming into someone's private residence and thrashing a young Muslim for being allegedly found in an obscene position inside a room with a Hindu girl. Accusing the boy of 'intending to convert the girl by trapping her into a love affair', the Vahini's Meerut district chief chose to turn prosecutor and judge himself. While the girl was handed over to her family, shockingly, the local cops booked the young boy for 'committing obscene acts in a public place'.[25]

In yet another incident, Vahini toughs intimidated a group of foreigners who had driven down from Nepal and halted at a church in Maharajganj. They sought to accuse the innocent foreign tourists returning from Nepal after visiting the famous Buddhist centre at Lumbini, of conspiring to 'convert' some Hindus in the church. However, in the absence of any evidence the police allowed the foreigners to go.[26]

At the same time there were a few members who harboured political ambitions. Yet Yogi asserted that is a 'social organization and there are no plans before it to join politics.'[27] He also warned that action would be taken against all those venturing into politics 'as this is illegal and against the ideals and policies of HYV'. It was after this warning that he sacked Sunil Singh.

In view of a series of violent incidents, Yogi felt the need to go in for some drastic steps and summoned P.K. Mal from the Vahini headquarters in Gorakhpur. The latter drove down the next morning along with over a dozen of his core team members, who were accorded a prompt entry into the official Kalidas Marg residence of the chief minister.

But the moment they got an audience with the chief minister, they were in for a huge shock. Unlike in the past when Yogi would give them a mild tongue lashing, which they naturally took lightly, here was a chief minister ready to blast the hell out of them. According to an eyewitness, the Yuva Vahini men received a dressing down they had, perhaps, never experienced before. They were also told to return to Gorakhpur and spread the word around to the entire rank and file that if they failed to behave, they would be dealt with most severely. 'You all are giving a bad name to my government. I will not spare any one of you if you dare take law into your hands,' he warned them.

On the other hand, Sunil Singh, his former trusted lieutenant, turned rebel and formed a parallel outfit, Hindu Yuva Vahini (Bharat), in May 2018. Sunil Singh was elected national president of the newly formed HYV-B at a meeting of its national executive in Lucknow on 13 May.

So upset was he with Yogi that he decided to work against the all-powerful mahant during the Lok Sabha elections of 2019. The new organization was launched because he and some others were sidelined for demanding tickets. He was arrested under the National Security Act after an altercation with the original HYV members in 2018. Upon his release from jail, he told the authors, 'Now I and my workers will destroy BJP in the coming elections . . . ' That, however, did not happen. He could not contest the election as his 'papers were rejected despite their being in order'.

On the eve of voting in Gorakhpur, Singh expressed his helplessness in being unable to meet the authors as the 'police had rounded up his workers and were also restricting his movement'.

As chief patron of the HYV, Yogi Adityanath had appointed Singh its first president in 2002. The social and cultural outfit earned notoriety for using strong-arm tactics to propagate Hindutva, protect cows, tackle love jihad and enforce ghar wapsi. He is a firm believer in an aggressive form of Hindutva.

While Singh's move to challenge Yogi's authority in Gorakhpur and other parts of eastern Uttar Pradesh was crushed, he himself clarified that his organization would only carry forward Yogi's agenda of Hindutva, which was his life's mission with power being only a 'commercial break'.

He told the authors that he would work towards the creation of a Hindu Rashtra, which was also the dream of Mahant Avaidyanath, Yogi's guru. Sunil Singh said that the HYV had moved away from Hindutva, and its members were now more into land grabbing and contractual work from government. According to him, the HYV-B had a presence in all the districts of the state and a sizeable membership.

Meanwhile, HYV's general secretary P.K. Mal alleged that Singh was playing into the hands of SP, and that his organization had nothing to do with either Singh or the HYV-B.

The Vahini activists have been lying low ever since they were chastised by Adityanath. But for how long will they remain tamed is a million-dollar question. After all, it was Yogi who showed them the path of muscular Hindutva politics—that eventually took him to the power pedestal, where any saffron-clad head of a temple trust could never dream of reaching. Surely, taming the tiger has been no mean and easy task.

Though Yogi and Vahini convener P.K. Mal blamed every act of vandalism on 'some saffron scarf wearing scoundrels' with the intent of giving a bad name to the Vahini, they seemed to have no explanation about the common allegation that it was the Vahini activists who drove away Muslim yogis from the precincts of the Gorakhnath temple. It is common knowledge that these Muslim yogis in eastern Uttar Pradesh who donned saffron attire and sang Ram bhajans were an active part of the Gorakhnath temple. The fear of lynch mobs has in fact muted those voices and ensured that Muslim followers of Gorakhnath give up their passion for singing bhajans, which was a unique example of communal amity.[28]

What Yogi and his Vahini practise is contrary to the tenets of Gorakhnath, who was 'against distortions in Brahminism and Buddhism in terms of polytheism and extremism. He laid the foundation of Hindu–Muslim unity and opposed caste discrimination and other evils'.[29] But that is not how Yogi may want to run the Nath order.

6

POLITICO-RELIGIOUS TRANSFORMATION OF AN EGALITARIAN ORDER

How did a sect that inspired someone like Kabir and Guru Nanak to give birth to Sufism, turn into a body that would refuse to look beyond aggressive Hindutva? And what purpose was it serving in doing so? After all, what Gorakhnath (the founder of the Nath sect) preached was a religion beyond religion that also believed in transcending considerations of caste or creed—something that was imbibed by both Kabir and Guru Nanak.

Be it the Nath sect founder Matsyendranath or his most widely known disciple Gorakhnath, who gave birth to the all-important Goraksh Peeth (seat of cow protection) and name to the town we known today as Gorakhpur, they practised true secularism. Gorakhnath always believed in cutting across caste and religious lines.

Gorakhnath encountered several social changes during his period. Islam had already arrived and Muslims were well entrenched within the Indian social ethos. Buddhism had received a setback with the revival of the Brahmanical order. Gorakhnath, therefore, found it convenient to mobilize the disgruntled and socially deprived to get attracted to his ideology that was based essentially on yoga. Interestingly, because of his 'no discrimination' approach he also attracted a number of Muslims to his congregation.

According to renowned Hindi writer and historian Padma Bhushan Hazari Prasad Dwivedi, Gorakhnath revolted against the distortions in Brahminism and Buddhism in terms of polytheism and extremism.[1] 'He laid the foundation of Hindu-Muslim unity and opposed caste discrimination and other evils. As a result members of untouchable castes isolated by the sanatan dharma joined the Nath sect in large numbers. Many of the followers were opposed to the *varna* system,' Dwivedi has pointed out.

No wonder that even to this day there are Muslim yogis, who are devout followers of Gorakhnath, and continue to formally describe themselves as part of the Nath sect. They call themselves devotees of Gorakhnath and Bhartrihari and associate themselves with the Nath sect. Many of them inhabit villages of Gorakhpur, Kushinagar, Deoria, Basti, Sant Kabir Nagar, Azamgarh and Balrampur districts of eastern Uttar Pradesh.

In the past, Muslim yogis were not only seen as regular visitors to the Gorakhnath temple but were also widely known to be organizing 'bhandaras' *in* the temple's precincts. They would also engage in other forms of charity and voluntary service in the temple trust. But several of these Muslim yogis had given up their connections with the temple, largely on account of the tensions created by those heading the temple trust.

The seat of the Nath sect in Gorakhpur showed its first signs of drift from the secular path in 1935, soon after Digvijay Nath became the temple's mahant. He moved heaven and earth to turn the temple into a seat of Hindutva politics. Having done that, it became easy for Digvijay Nath's successor Mahant Avaidyanath as well as the latter's successor Yogi Adityanath to march ahead on the new path. The aggression with which they pushed the new-found agenda led many Muslim Yogis to distance themselves from the sect.

Gorakhnath has been widely hailed through the centuries. Even the twentieth-century spiritual guru Acharya Rajneesh Osho praised him as an unparalleled icon. Osho recalls how he placed Gorakhnath as among India's greatest of spiritual leaders.[2] According to him, when renowned Hindi poet Sumitranandan Pant once asked him to name 12 most important spiritual figures of India, Osho named Krishna, Patanjali, Buddha, Mahavir, Nagarjun, Shankar, Gorakh, Kabir, Nanak, Mira and Ramakrishna. Sumitranandan Pant then told him to cut down the list to seven, five and then four. Osho removed several names but retained that of Gorakhnath. When Pant asked him to further shorten the list and pick only three, Osho refused. Why could he not leave out Gorakh, the poet asked. Osho replied,

> I cannot leave him because Gorakh opened a new avenue in the country and gave birth to a new religion. Without him, there would be no Kabir or Nanak. There would neither be Dadu, nor Wajid, Farid or Meera. The entire Sufi tradition of India is indebted to Gorakh. Nobody equals him in his teachings that lead to the discovery of the inner soul.

Gorakhnath penned down as many as 40 books largely in Sanskrit and a few in Hindi. According to Hazari Prasad Dwivedi, Gorakhnath's Hindi works are in the form of a dialogue between Gorakhnath and his guru Matsyendranath. The shlokas (verses) coined by him reflect his generously secular philosophy.

In his book *Gorakhnath and the Kanphata Yogis*,[3] twentieth-century Cambridge-educated English hymn composer and Anglican clergyman George Weston Briggs puts the number of yogis in India at 214,546 with reference to the 1891 census. In Agra and Awadh province, there were 5,319 Oghars, 28,816 Gorakhnathis and 78,387 yogis. The data also included a large number of Muslim yogis. According to a report from Punjab, the number of Muslim yogis was 38,137 that year.

'According to the census held in 1921, there were 629,978 Hindu yogis, 31,158 Muslims and 141,132 Hindu Fakirs. The census also gave the number of male and female yogis separately. However, in the census conducted in later years, a separate mention of the community was not made,' points out Briggs. He mentions a long list of Muslim yogis residing in different villages of Gorakhpur and in the adjoining districts of eastern Uttar Pradesh.

Recalling his visit to Badgo village in Gorakhpur, social activist Manoj Singh has written in The Wire how activists of Yogi Adityanath's HYV went about opposing the continuance of Muslim yogis in the Gorakhnath tradition. He says,

We reached there and met several young men outside the village. When we asked them about the yogis, they expressed their disdain at the fact that the yogis wore saffron clothes despite being Muslims. They wished that the Muslim yogis would leave this practice. They were all Hindu men, some of whom were members of the Hindu Yuva Vahini.[4]

Singh goes on to write:

> [I]n Badgo village, 75 households belong to Muslims with almost 24 belonging to yogis. Bakshish is one of them. When we met him, he was working in a field. This 35-year-old yogi's father Dilshafi and father-in-law Ali Hasan are yogis too. They taught Bakshish the songs glorifying Bhartrihari and Gopichand as well as Kabir's bhajans. Bakshish does not have any land for farming. He no longer wishes to be a yogi because other members of the community do not like it. He possesses a sarangi which has been with the family for the past two generations but he refused to show it to us. After much enquiry, he informed us that his wife, who has gone to her parents, has locked the sarangi in a room and taken away the key as she does not want him to go out in the streets in her absence singing devotional songs and bhajans.

Singh adds:

> the village head Mukhtar Ahmed also seems to agree that Bakshish and other yogis should end the tradition of singing bhajans and look for other work. He said that he was issuing them job cards so that they leave their sarangis and pick up tools instead. Upon much insistence, Bakshish agreed to sing to us a bhajan which was a folktale about Raja Bhartrihari who left his kingdom to become a sanyasi. He began by humming a stanza in praise of Gorkhnath which he called jhaap . . .

Singh's foray into an adjoining village was even more revealing. He writes:

> We were informed that in a neighbouring village there is a yogi Hameed who sings really well. When we reached Hameed's house, his wife received us. We were told that Hameed passed away some four years ago. Throughout his life he sang bhajans of Gopichand and Bhartrihari. He owned a very old sarangi. When he fell ill, he asked his wife what should be done with the sarangi because the young generation would not take the tradition forward. He handed it to his patidar (distant relative) with the hope that he would continue the tradition. Hameed's son is a hawker who sells utensils.

In eastern Uttar Pradesh, dozens of villages are inhabited by Muslim yogis who, like members of the Nath sect, wear saffron 'gudri' or 'kantha' (robe) and wander through villages singing folklore on their sarangi, narrating how Gopichand and Raja Bhartrihari became sanyasis under the influence of Gorakhnath. Villagers offer them food and money and passionately listen to them while they glorify Gorakhnath in their songs. Singh goes on to add,

> We met Kalu Jogi, a resident of Badgo village while he was singing a folk tale about Bengal's Raja Gopichand. When we told him we were covering a story on the yogi tradition, he reluctantly agreed to sing for us. He was miffed when we asked him to take on his yogi garb. He put down his sarangi and asked, 'Why do you want me to do it? What if something happens?' On being asked, 'What could happen?' he said, 'You will not understand.'

According to Manoj Singh, when after much persuasion he
agreed to play the 'sarangi', his wife rushed out to stop him. He
took some time to convince his wife to let him take the risk of
playing for us.

Interestingly, the 'bhajan' which he sang went as follows:

Arre Ram ke Maai banwa bhejwalu
Bharat ke dehlu rajgaddi
Batao Maai Ram kahiya le aiyya
Arre Patjha bagiya mein phulwo na phulela
Bhanwron ne khilela
Batao Maai Ram kahiya le aiyya

[Hey Mother! You exiled Ram to the forest and gave the
throne to Bharat. I am pained. When will Ram come back?
Nothing gives me joy without him. It seems that flowers
have stopped blooming in the garden; I do not even see a
bee around the flowers; therefore, my mother, please let me
know, when will Ram return?]

According to Singh, in addition to Gopichand–Bhartrihari
folklore, the yogis also sing on request from listeners. Some of
them also sing about Shankar–Parvati's wedding and the Rama
Katha. But the focus always remains Gorakhnath, Gopichand
and Bhartrihari.

Yet another yogi, Qasim, told Manoj Singh how times had
turned for the worse for Muslim yogis:

We are Muslims but we keep the Ramayana in our homes
alongside the Quran. We narrate the tales of Baba Gorakhnath
and his disciples Gopichand and Bharthari. Earlier, we were

only jogis. Nobody asked us whether we were Hindus or Muslims. But nowadays, there is a lot of fear. Wherever we go, we are asked about our religion.

We are afraid that something might go wrong or somebody might ask us why we wearing saffron or singing praises of Gorakhnath on a sarangi? Today, I have picked up the sarangi after 12 years.

Singh also writes that it is believed that the sarangi Muslim yogis play was invented by Gopichand, the son of Bengal's Raja Manikchand who comes from the lineage of the Pallavas.

In his book, Dr Mohan Singh[5] has written a section titled 'Udaas Gopichand Gatha, Gorakhpad' in the form of a dialogue between Gopichand and his mother based on several manuscripts currently available in Punjab University library. Most of the Muslim yogis narrate it in their songs. In some folklores, Gopichand has been portrayed as the king of Bengal. His mother Maynawati took initiation from Gorakhnath and inspired her son to become a yogi after he ascended the throne.

Raja Bhartrihari[6] was married to Sinhalese princess Samdei. After meeting Gorakhnath, Bhartrihari became a yogi. The folklore contains dialogue between Bhartrihari and Samdei. In one of the songs, Samdei remonstrates Bhartrihari for having forsaken the bond of marriage by becoming a yogi.

Singh's article (in the Wire) also talks about 72-year-old yogi Sardar Shah from Kushinagar's Hata village. According to the latter, Muslim yogis set out individually or in groups of four or five and wander in states of Bihar, Jharkhand and West Bengal. He himself travelled long and far when he was younger. Sardar Shah's son and grandson were least interested in carrying forward the family's spiritual path. His son is happier driving a

cab and has absolutely no inclination to spread the Gopichand–
Bhartrihari folklore by playing the sarangi. Left to the son, he
would not allow his father to be risking his life by continuing
to play the sarangi in pursuance of the Gorakhnath tradition.
But Sardar Shah refuses to get cowed down by the alleged
intimidation and plans to continue pursuing the tradition to his
last breath.

In Juharia village of Basti district (barely 50 km from
Gorakhpur), the authors came across yet another family of
Muslim Jogis, who were initially reluctant to talk to journalists.
It was only after much persuasion that the family head Maqbool
agreed to open up. 'Yes, I am a Jogi and I enjoy singing Ram
bhajans and songs devoted to the life and times of Raja Bharthari
and Gopichand,' he admitted.[7]

But to finally cajole him into rendering the bhajans, it again
took some time. After a lot of prodding, he agreed to get into
the traditional clothing of a Jogi—saffron kurta and a matching
lungi. Even convincing him to take out his sarangi from a faded
saffron-coloured soiled cloth bag was not easy. The instrument
looked as worn out and ancient as the bag, yet the melody that
Maqbool created with every move of the bow on the twin strings
was divinely mesmerizing. And the flow of his singing seemed to
be pouring out of his heart.

And once he took off with the first bhajan telling the story
of Raja Bharthari's decision to turn into a hermit, it became
easier to draw more out of him. One after the other, he
rendered as many as seven Ram Bhajans. Eventually his wife
had to intervene to remind him that it was time for him to reach
another village where he was scheduled to perform at a local
function in a Hindu family. 'Well, that is how he makes our
two ends meet', explained the frail 50-year-old wife, who also

hastened to add, 'Now he is the sole breadwinner of the family as neither of our three sons was interested in continuing the traditional Jogi profession.'

However, there was no way that Maqbool would either confirm or deny his association with the Gorakhnath temple. 'I will not say anything on that,' was his persistent reply to any query on his link with the Gorakhnath temple. The only acknowledgement was, 'all of us hold Baba Gorakhnath in very high esteem'.

Gorakhnath's non-Brahmanical order witnessed a smooth expansion through the centuries in eastern Uttar Pradesh largely because of its non-casteist and democratic approach that also believed in cutting across religious lines. Evidently, the order grew because it threw open its doors to the downtrodden Hindu castes who were denied access to upper caste–dominated Hindu temple. Academics in Gorakhpur, who have gone into the depth of Gorakhnath's poetry, point out that the legendary icon rarely mentions Ram.

According to them, he was also against the idea of power. It was nearly eight centuries later that Mahant Digvijaynath turned to politics, and Digvijaynath's successor Mahant Avaidyanath concentrated on consolidating political power, which was further reinforced by Yogi Adityanath.

To mark the beginning of a new trend, it was Mahant Avaidyanath who created the Digvijaynath Smriti Bhawan, which houses 79 life-size statues of holy Hindu men including the Nath panthis as well as spiritual leaders such as Buddha, Kabir and Sant Ravidas. Significantly, each of them stands out as some kind of 'rebel' against the Brahmanical order. The Smriti Bhawan also has a women's section displaying the idols of Sita, Mirabai and others.

Professor Chittaranjan Mishra of Gorakhpur University considers building of Smriti Bhawan as a sharp deviation from the path laid down by Gorakhnath. He is strongly of the view that 'Gorakhnath was against the system of avatars, hence this is clearly not a part of his tradition.' The hall was built in the 1980s in Gorakhpur by the late Mahant Avaidyanath (Yogi Adityanath's guru) to honour his own guru, Digvijaynath. Interestingly, the Gorakhnath temple is perhaps among the rare temples in India where a majority of the successive priests happen to be non-Brahmin. In fact, the last three Mahants have been Thakurs and so is Yogi Adityanath, who evidently has a soft corner for the community.

Digvijaynath, who cast the Goraknath panth into a new mould, switched to active politics in the 1920s, but very skillfully he also retained his religious position as head of the Gorakhnath temple trust. His popularity among the lower castes rose essentially because he advocated the entry of all castes into the temple. And to keep the upper-caste Hindus too in his loop, he made it a point to raise his voice for 'cow protection', which eventually helped him to ensure overall Hindu consolidation in his favour.

In his book *Gita Press and the Making of Hindu India*[8] (on the city's oldest and leading religious publishing house), journalist Akshay Mukul says there was 'a close alliance' between the Mahants of Gorakhnath temple and the Bania-run Gita Press management. Interestingly, once again, it was the downtrodden castes which formed the biggest clientele for these religious books.

Yogi Adityanath's team, however, flatly denies any of this. Dwarka Tiwari, chief manager of the Gorakhnath temple, urges, 'don't see caste and religion everywhere.' However, when confronted with a simple query about how many Brahmins have headed the Gorakhdham math over the centuries, Tiwari cannot give you more than one name—that of Mahant Brahmnath. Yet, he loves to assert that 'the Nath panthis are certainly not anti-Brahmin.' Significantly, no matter how much it may proclaim to be completely open to lower castes, Tiwari cannot name a single lower-caste person to have held a key office in the temple, even as the larger chunk of the following of the math comes from that downtrodden section of society.

The fact of the matter is that ever since the 1920s when Digvijaynath assumed office as mahant, the temple has remained in the hands of upper-caste Thakurs only. On the other hand, it was Brahmnath—a Brahmin chief—who installed Digvijaynath as mahant. But that was a rare case.

Digvijaynath joined the Hindu Mahasabha shortly after Vir Sarvarkar became its president in 1937. He first shot into the spotlight by raising his voice against voting rights to Muslims. Digvijaynath went about calling for withdrawal of voting rights of Muslims until they 'proved their loyalty'.[9] And that was what gave Digvijaynath a prominent place and eventually a seat in Parliament.

Gorakhnath is revered by Hindus and Muslims alike even to this day. Evidently, Gorakhnath was unique in many ways. His mythical existence defies age and cuts across time—when his followers speak of his influence on Kabir, Guru Nanak, Tulsidas as well as on Sant Ravidas, the champion of the cause of lower castes. It was the focus on inclusiveness that attracted the deprived lower-caste Hindus to this sect.

It was around the thirteenth century that a group of yogis began to form a community around the teachings and narratives of Gorakhnath. The community was not limited to Hindus. The doors were thrown open to Buddhists, Jain and even Muslims. At the core of this new group was the theory of 'One God'. The Gorakhbani, or teachings of Gorakhnath, formed the basis of this new order, which grew by leaps and bounds through the centuries.

According to the Gorakhbani, this order defined itself as neither Hindu nor Muslim, but distinctly as 'Jogis'. While the theological tenets of this group were laid out on both Hindu and Islamic ideas, the 'jogis' were also free to subscribe to or reject the teachings of both communities.

Acknowledging the importance of Hindu deities and Muslim prophets, as well as the wisdom of 'pandits' and 'pirs', Gorakhbani illustrates how the early modern community incorporated the best out of the various religions of the day. Gorakhbani goes to the extent of stating that neither the Vedas nor the Quran was sufficient to provide complete knowledge. It sought to emphasize that Guru Gorakhnath's teachings were enumerated as 'shabad' that was described as the ultimate truth.

Utapati hindu jaranan jogi akali pari musalmananin
te rah cinhon ho kaji mula brahma visnu mahadev mani
manya sabad cukaya dand, nihacai raja bharathari parchai
    gopichand
nihacai naravai bhae niradand, parachai jogi paramanand.

[You are Hindus by birth, Muslims by wisdom, and Yogis by absorption.
Oh, Qazi and Mulla, acknowledge that path which Brahma, Vishnu, and Mahadev have already accepted.
Whoever has accepted the sabad, the word of Gorakh, duality has ended.

Through the determination of the sabad Bharatrihari was
　　made king,
through its knowledge Gopichand experienced truth.
With its persistence kings transcended duality.
With its knowledge yogis obtained ultimate happiness.]

Gorakhbani also talks about how the yogis had mastered the art
of complete control over their body. It was also widely believed
that they could even exercise control over life and death, forces
of nature, and for that matter, also over the minds of others. In
short, their ability to rise above duality allowed them to become
god-men within the world. Not only were others able to relate
to their teachings but they were also eager to employ their
supernatural abilities.[10]

Adityanath grew up in the Digvijaynath mould where
Hindu consolidation was the prime focus. And he found it
convenient to achieve this goal by drawing the huge population
of the lower castes who were the outcasts in the traditional
Brahmanical order. Sure enough, the panth's number swelled
by leaps and bounds. But at what cost? The panth began to
forget what it originally stood for and the values laid down by
its founder Gorakhnath.

Political goals began to dominate over the spiritual agenda.
To everybody's surprise, what became Adityanath's strength was
his complete deviation from the path paved over the centuries by
Gorakhnath. Yogi Adityanath remained a part of Gorakhnath
lineage only by virtue of the fact that he was a 'kanphata' (with
torn ear lobes). Otherwise, there was clearly very little that he
had imbibed from the line of Gorakhnath. He preferred to walk
in the shoes of his guru Avaidyanath's guru Digvijaynath, who
laid the foundation of using religion for political gains.

The popularity earned on account of the religious following of the Gorakhnath temple made the task simpler for him. It also allowed him greater leeway to cast himself into the mould of an aggressive Hindutva icon. Perhaps realization dawned on him that time was ripe for playing the politics of polarization and the best way to do it could be by adopting a hard anti-Muslim stand. Evidently, that was in sharp contrast to the clearly secular ethos cultivated by the panth founder Gorakhnath. That is what gave Adityanath the image of a rabid Hindu leader.

While it was his guru Avaidyanath's popularity that initially got him votes, in the later years he was able to build his own following by pursuing the path of aggressive Hindutva. He raised the HYV to push his agenda that was a clear-cut deviation from not only Gorakhnath's ideology but also from BJP's declared political path. No wonder, when the time came, Yogi Adityanath did not hesitate to blast the BJP left, right and centre. And interestingly, he could get away with all that simply because he had been able to emerge as a leader in his own right—thanks to the math he represented.

7

THE LEGACY OF GORAKHNATH TEMPLE

Once in the Shaivite tradition, Ajay Singh Bisht's Guru Mahant Avaidyanath rechristened the young sanyasi Adityanath. The term 'nath' came to be used as a suffix sometime during the twentieth century, along with the prefix of 'yogi'.

In *Gorakhnath and the Kanphata Yogis*, George Weston Briggs describes the initiation ceremony of a Nath yogi thus:

> The essential parts of the ceremony is the splitting of the ear, tonsure, the covering of the body with ashes and giving of the mantra . . . In the final stage of their ceremony of initiation a specially chosen guru, or teacher, splits the central hollow of both ears with a two edged knife (or razor). The slits are plugged with sticks of nim-wood; and after the wounds have healed, large rings (mudra) are inserted. These are a symbol of the Yogi's faith.[1]

Briggs says that 'wearing of the earrings is of great importance' and a yogi cannot partake of food, or perform his religious duties without it.

At age 22, Ajay Bisht joined the Nath panth. For Mahant Avaidyanath, Ajay was the chosen one and deserved to be his successor. Within a few months of being appointed a full-time disciple in the latter half of 1993, Mahant Avaidyanath initiated him into the sect. On 15 February 1994, which happened to be the auspicious Basant Panchami day, Ajay was given deeksha (whispering of mantra in his ear) by his guru, at a simple ceremony, which included piercing of his ears as per the Nath tradition in which he wore ashtadhatu rings. (His 2017 Assembly election affidavit showed that Adityanath replaced the ashtadhatu rings with gold kundals [earrings] weighing 10 gm each.[2]) To complete the initiation process, he was given the new name of Yogi Adityanath.

The daily routine of sanyasi Yogi Adityanath included learning of Hindu scriptures, practising Hatha yoga, tending and protecting cows, besides carrying out his guru's instructions.

Following Mahant Avaidynath's death on 12 September 2014 after a prolonged illness, Yogi Adityanath was anointed Mahant of Gorakhnath temple. Two days later, on 14 September, Yogi Adityanath was made Peethadheeshwar (temporal head) of the Guru Gorakhnath temple amid traditional rituals of the Nath sect in which seers from other parts of the country, including Haryana and Rajasthan, took part, given the importance of Gorakhnath temple which contains Gorakhnath's gaddi (seat). As per the tradition, the anointment took place just before the body of the former Peethadheeshwar Mahant Avaidyanath was laid to rest (Hindu saints of high order are not cremated).

The Gorakhnath temple takes its name from Baba Gorakhnath, who chose to make it the seat of Nath sampradaya (monastery or order).

The temple has a tremendous following in large parts of eastern Uttar Pradesh and Bihar, and its influence extends right up to Nepal, where the legendary guru Matsyendranath had established the first few temples of the order.

Located on the banks of the Rapti and Rohini rivers at an elevation of 77 m from the sea level, Gorakhpur was earlier famous as Ramgarh. It served as the capital of the Koliyas in the ancient days. However, subsequently it was named after Gorakhnath, the founder of the Nath sampradaya. It was through his revolutionary preaching that he inspired people coming from the lowest social strata to follow the order. Dalits and other socially downtrodden castes which were denied entry into the traditional Brahmanical Hindu temples, were welcomed in the new temple created by Gorakhnath. Sure enough, the following of the temple grew by leaps and bounds.

Gorakhnath temple epitomizes the identity of the city. It is said that this temple is erected at the spot where Gorakhnath did meditation in Treta Yug. Standing on 52 acres of land, this famous temple is located in the heart of the city on the Gorakhpur–Sonauli state highway.

In the pond adjoining the temple is a statue of Bhima (one of the five Pandava brothers in the Mahabharata) in the lying position. Suggesting that Gorakhnath was omnipresent in different ages, legend has it that Bhima had come all the way to this place to request Gorakhnath to perform a particular yajna (ritual sacrifice) for the Pandavas. Since Gorakhnath was praying at that time and could not be disturbed, Bhima lay down on the ground. The ground sank under his weight, leading to the creation of a pond at the spot. Bhima's statue is a reminder of that legend.

In the subsequent years, many Nath temples came up in different parts of India as well as neighbouring countries, including Pakistan, Afghanistan and Nepal, where the Nath sect continues to have significant presence. Nath temples are well preserved in Uttarakhand, Rajasthan, Punjab, Maharashtra, Gujarat, Andhra Pradesh, West Bengal and Odisha.

The parity given by the temple to members of each and every community can be seen at any point of time. The 'no discrimination' approach of the temple is visible in the janata darbar (audience to common public), that is held religiously every day in the main quarters of the sprawling temple compound.

The practice was started by Mahant Avaidyanath. And even after Adityanath moved to Lucknow in his new role as Uttar Pradesh chief minister, a dedicated team led by his key representative Dwarka Prasad Tiwari runs the show with the same zeal and commitment. The sight of hundreds of people (referred to as 'fariyadees' or petitioners) is not uncommon on any given day. Mostly illiterate people—victims of poverty and deprivation—converge at the temple with their woes, without even a written text. But that is where the saffron-clad monk-turned-politician deserves appreciation for taking care of this class of people who, naturally, hold him in awe.

In the hall, where the erstwhile MP Adityanath used to hold his daily janata darbar, there are at least seven desks with clerks, whose job is to pen down applications on behalf of the poor and the underprivileged, who are not even equipped to spell out their grievance in black and white. Once that is done and the signature or thumb impression of applicants is taken down, they move to the adjoining room where Dwarka Prasad Tiwari sits with his old-fashioned typewriter and his assistant with a laptop.

Depending on the nature of the request, Tiwari takes a call on whether to make a phone call or to shoot off a letter to the official concerned to whom the grievance is addressed. His recommendations are then typed on a letterhead saying: Camp office, Yogi Adityanath, Mukhya Mantri, Uttar Pradesh. Surely, that means a lot for any government functionary operating from anywhere in the hinterland of this sprawling state. Apparently, the system works, as was borne out by several fariyadees perched there. Some of them had come from Deoria and Padrauna in the easternmost corner of the state, while there were some from as far as Mirzapur (in the southeastern corner of the state).

Their grievances seemed to be mostly arising on account of land disputes, harassment by police, and inaction or biased and ill-motivated action by lower revenue officials. Interestingly, some of the applicants were seen carrying complaints against their spouses (mostly husbands). The temple administration spends the larger part of the day attending to the public grievances. And their burden has increased ever since their boss got elevated as chief minister. 'Earlier the complainants were mostly from Gorakhpur and a few adjoining districts, but now people come here even from far off places, perhaps because they consider it easier to get their grievances addressed from Gorakhpur than from Lucknow,' pointed out Dwarka, who has been associated with the temple for several decades, to the authors when they met him at the Gorakhnath temple.

Until March 2017, before Yogi Adityanath rode on to high office in Lucknow, attending the janata darbar was a part of his daily routine which, according to Tiwari, would start around 3.30 a.m.

Once through with his personal morning chores, including a long yoga session and puja, Yogi Adityanath would sit down in the hall, listening to grievances of common people. According to insiders, it was like a private court where he would pass judgments on disputes brought to him. And more often than not, the disputing parties would abide by his verdict.

Ironically, it can be compared to a similar private court held by the erstwhile feudal-lord-turned-politician Raghuraj Pratap Singh (better known as Raja Bhaiya), who remained minister under different regimes led by diverse leaders like Kalyan Singh of the BJP and Mulayam Singh Yadav of SP. Evidently, the feudal element is what eventually led people to accept the verdict of the Yogi, who is held in the same awe as any lord of a princely state. Just as it was said about Raja Bhaiya that a verdict passed by him in a dispute carried more weight than a judgement issued by a court of law, so was it said about Yogi Adityanath.

As chief minister, Adityanath resumed the janata darbar in Lucknow where he drew huge crowds at least four days a week. But the practice did not last long. Towards the end of 2019, he even went to the extent of—on the days that he was unable to attend to the people—allegedly assigning the task to one of his cabinet colleagues. In addition to that, a separate people grievances cell functions on a daily basis at the BJP state headquarters. The chief minister has fixed a roster for every minister to attend to this second janata darbar.

It was after a prolonged gap, in July 2021, that Yogi Adityanath resumed his janata darbar at the chief minister's official residence in Lucknow. This time it was organized with much fanfare and wide publicity, aimed at spreading the word that the chief minister's janata darbar had remained suspended for some time only because of the Corona pandemic.

Just as his ministers were ready to give themselves full marks for running this grievance redressal system at the party office, so were the functionaries at the Gorakhnath temple convinced about the effectiveness of their janata darbar. It was felt that the temple grievance redressal system was far more prompt and ran more efficiently than the one at the chief minister's official residence in Lucknow, on account of 'lesser bureaucracy' in Gorakhpur.

Significantly, even now whenever Adityanath is in Gorakhpur—and that is not infrequent—he still makes it a point to throw open his doors to public audience. Once word spreads that he is around, the janata darbar draws bigger crowds, even if he is not able to devote as much time under the changed circumstances. The local people are also aware that Yogi Adityanath is no longer in a position to lead his band of HYV activists into a government office to get their work done. Known for his aggression, it was quite common for him in his earlier days to storm into a government office and reprimand lethargic and corrupt officials for sitting over grievances of common people.

On the other hand, given his new role as chief minister, the expectations of common people have risen higher. 'Some people have started expecting too much and sometimes they seek the moon, but then they have to be told that they will get only what is within the limits of official framework,' said one of the functionaries at the temple office. But those coming in the hope of getting their grievances redressed are now even more confident that their petitions will not go unheeded.

Interestingly, even as Yogi Adityanath is better known for his vehemently anti-Muslim stance, no Muslim is denied audience or response at the temple janata darbar. What seems equally incredible is that there is no discrimination in dealing with the complaints. The sight of burqa-clad women is not uncommon on any given day. Such contradictions appear to be strange in an environment where communal divide was on the rise—thanks to a well-thought-out strategy of the man at the helm to polarize the electorate.

Remarkably, a few key tasks in the temple trust are entrusted to Muslims, whom Adityanath often showcases to prove his secular credentials. These include the posts of chief accountant, the in-charge of 'gaushala' as well as head of constructions. 'You can see for yourself that these Muslims are entrusted with some major assignments in the temple trust; and they have been with us for decades; so where is the question of discrimination with the minorities?' asks Professor U.P. Singh, the 85-year-old former vice chancellor of Gorakhpur University, who now heads the temple trust administration.

The temple trust is known to have been helping out weavers, who form a large part of the population around Gorakhpur. As is to be expected, most of them are Muslims.

Temple Trust Activities

The temple trust activities are not limited to running the temple alone. Beyond the temple's 56-acre campus, there are several institutions run by the trust. And foremost of these is a 300-bed hospital that caters to the needs of thousands of people who converge on Gorakhpur from the poverty-ridden backward areas of a sprawling eastern Uttar Pradesh. Strangely, the hospital does not provide free treatment, which the rich temple trust could easily afford. But there is no denying that the charges at the hospital are fairly lower than those at the local commercially run private hospitals, widely known to be fleecing the poor and the illiterate. 'Our objective is to provide affordable treatment to the underprivileged and we do have facility for free treatment to the poor and the destitute,' points out U.P. Singh.

The 300-bed hospital at one end of the sprawling temple estate is run under the leadership of a retired brigadier. The hospital is a boon for millions of underprivileged and downtrodden from all across eastern Uttar Pradesh, who converge here in search of good treatment at an affordable price. Significantly, some leading doctors in the BRD Medical College have been providing voluntary service in the temple trust hospital.

'We have all the specialties and are in the process of converting this hospital into a medical college,' says Singh, who goes on to add, 'a school of Nursing and Pharmacy is already in place for several years.' The hospital is now in the process of being upgraded to a medical college.

The trust runs a number of educational institutions including two degree colleges under the aegis of Maharana Pratap Shiksha Parishad, constituted by Adityanath's guru's guru Mahant Digvijaynath, way back in 1957.

The temple's influence in the region has grown by leaps and bounds. And that is largely attributable to its decision to throw open its doors to those downtrodden castes who did not have easy access to temples of the traditional Brahmanical order. No wonder, today the bulk of its devotees happen to be Dalits or those drawn from other lower social orders.

The trust also runs a number of educational institutions as well as schools for vocational training. The bulk of these institutions were started by Mahant Digvijaynath, who is widely perceived as a visionary. In fact, when he created a polytechnic in Gorakhpur way back in 1957, it was the first of its kind in entire eastern Uttar Pradesh. And notwithstanding Adityanath's views against reservation for women (even expressed in Parliament), he has promoted a co-education system in several of these institutions.

Still earlier, in 1932, Digvijaynath constituted the Maharana Pratap Shiksha Parishad, under whose umbrella as many as 48 institutions have come up over the years.

In *Gorakhnath and the Kanphata Yogis*,[3] Weston Briggs dates the construction of the Gorakhnath temple in its present form to the year 1800, even though its history is traced back to the eleventh century. Briggs visited Gorakhpur in 1914. Prior to the construction of the existing white marble structure, it is said that the place was known as the site where the highly revered Gorakhnath had offered prayers ages ago when he first landed on this soil. He lit a flame (dhuni) that has been kept alive through the centuries with smoke emerging out of smoldering wood. People would take a round of the site, seeking blessings of Gorakhnath to fulfil their wishes.

Digvijaynath

Digvijaynath's background is quite interesting. He was born in 1894 in an ordinary Rajput family of Udaipur, as Nanhu Singh. Shortly after his parents passed away, his uncle chose to hand over the then eight-year-old Nanhu to the Nath panth. He was taken to the Gorakhnath math in Gorakhpur, where he was groomed into a yogi.

However, the liberal ways of the math in those days allowed him to seek formal education at the Christian missionary–run

St Andrews College in Gorakhpur. It was here that he displayed his talent as a sportsman and earned a name in hockey, lawn tennis and riding. Despite being a mahant, Digvijaynath continued his favourite pastime of playing lawn tennis as well as his political activities.

But his increasing inclination towards politics led him to abandon studies and join public life in 1920. The non-cooperation movement launched by Mahatma Gandhi drew Digvijaynath towards the Congress; he was arrested for his active participation in the 1922 Non-cooperation Movement. But the violence that was resorted to by the demonstrators who burnt down the Chauri Chaura police station and killed 23 policemen, provoked Gandhi to call off the entire movement.

Digvijaynath refused to subscribe to Gandhi's ahimsa and got disillusioned with him because of his decision to abandon the Non-cooperation Movement. Perhaps, he felt that violence perpetrated by the British could be answered only by violence.

The leadership of Gorakhnath math eventually passed to Digvijaynath, who was anointed as mahant on 15 August 1935. While he concentrated on the Gorakhnath math, he simultaneously returned to politics, but took an ideological U-turn and joined the Hindu Mahasabha in 1937—soon after V.D. Savarkar took over as its president.

Using his position as head of the Gorakhnath temple—which always had a huge following—Digvijaynath did not take time to become a popular political entity. Also, the realization that a Hindu–Muslim divide could make him some kind of a hero led him to turn so virulently anti-Muslim that he went to the extent of once declaring in a press interview in 1952 that he would not hesitate to take away the voting right from Muslims for five to ten years—'until they proved their loyalty to India.'

According to authors Krishna Jha and Dhirendra K. Jha, just three days before Mahatma Gandhi's assassination on 30 January 1948, Digvijaynath 'exhorted Hindu militants to kill the Mahatma'.[4] The revolver used by Nathuram Godse to kill Gandhi also allegedly belonged to Digvijaynath. These accusations landed him in jail, but he was let off after nine months.

The profile of a Hindu bigot, which he acquired as head of the Gorakhnath temple, led him to win the 1967 Lok Sabha election and become an MP from Gorakhpur. In recognition of his 'achievements', Digvijaynath was elevated as national general secretary of the Hindu Mahasabha.

Interestingly, Digvijaynath was quite a mixture of opposites. On the one hand, he played the Hindu card to fuel divisive politics in the land of a highly secular Gorakhnath, where he built his political empire; on the other, he maintained good relations with prominent local Muslims. According to Mian Saheb Farooq, who heads Gorakhpur's oldest Islamic institution of the Imambara, Digvijaynath was a regular lawn tennis partner of his grandfather, who then headed the institution.

The relationship was maintained even after Digvijaynath's aggressive Hindutva came to the fore with the installation of Lord Ram's idol inside the sanctum sanctorum of the Babri Masjid in Ayodhya in 1949, in which he is believed to have played a key role.

Digvijaynath also worked with Swami Karpatriji, founder of the Ram Rajya Parishad, which, like the Hindu Mahasabha, had always kept a distance from the Sangh Parivar, and vice versa. Digvijaynath and Karpatriji were still working together when the Sarvadaliya Gauraksha Maha-Abhiyan Samiti (Committee for the Great All-Party Campaign for the Protection of the Cow) was set up in 1966 by the VHP. The campaign brought Digvijaynath closer to the VHP, but he remained part of the Hindu Mahasabha till his death in 1969.

He became a hero of sorts in December 1949, when he joined hands with the Akhil Bhartiya Ramayana Mahasabha to ensure the surreptitious installation of Lord Ram's idol inside the disputed Babri mosque in Ayodhya.

Yet, Digvijaynath could not build himself into a Hindu icon as despite all his attempts to polarize election after election, he failed to win. It took him a good 18 years to make his mark through his maiden electoral victory in 1967, when he won the Gorakhpur Lok Sabha seat. However, he could not enjoy a long stint as a parliamentarian, due to his sudden death in 1969.

Avaidyanath

Avaidyanath, whom Digvijaynath had anointed as his successor, took over the command of the grand empire Digvijaynath had built around the temple. All he needed to do was to consolidate that fiefdom, which he did with considerable ease. After all, as inheritor of Digvijaynath's legacy, things were simpler for him. Mahant Avaidyanath, who described Digvijaynath as being a 'father' to him in the Lok Sabha Who's Who, 1991, had a similar career.

Mahant Avaidyanath was looked upon as a huge Hindutva icon. But it was not overnight that he built his larger-than-life profile. Avaidyanath was elected MLA three times—1962, 1967, 1968—before he won a Lok Sabha seat for the first time in 1970. Thereafter, he got re-elected to the state assembly twice, before once again entering the Lok Sabha—as a Hindu Mahasabha representative in 1991 and as a BJP nominee in 1996.

In fact, it was in the late eighties that he threw himself whole hog into the Ramjanmbhoomi campaign that was at its peak at that time. And that was what helped raise his profile and let him make deeper inroads into Hindutva politics. He soon emerged as one of the key players in the Ayodhya movement, that was already on the boil. Top BJP leadership roped him into the Ayodhya Ramjanmbhoomi temple movement which got a big boost on account of his association.

It was the rise of a simple man born as Kripal Singh Bisht on 28 May 1921 in a remote hilly village of Kandi in Pauri Garhwal district of what is now Uttarakhand state. Perhaps, he had never imagined that one day he would brush shoulders with top political leaders of the country including former Prime Ministers Narasimha Rao and Atal Behari Vajpayee as well as former Deputy Prime Minister Lal Krishna Advani—thanks to his active role in the Ayodhya movement. He was known to have even gone to the extent of criticizing some top BJP leaders, including former Prime Minister Atal Behari Vajpayee, for not being proactive in the Ayodhya movement.

Mahant Avaidyanath founded the Sri Ramjanmabhoomi Mukti Yagna Samiti (Committee for Liberation of Ram's Birthplace) in 1984. He was also responsible for launching the much publicized 'yatra' from Sitamarhi in Bihar to Ayodhya, in pursuance of the mission 'to liberate the Ram temple'. All along the 410-km route, Avaidyanath remained busy exhorting people to vote only for political parties who were ready to push their demand for liberation of not just Ramjanmhoomi, but also two other prominent Hindu shrines—the Krishna janmbhoomi (birthplace of Lord Krishna) and the Kashi-Vishwanath temple in Varanasi.

Mahant Avaidyanath died at the age of 93 in Gorakhpur on 12 September 2014. By that time Yogi Adiyyanath had already done four terms as MP, so his ascendance as a natural successor to Avaidyanath's religious throne was even smoother.

Strangely, however, no senior BJP leader cared to attend Mahant Avaidyanath's last rites, barely four months after Narendra Modi became Prime Minister. All that Yogi Adityanath received from Modi and Rajnath Singh were oral tributes for his 'guru'-cum-foster-father.

Having been entrusted with the legacy of Mahant Avaidyanath well during the latter's lifetime, Yogi Adityanath made it a point to impress upon his mentor that he had made no mistake by making him the sole inheritor. Even as Avaidyanath's understudy, he made himself known as a rabble-rouser who could whip up Hindu passions at the drop of the hat across large parts of eastern Uttar Pradesh.

Yogi's inflammatory speeches—pointedly anti-Muslim and anti-Christian—continued to help him consolidate his Hindu vote bank. Once he saw the strategy working, he formed his own private organization under the banner of HYV (see Chapter 6). With young elements from the saffron ranks rallying behind him, the HYV gained so much currency that it could challenge the BJP against whom Adityanath often fielded candidates in several elections. There was precious little that the BJP leadership could ever do to cow him down.

Though the huge following of the Gorakhnath temple was a major factor behind his increasing political clout, there can be no doubt about Adityanath having made it big on his own steam too. No wonder, he rarely missed any opportunity to keep the BJP on tenterhooks, so much so that often the top BJP leadership had to shrug themselves away from the provocative utterances made by him. BJP spokespersons were often seen disowning his remarks, such as,

> Whenever a Hindu visits Kashi Vishwanath Temple, the
> Gyanvapi masjid looks at him with ridicule; if I were to
> be given a chance, I would get idols of Gauri, Ganesh and
> Nandi installed in every mosque.[5]

It is at the Gorakhnath temple where the activities of the HYV
seem to merge with the day-to-day functioning of the temple.
Ostensibly, the Vahini has an independent office in a building
called Hindu Bhawan near Gorakhpur railway station. But it
would not be wrong to perceive that the organization is run
from the premises of the Gorakhnath temple.

Fundamentally, the two bodies may lie in sharp contrast
to each other, yet the two coexist here solely because both are
headed by Yogi Adityanath. And this despite the fact that while
the temple welcomes every human being irrespective of caste,
creed, sect or religion, the HYV clearly has no room for Muslims
or Christians.

The Vahini's aversion to the minority community is not
only spelt out in the constitution of the organization, but is also
aggressively asserted in its acts of omission and commission.
That this goes in sharp contrast to the fundamental ideology
of Gorakhnath is amply visible. Gorkhnath's secular credentials
need no scrutiny. There could be no better testimony to that
than the fact that both Kabir and Guru Nanak took their
inspiration from the teachings of Gorakhnath.

8

AYODHYA BECKONS

The Gorakhnath math has been at the vanguard of the Ram Janmbhoomi movement. Mahant Avaidyanath's guru, Mahant Digvijaynath, was the one who is said—rightly or wrongly—to have had a role in the manifestation of Ram idol inside Babri Masjid.

The math's role received prominence for the first time in December 1949, when a nine-day non-stop recitation of the Ramayana was organized on Ram Chabootra—the raised platform in front of the Babri mosque. The sixteenth-century mosque was believed to have been built over the debris of a temple erected to mark the birthplace of Ram. Hindus were led to believe Mughal Emperor Babur's army commander Mir Baqi pulled down an ancient temple that stood there and constructed the mosque, as a tribute to the emperor in 1528.

While claims and counterclaims were being made by the two sides for years and some conflicts had taken place between Hindus and Muslims, Digvijaynath allegedly led a band of Hindu Mahasabha activists inside the Babri Masjid and remained in the forefront with aggressors who planted Ram's deity inside the disputed mosque on the fateful night of 22–23 December 1949.[1] As word was spread that the idol of 'Ram Lalla' (infant Ram) had appeared miraculously inside the mosque, a large number of Hindus converged there and began offering prayers before the newly installed idol.

Word was spread that the idol was a divine occurrence, preceded by some 'akashvaani' (sound from the heavens) amidst a sudden beam of light. Even the police constable on duty at the site that night, later deposed that he was a witness to all the celestial occurrences.

Then Prime Minister Jawaharlal Nehru and Home Minister Sardar Vallabhbhai Patel told the then Uttar Pradesh Chief Minister Govind Ballabh Pant and Home Minister Lal Bahadur Shastri to get the surreptitiously planted idol removed from the mosque. But the local administration led by Faizabad District Magistrate K.K. Nayar (an Indian Civil Service officer) expressed his inability to carry out those directives. Meanwhile, a suit was filed in the lower court following which the place was locked and status quo maintained for nearly four decades until 1986, when the Faizabad district judge ordered unlocking of the gates, that led to opening the Pandora's box.

Nayar took voluntary retirement from the prestigious ICS in 1952 and was rewarded with a Bhartiya Jana Sangh (now BJP) ticket for Parliament. He won the neighbouring Bahraich Lok Sabha seat in 1956 essentially because of religious polarization.

Simultaneously, Digvijaynath's stock rose among that section of Hindus who were already enamoured by his policy of aggressive Hindutva. He was shortly thereafter elevated as the Hindu Mahasabha national general secretary.

The placing of idols inside the mosque marked the beginning of a long-drawn acrimonious legal and political battle over the ownership of land on which Babri Masjid was located and whether a temple actually existed at the site where the Babri Masjid stood until its demolition by kar sevaks on 6 December 1992. The matter was finally decided in favour of the temple by the Supreme Court of India on 9 November 2019. The Supreme Court cleared the way for the construction of a Ram Temple at the disputed site at Ayodhya and directed the Centre to allot a 5-acre plot to the Sunni Waqf Board for building a mosque.[2]

The bench, comprising Chief Justice Ranjan Gogoi, Justice S.A. Bobde, Justice D.Y. Chandrachud, Justice Ashok Bhushan and Justice S. Abdul Nazeer, unanimously ruled that possession of the disputed 2.77-acre land rights will be handed over to the deity Ram Lalla, who is one of the three litigants in the case. The possession, however, will remain with a central government receiver.

In one of the most important and most anticipated judgements in India's history, the five-judge Constitution bench led by Chief Justice Ranjan Gogoi put an end to the more-than-a century-old dispute that has torn the social fabric of the nation. The Supreme Court's landmark judgment said there will be a Ram Mandir at the disputed site and Muslims will be given an alternative 5-acre plot of land for their mosque.

The special bench of the Supreme Court heard the long-pending Ayodhya dispute for 40 days at a stretch and pronounced the historic verdict on 9 November 2019. Chief Justice Ranjan Gogoi who had always maintained that he would decide the case before his retirement, eventually kept his word by doing so barely eight days before demitting office. Four months later he was nominated as member of the Rajya Sabha.

Ten key takeaways from the judgment:

1. Supreme Court has granted the entire 2.77 acre of disputed land in Ayodhya to deity Ram Lalla.
2. Supreme Court has directed the Centre and Uttar Pradesh government to allot an alternative 5-acre land to the Muslims at a prominent place to build a mosque.
3. The court has asked the Centre to consider granting some kind of representation to Nirmohi Akhara in setting up of a trust. Nirmohi Akhara was the third party in the Ayodhya dispute.
4. The Supreme Court dismissed the plea of Nirmohi Akhara which was seeking control of the entire disputed land, saying they are the custodian of the land.
5. Supreme Court has directed the Union Government to set up a trust in three months for the construction of the Ram Mandir at the disputed site where the Babri Masjid was demolished in 1992.
6. The Supreme Court said the underlying structure below the disputed site at Ayodhya was not an Islamic structure, but the ASI has not established whether a temple was demolished to build a mosque.
7. The court also said that the Hindus consider the disputed site as the birthplace of Lord Ram while Muslims also consider the Babri Masjid as their heritage. They believe that once a mosque, always a mosque; so, they were unwilling to part with it. Their contention was that the mosque has been there since the sixteenth century and Islam does not permit construction of mosque on a disputed land. They, therefore, rule out that the mosque could have been built after demolition of a temple at the site.

8. The Court also said that the faith of the Hindus that Lord Ram was born at the disputed site where the Babri Masjid once stood cannot be disputed.

9. The Supreme Court also said that the 1992 demolition of the sixteenth-century Babri Masjid (Babri mosque) was a violation of law.

10. While reading out its judgment, the Supreme Court said that the Uttar Pradesh Sunni Central Waqf Board has failed to establish its case in the Ayodhya dispute case and Hindus have established their case that they were in possession of outer courtyard of the disputed site.[3]

Coming back to Ayodhya's history, Mahant Avaidyanath, who succeeded Digvijaynath, also played an active role in the temple movement following which he was roped in by the RSS to further its Hindutva agenda. To capitalize on the Gorakhnath temple's appeal among the masses, the BJP decided to field Avaidyanath from Gorakhpur Lok Sabha constituency in 1991 and 1996. In 1989, when a 'shilaniyas' (foundation stone–laying) ceremony was performed at the Ram Janmbhoomi in Ayodhya, Avaidyanath was an MP on the Hindu Mahasabha ticket from neighbouring Gorakhpur.

If Digvijaynath was involved in the dramatic events of 22 December 1949 in Ayodhya, Avaidyanath played an equally proactive role in the temple movement, by founding the Sri Ram Janmbhoomi Mukti Yagna Samiti (Committee to Liberate Ram Janmbhoomi) in 1984. In September that year, the committee started a religious procession from Sitamarhi in Bihar to Ayodhya for the 'liberation' of Ram Janmbhoomi.

Avaidyanath went around exhorting people to vote for only those parties which promised to liberate all the sacred places of

Hindus. And among these, besides Ayodhya, were Varanasi and Mathura. At both these places, mosques were built on part of the land of famous temples—Kashi Vishwanath in Varanasi and Krishna Janmbhoomi (birthplace of Lord Krishna) in Mathura.

Avaidyanath's speech at a meeting of sadhus—the Dharma Sansad (religious parliament)—organized by the VHP at the 1989 Kumbh Mela in Allahabad (now Prayagraj) laid the foundation for bringing the two saffron traditions closer. While several resolutions were passed at the Dharma Sansad, its main thrust was on construction of a Ram temple at the disputed Ram Janmbhoomi–Babri Masjid site for which a separate resolution was passed.

Writer Dhirendra Jha has quoted *The Statesman* as saying in its edition of 1 February 1989, that

> most of the clergy who spoke today took a strong anti-Muslim and anti-government tone. Mahant Avaidyanath of Gorakhpur pointed out that the Quran prohibited Muslims from constructing mosques at the holy places of other religions. 'And telling us to construct the temple in another place to avoid conflict is like telling Lord Rama to wed another Sita to avoid war with Ravana'.[4]

On Avaidyanath's role in the destruction of Babri Masjid, the Liberhan Inquiry Commission noted the following:

> There is sufficient and believable evidence on the record [. . .] that provocative speeches were delivered by Uma Bharti, Sadhvi Ritambhara, Paramhans Ramchandra Dass, Acharya Dharmendra Dev, B. L. Sharma [. . .] Mahant Avaidyanath etc . . .

There is no manner of doubt admissible in the culpability and responsibility of the Chief Minister (Kalyan Singh), his ministers and his cohorts, who were handpicked to occupy selected posts. Paramhans Ramchander Das, Ashok Singhal, Vinay Katiyar, Vishnu Hari Dalmia, KS Sudershan, HV Sheshadri, Lalji Tandon, Kalraj Mishra, Govindacharya and others named in my report formed this complete cartel led by Kalyan Singh and supported by icons of the movement like LK Advani, MM Joshi and AB Vajpayee . . .

The conundrum which faced the Commission during its long hearings and extensive fact finding efforts was to reconcile the stance of the public face of the Sangh Parivar with the actions which defied law, morality and political ethics. Leaders like AB Vajpayee, MM Joshi and LK Advani, who are the undeniable public face and leaders of the BJP and thus of the Sangh Parivar, constantly protested their innocence and denounced the events of December 1992 . . . It cannot be assumed even for a moment that LK Advani, AB Vajpayee or MM Joshi did not know the designs of the Sangh Parivar. . . . These leaders cannot be given the benefit of the doubt and exonerated of culpability.[5]

As chief minister, Yogi can now boast of accomplishing his responsibility to concretize the dreams of his guru, and his guru's guru, by ensuring construction of the much-debated Ram temple at Ayodhya.

As if to prove that he was just as committed towards the cause of the Ram temple as his guru was, Yogi offered prayers at the makeshift temple at the disputed site on 31 May 2017, a day after a CBI court at Lucknow framed criminal charges against top-rung BJP leaders like Lal Krishna Advani, Murli

Manohar Joshi, Uma Bharti and nine others for conspiring to raze Babri Masjid. Adityanath also called on each of these senior BJP leaders and expressed his support to the cause they had once championed.

By offering prayers at the makeshift Ram temple, Adityanath became the second chief minister after Rajnath Singh to do so. As chief minister, Rajnath offered prayers at the makeshift shrine in 2002. No other BJP chief minister, including Kalyan Singh during whose tenure the Babri Masjid was razed, nor any of the non-BJP chief ministers—Mulayam Singh Yadav, Mayawati and Akhilesh Yadav—ever visited the disputed site.

The demolition of the structure proved catastrophic with communal riots engulfing large parts of the country leaving over 3,000 people dead. Simultaneously, it played a major role in shaping the political destiny of not only Uttar Pradesh but also that of the country.

On his maiden visit to Ayodhya as chief minister, Adityanath did not talk about the temple but announced Rs 350 crore grant for sprucing up the pilgrim city under his government's PRASAD (Pilgrimage Rejuvenation and Spiritual Augmentation) scheme. Projects worth Rs 137 crore for the development of Ayodhya have been cleared by the state government. Amongst its notable decisions was to upgrade the Ayodhya civic body to a municipal corporation for fast-tracking the pilgrim town's development.

A Ramayana circuit is planned at a cost of Rs 133 crores. The Ram Katha Park, an urban haat (market) and a Korean temple along the Saryu riverfront will be part of the Ramayana circuit, which will depict events from *Ramcharitmanas*—the epic poem on Ram by the bhakti poet Tulsidas. Ramleela (enacting the story of Ram's life) is to be performed throughout the year.

All these Ayodhya-centric developmental activities are taking place at a time when many of Uttar Pradesh's cities like Lucknow, Kanpur and Prayagraj (Allahabad) are waiting to be smartened up.

Even before the temple row was resolved, the Adityanath government went all out to put Ayodhya on the tourist map more prominently than ever before. The showcase of his efforts was the special Diwali celebration with the lighting of nearly 2,00,000 diyas (earthen lamps) on 18 October 2017 in the ancient temple town.

Yogi Adityanath's idea was to portray the arrival of the legendary Lord Ram back in his kingdom of Ayodhya after a 14-year exile and the devastation of demon king Ravana and his Lanka. The government went to ludicrous lengths to re-enact the moment with one helicopter showering petals over the other chopper (modern version of the mythological Pushpak Viman) carrying artistes playing Ram, Sita and Laxman for Ramleela. 'The idea is to show to the people how Shree Ram Chandra ji took the Pushpak Viman to return to Ayodhya which is lit up like never before,' said a spokesman of the Uttar Pradesh government which provided its helicopter for the very special ride.

These performers, dressed as mythological characters of Ram, Sita and Laxman, were received by Chief Minister Adityanath as well as Uttar Pradesh Governor Ram Naik. All approach roads to the Ram Katha Park were spruced up for the occasion.

Yes, it was an official show, obviously to impress upon all, including the ordinary Hindu, how dedicated the saffron-clad Uttar Pradesh chief minister was to the cause of Ram. So what if the much-debated Ram temple could not be built without the verdict of the country's apex court? The whole idea obviously was to show that Yogi was leaving no stone unturned to pay obeisance to the most-revered Hindu God on the soil of his birthplace. To further demonstrate his devotion to Lord Ram, the chief minister also announced his proposal to have a 100 m tall statue of the deity erected on the banks of the Saryu river.

Yogi Adityanath skillfully and discreetly played on the sentiments of the people without raising the usual fervor associated with this city, believed for ages as the birthplace of Lord Ram. Understanding the pulse of the people, he did not bother to disguise his efforts to bring Ayodhya back to the centre stage of Indian politics.

What had become visible during the much-hyped Ayodhya movement in the 1980s and early 1990s, until its demolition in 1992, was largely on account of Hindu activists converging at the temple town from different corners of the country. And every attempt to revive the temple issue was fraught with much tension, and would end up disrupting the normal lives of locals. 'Leave us alone' was the cry of most people who were often heard asking, 'Why can't these politicians let us live in peace?'

The grand celebrations on Chhoti Diwali, on 18 October 2017, was one of those rare occasions when locals looked cheerful and actively participated in the event right from the morning. For a change, the city—like any other Uttar Pradesh town usually, laden with filth and squalor—was swept clean for the mega event.

The morning began with a heritage walk by local sadhus. And quite discreetly, they kept a safe distance away from the contentious Ram Janmbhoomi–Babri Masjid site, where the makeshift Ram Temple continues to attract large number of Hindus every day.

The real celebrations began with the arrival of the 'Pushpak Viman', carrying the symbolic Ram–Sita–Laxman trio. The chief minister seemed to be playing the symbolic Bharat, by receiving them at the helipad. Uttar Pradesh Governor Ram Naik and Yogi's entire cabinet remained in tow, perhaps to symbolize the 'Treta Yuga' elite, who welcomed Ram on his return to Ayodhya in that era. With that, began the unprecedented grand celebrations all along the beautifully decorated and brightly illuminated Ram ki Pairi (series of ghats on the banks of the Saryu river), where a laser show provided a breathtaking spectacle for the local masses who had never even imagined anything like that.

The chief minister's arrival was marked with the simultaneous lighting of some 2,00,000 diyas on the steps along the river ghats—a feat that a team from Guinness Book was also invited to witness.

The deftness with which Yogi carried out his obvious agenda must be admired. No matter how much he could be targeted for lapses in his governance, he knew that questioning him for celebrating Diwali in Ayodhya could prove counterproductive for the Opposition.

But what he apparently failed to explain was why did he choose to celebrate Diwali on Chhoti Diwali, which neither has any mythological nor historical significance. Apparently, Yogi found it more convenient to put up the mega show a day earlier because he could not afford to be away on the auspicious Diwali day from his first love—the Gorakhnath temple. Evidently, notwithstanding his loud assertions about his dedication to Ram Nagri, when it comes to choosing between Ayodhya and Gorakhpur, his preference was surely for the latter.

Yogi Adityanath, undoubtedly, is a master of playing his cards well. The entire BJP–RSS combine went to town vehemently denying any political undertones to the high-profile event, which according to them was only a reflection of their devotion to Lord Ram. But that begs the question—what stopped them from celebrating Diwali in Ayodhya all those years when the BJP was at the helm in the state as well as when other parties ruled the state? BJP stalwart Kalyan Singh—widely portrayed as architect of the Babri demolition—ruled Uttar Pradesh twice, while Rajnath Singh (the present Union defence minister) also had two tenures as chief minister of Uttar Pradesh. This was in addition to a brief stint by Ram Prakash Gupta.

Surely no one could have dared to stop them if they had given a call to celebrate Diwali even without being in power. The party could have easily mobilized popular support and funds for such a celebration. That would have demonstrated their true passion for Lord Ram and his legacy. Who would believe that any political party—much less the BJP—requires state funding for a celebration of this kind?

The fact that Diwali celebrations in Ayodhya came up so suddenly arouses suspicion about a hidden agenda—to bring the Ayodhya temple from the back burner to the centre stage of politics. And there could be two key reasons for that—either building a people's narrative around Ayodhya well before the long-pending dispute was taken up for fresh hearing by the country's apex court, or using the temple card while continuing to harp on 'development' as their mainstay, so that it could ensure the much-desired polarization of votes in 2019 when the nation went to poll. After all, it has been part of BJP's election manifesto since 1991, so much so, that the party came to be the butt of ridicule for its failure to deliver the temple promise.

As each election time gets close, the VHP and the sadhus of Ayodhya start turning restive on the issue. They fear that the

BJP will once again let them down and cite the pendency of the case in the Supreme Court for putting off the construction of their much-awaited Ram temple. Left to themselves, the sadhus would want to defy the law of the land. However, the seers always had their own limitations and it would not be possible for them to fulfill their mission without government support. As the seers clamoured for bypassing the judiciary, seeking issue of a special ordinance for temple construction, Yogi Adityanath urged them to be patient for some more time.

The BJP got a boost on 1 October 2010 when a three-judge bench of the Allahabad High Court[6] said that the central dome below which the makeshift temple exists belongs to Hindus. While Justice S.U. Khan ruled that no temple was demolished to construct the mosque, two other judges—Justice Sudhir Agarwal and Justice D.V. Sharma—held a contrary view.

In a 2–1 majority verdict the court ordered a three-way split of the disputed land, with one-third each going to the Sunni Waqf Board, Ram Lalla (infant Ram) and Nirmohi Akhara, a religious denomination which is party to the case.

For Ravi Shankar Prasad, then Union law minister and senior advocate who represented one of the litigants, the important part of the majority verdict was that the birthplace of Ram lies precisely where his idol is installed—and that is what he feels 'the Hindus believe'. Prasad further pointed out that Justice S.U. Khan had also said that Ram Lalla will not be shifted even when the land is divided between the three contesting parties.

The Sunni Waqf Board and the chairman of the Sri Ram Janmbhoomi Trust, Mahant Nritya Gopal Das, disagreed with the judgment and said they would go in to appeal. Consequently, the matter went before the Supreme Court.

None of the Hindu groups which were party to the case, wanted any share of the disputed land to be given to Muslims. Even before the start of daily hearings in the Supreme Court, BJP leaders and seers started asserting that construction of the promised Ram temple would begin by the end of 2018. Perhaps, that was because they hoped to use the issue for political dividends in the 2019 Lok Sabha elections.

No one was ready to bet on exactly when the temple construction would begin, barring the BJP's Rajya Sabha MP Subramaniam Swamy and a seer, Acharya Ram Bhadracharya, who claimed that the temple dream would be realized by 6 December 2018, the 26th anniversary of Babri Masjid demolition.

These developments must be viewed along with the arrival of stones for the temple. On 21 June 2017 two trucks carrying huge stones for use in the proposed Ram temple reached Ayodhya.

A little over a fortnight later, on the morning of 5 July 2017, three more truckloads of stone reached Ayodhya, while another six were on the way. Preparations, obviously, were in full swing.

In 2015 the SP government had stopped the transportation of stones to Ayodhya, inviting condemnation from the VHP.

In 2015, Triloki Nath Pandey of the VHP, who calls himself as the 'best friend' of the makeshift temple's presiding deity Ram Lalla, said that the transportation of stones for the temple had gained speed. According to Pandey there were sufficient stones for beams and pillars but more were needed for the ceiling and the first floor. These stones were mined and transported from Bharatpur, he said.

'Stones have been coming since 1991 and it was only during Akhilesh Yadav's rule that the flow was stopped. The supply, along with financial donations from the devout, has now resumed,' Triloki Nath said.

About the possible date for the temple construction to begin, Sharad Sharma, the VHP's most active and well-informed spokesperson in Ayodhya, had said that he was not in a position to make a guess.

When told that Acharya Ram Bhadracharya and Subramaniam Swamy had said that the temple would be constructed in 2018, Sharma said, 'they were the right persons to talk to about it.' He had added, 'or else, let the Central government move a legislation to allow the construction of the temple.'

According to Sharma there were 110,000 cu ft of stones cut and carved for use in the proposed temple. Work at the karyashala (workshop) in Ayodhya has continued uninterrupted over the years, he said.

Although the available stock 'is sufficient to build the ground floor', Sharma said that about 70,000 cu ft more was required to build the first floor of the temple in which no reinforcement, mortar or cement was to be used. The entire temple was proposed to be erected by interlocking of sculptured stone blocks—a technology used in many ancient Indian temples as well as in Delhi's famous Akshardham temple, built in 2005.

Adityanath ruled out temple construction through consensus at this stage. Commenting on Art of Living founder Sri Sri Ravishankar's mediation effort to resolve the dispute, Yogi Adityanath said that it was now too late for a negotiated settlement. 'There was no discussion with him on any formula pertaining to this issue, nor am I aware of it. If the issue could be resolved through consensus then it would have been done

long ago,' Adityanath said after meeting Sri Sri Ravishankar in
Lucknow in November 2017.

Then Union Minister Ravi Shankar Prasad advocated
building consensus in the society to resolve the Ram temple issue,
a day after Subramanian Swamy went ahead with a seminar in
Delhi university on the matter, and asserted that nothing would
be done forcibly or against the law.[7] 'It is part of our manifesto.
The matter is in Supreme Court. Let's await its decision,' Prasad
told reporters there.

'There has to be a consensus in the society and the matter
can be resolved through dialogue,' the minister said.

'Construction of Ram temple in Ayodhya is "mandatory"
for revival of our culture. We have started and we will not give
up until it is made but nothing will be done forcibly and against
the law. We have full faith that we will win in the court,' Prasad
said in his inaugural address at the two-day seminar.

Why then the flip-flop over Ravishankar's consensus-
building effort by Adityanath?

The VHP also doubted the success of Sri Sri Ravishankar's
conciliatory mission. Surendra Jain, joint general secretary of
VHP, said the issue of construction of Ram temple could never
be resolved through talks.

Sunni cleric Maulana Khalid Rashid, who is an executive
committee member of All India Muslim Personal Law Board
(AIMPLB), said that he had received Ravishankar not as member
of AIMPLB, but as the imam (one who leads the prayers) of
Lucknow's Aishbagh Eidgah.

The Muslim organization, referred to by Yogi in his May
2017 Ayodhya speech, could have been the Uttar Pradesh Shia
Central Waqf Board, which took a line different from the Sunni
Waqf Board, one of the original litigants in the case. In an

affidavit filed before the Supreme Court, the Shia Waqf Board stated that a mosque could be built in a Muslim-dominated area at a reasonable distance from the disputed site. This Board also suddenly staked claim over the disputed land, which according to its chairman Waseem Rizvi, is a property of the Shia waqf.

'The demolished mosque belonged to the Shia Waqf and neither the Sunni Waqf Board not the All-India Muslim Personal Board has any right to take a call on the issue,' declared Rizvi, who went to the extent of suo moto offering the disputed Babri Masjid land for construction of the Ram temple. 'I will also gift ten silver arrows for Ram's statue to be installed in Ayodhya,' he said.

However, the Sunni Waqf Board dismissed the Shia Waqf Board affidavit as 'politically motivated' and 'without locus standi'. Counsel for Sunni Waqf Board Zafaryab Jilani pointed out that this stand was never taken when the Allahabad High Court was hearing the case. He said that despite being impleaded by the VHP in its 1989 petition, the Shia Waqf Board did not spell out its stand and even when evidence was being submitted before the High Court, the Shia board did not care to become a party to the case. 'The affidavit sworn now, has no legal validity as it was not submitted before the high court,' Jilani emphasized.[8]

Rizvi continued to insist that the Shia Waqf Board was 'very much a party to the case', though he is unable to explain the basis of his assertion. In fact, way back in 1944, the Shia Waqf Board had sought to stake its claim to the mosque before a local court in Faizabad, under which Ayodhya falls. But the court turned down its plea, following which a notification was issued declaring the mosque as a Sunni waqf.

Thereafter, the Shia Waqf Board never raised the issue until Waseem Rizvi suddenly emerged out of the blue and went to the extent of offering the disputed land for construction of the temple.

What took the Shia Waqf Board to realize that the disputed property does not belong to Sunnis? A background check of Waseem Rizvi would probably reveal the answer. Rizvi, who was first appointed chairman of the Shia board in 2008, has been embroiled in controversies.

Once a close ally of popular Shia cleric Kalbe Jawad, Rizvi became his adversary as he switched loyalties to Azam Khan, senior SP leader and top minister in successive SP governments. The war turned bitter after Jawad filed a complaint against him, following which the Akhilesh Yadav government directed the Crime Branch of CID to probe the alleged misappropriation of Waqf property by him.

A widely acclaimed Shia cleric, Jawad, who is the general secretary of Majlise-e-Ulama-e-Hind, said that Rizvi supported the BJP on the Ram temple issue only to please the ruling party and to save his skin in the CID probe.

Together with Rizvi there were several others who suddenly evinced interest in the Ayodhya case, ever since the apex court suggested that the parties involved in the age-old dispute should explore possibilities of a negotiated settlement.

Interestingly, the Shia Waqf Board's claim also received full support from BJP quarters. BJP spokespersons participating in debates on various television channels openly batted for the Shia Waqf Board and its chairman Rizvi.

Rizvi's sole contention was that even though Mughal emperor Babur—after whom the mosque was built—was a Sunni, his army commander Mir Baqi, who actually erected the shrine, was a Shia.

Much on Rizvi's lines, and far from any of the involved Hindu parties, it was the 'Art of Living' maestro Sri Sri Ravishankar, who took a plunge into the cesspool of a proposed out-of-court settlement. Like the Uttar Pradesh Shia Waqf Board chief Waseem Rizvi, the Art of Living guru, too, was a rank outsider to the long-drawn legal battle for the Ram Janmbhoomi. However, his initiatives towards a negotiated settlement drew as much applause from BJP circles as the excitement in the saffron ranks about the Shia Waqf Board's stand regarding the temple.

It was no secret that Sri Sri Ravishankar was representing the Hindus. The settlement he was seeking to strike was with those representing Muslims. Because of the goodwill he enjoyed with both communities it was felt that he could make them arrive at a common ground. Both Nirmohi Akhara and VHP spokespersons were quite critical of Sri Sri's initiative for an amicable out-of-court settlement to the dispute.

Earlier, BJP leader Subramaniam Swamy who went out of his way to initiate a negotiated settlement of the long-pending legal battle, had moved the apex court for expediting the Ayodhya case.

It was unlikely that the proximity between Sri Sri Ravishankar and the BJP, and the simultaneous affinity between BJP and the Shia Waqf Board, were merely coincidences. Therefore, there was reason to suspect that there was something more than what met the eye.

Subsequently, in March 2019, the Supreme Court decided to give mediation a try. However, by August, it chose to reverse its own decision and snapped the mediation process as suddenly as it had resolved to entrust it to a three-member mediation panel.

Several persons who had participated in the mediation process ever since it took off were of the view that the exercise did actually make some meaningful headway. They believed that it was moving in a positive direction with most of the parties on either side showing their inclination to take it forward.

It was on 8 March 2019 that the apex court appointed a panel comprising former Supreme Court Judge Justice Khalifullah, well-known mediator and senior advocate Sriram Panchu and Sri Sri Ravishankar, who got down to business within the next seven days.

Evidently, the process had to face many stumbling blocks from day one. 'It was no mean task to get different parties to agree to come to the mediation table; and once that was done, it lent much hope, but no one knew that the allotted time frame would be cut short so abruptly,' said a well-known participant in Lucknow.

Meanwhile, the common suspicion among political analysts was that bringing Ayodhya back to the centre stage could help BJP make some gains in poll-bound states, as also pave the way for Hindu polarization well before the crucial 2019 election—which would determine the political destiny of Prime Minister Narendra Modi as well as Yogi Adityanath.

It may be pertinent to mention here that while Muslims were very categorical in stating that they would relinquish their claim to the disputed site if the apex court verdict went against them, hardcore Hindu groups went about openly asserting that verdict or no verdict, the Ram temple would be built where the makeshift temple stands—on the debris of the Babri Masjid.

Perhaps that was the reason why Muslims were generally against the idea of an out-of-court settlement. Their apprehensions were quite natural. Any negotiated settlement could open the pandora's box for a similar settlement on two other vexed issues—the Kashi Vishwanath temple in Varanasi and the Krishna Janmbhoomi in Mathura.

After all, there could be no denying that the Ayodhya verdict going in favour of the temple would prove to be a big boon for BJP at the hustings.

However, there is one marked difference between Ayodhya and these two shrines. Unlike in Ayodhya, a temple and mosque have coexisted for centuries, both in Varanasi as well as in Mathura. But what is glaringly visible in these two places—again unlike Ayodhya—are temple remains jutting out of some of the walls of the mosques, built during the seventeenth century.

As for the Varanasi shrine, a dispute has been pending before the local district court, with Hindus and Muslims making their respective claims.

It was therefore no surprise when Lucknow-based lawyer Ranjana Agnihotri moved an application before the additional district judge (ADJ) of Mathura seeking handing over of the Eidgah land to the Krishna Janmbhoomi temple. Unfazed by the rejection of this application by ADJ Chhaya Sharma in September 2020, she filed a review petition before the district judge.

The second attempt did not prove to be a futile exercise like the initial effort that was turned down on account of the Places of Worship Act 1991, which disallowed any change in the status of any place of worship from how it stood on 15 August 1947. Agnihotri's plea has not only been taken note of, but the District and Sessions Judge Sadhana Rani Thakur decided to issue notices to all concerned parties named in the petition. These included the Sunni Central Waqf Board, the Shahi Masjid Idgah Management Trust, as well as Shri Krishna Janmbhoomi Trust and Shree Krishna Janmsthan Sewa Sansthan.

In fact, the enactment was made during the Narasimha Rao regime, while the Ramjanmbhoomi–Babri Masjid movement was touching its crescendo and with the VHP staking loud claims to two other mosques—the Gyanvapi mosque in Varanasi and the Shahi Idgah mosque in Mathura. It was against such a backdrop that the Narasimha Rao government brought in the act in September 1991 with a view to clamping a freeze on the status of all places of worship as they were on 15 August 1947.

However, the Places of Worship Act excluded the Ayodhya shrine from its purview simply because the issue had already been pending before different courts of law for more than a century.

According to a report in *The Hindu*,

> the enactment was intended to pre-empt new claims by any group about the past status of any place of worship and attempts to reclaim the structures or the land on which they stood. It was hoped that the legislation would help the preservation of communal harmony in the long run.[9]

Taking a cue from the Ayodhya case where 'Ram Lalla Virajman' (the deity of Lord Ram) was recognized as a legal entity, Agnihotri moved her application together with four others in the name of 'Sri Krishna Virajman' (the idol of Lord Krishna).

Also, precisely on the same lines as in the Ayodhya case, these applicants have contended that Lord Krishna was born exactly where the mosque stands today. As such, their main demand is 'restoration' of the entire 13.37 acres of land in and around the shrine. They also want the annulment of a settlement arrived at way back in 1968 between the Krishna Janmbhoomi temple governing body and the mosque management committee to coexist in harmony.

While the next date of hearing the case has been fixed for 18 November 2020, the applicants are confident of mobilizing huge support for their plea. 'You will see this turning into a people's movement very soon,' asserts a confident Agnihotri, who was closely involved with the Ayodhya legal battle for many years.

Agnihotri and her team have left no stone unturned in citing similarities between Mathura and Ayodhya. Quite akin to Ayodhya, where Hindus alleged that Mughal emperor Babur's army commander Mir Baqi destroyed the original Ram temple, the Krishna temple at Agnihotri's birthplace, she has contended, was desecrated by Aurangzeb, the last of the great Mughal emperors.

9

FLIRTING WITH CONTROVERSIES

Adityanath has imbibed his strong views against Muslims from Mahants Avaidyanath and Digvijaynath. On becoming the Hindu Mahasabha general secretary in 1950, Digvijaynath had declared that if his party 'attains power, it would deprive the Muslims of the right to vote for five to 10 years, the time that it would take for them to convince the government that their interests and sentiments are pro-Indian', *The Statesman* reported on 23 June 1950.[1]

In his 2017 statement carried on www.news18.com, Yogi is reported to have said that 'opposing Hindutva is akin to opposing development, spirit of India'.[2] In a warning to those who were against his brand of radical Hindutva, Yogi said, 'Hindutva and development are complementary to each other. Those who are opposing Hindutva are in fact opposing development and Bharatiyata (Indianness)'.[3] He was speaking at the launch of BJP's campaign for local bodies' elections in Ayodhya on 14 November 2017.

Yogi's antipathy towards the minorities is often reflected in several articles, which do not carry the writers' names but are available on his official portal http://www.yogiadityanath.in/ and in his speeches, examples of which are provided further down in the chapter. His strong views against the Muslim minority community leave one wondering if there is a cleaver hidden somewhere in the monk's saffron robes. He also betrayed his sentiment against secularist Hindus in a tweet on 7 July 2018:

> Kadwa satya jo bhagwa dhwaj sanatan dharmiyon ko jodta hai uske tagde virodhi adhikansh Hindu hi hain. Parantu jis ISIS ne poori duniya mein aatank macha rakha hai uska virodh koi shantipriya kaum ka sadasya nahi kar raha. Ab bhi samay hai sudhaar kar lo Hinduon apne dharm ko pehchano warna shamshaan bhi naseeb nahin hoga.

> [The bitter truth is that the strong opponents of the saffron Hindu flag, which unites the followers of Sanatan Dharma, are mainly Hindus. But no member of peace-loving community is criticizing the terror unleashed by ISIS. Hindus, there's still time to improve, recognize your religion or else you would not find place even for cremation.]

In April 2017, two of Adityanath's tweets were taken down by Twitter on the directive of the Election Commission of India because of their communal content. Posted on 5 April, the tweets referred to the Indian Union Muslim League (IUML) as 'green virus'.[4] His remark 'if the Congress, the SP and the BSP have faith in Ali, then we too have faith in Bajrang Bali' also invited the Election Commission's (EC) ire.

A Twitter official was quoted by the *Economic Times* as saying, 'This Tweet from @myogiadityanath has been withheld in India in response to a legal demand.'[5]

Explaining why a peaceful coexistence between the two communities is becoming increasingly difficult, veteran journalist Peter Popham wrote in an article in the *Independent*:

> According to the secularists who, in the name of the Congress Party, have ruled India for most of the past 50 years, centuries of cohabitation have resulted in the weaving together of the Hindu and Islamic strands of India's cultural heritage, to a point where they form a single cloth and cannot be separated without violence.
>
> The Hindu nationalists, in contrast, argue that it is Islam's intolerance and claim to exclusive truth that has led to the destruction, over and over again, of Hinduism's treasures and the defilement of its holy places, and that India's fundamental problem has been the failure of Hindus to stand up and fight.
>
> That is what, through militant organisations like the Rashtriya Swayam Sewak Sangh (RSS) and the Vishwa Hindu Parishad, they have been trying for the past century to rectify. The demolition of Babri Masjid . . . in Ayodhya in 1992 was one way of doing that.[6]

Such was the impact of Hindutva wave and consolidation of Hindu votes in 2014 that the BJP, which in keeping with its old tradition did not field a single Muslim candidate, swept the polls by winning 73 of the 80 Lok Sabha seats. The SP and Congress just managed to retain their family pocket boroughs, while the BSP got a cipher. What was significant was that for the first time in Uttar Pradesh's electoral history not a single Muslim was elected to the Lok Sabha from the state.

Describing the impact of Hindutva politics, one of Yogi's college friends told this author that 'Modi and Yogi have shown Muslims their place' even as the prime minister and the Uttar Pradesh chief minister insist that they believe in development of all and appeasement of none.

On his first visit to Gorakhpur as chief minister on 26 March 2017, Yogi said that as 'envisaged by the prime minister and BJP President Amit Shah there would be no discrimination on the basis of caste, religion or gender. There will be development of all. But there will not be appeasement of any section'.[7]

During the election campaign, the BJP fed into the fears of the Hindus that successive state governments—headed earlier by the Congress and in the recent decades by the BSP and the SP—had been unfairly biased against the majority community and were overtly in favour of the Muslims. This prompted a large chunk of Hindus to wholeheartedly support the BJP.

The argument had some weight. The SP government's various actions, such as its order withdrawing cases against terror-accused, making budgetary provision for construction of boundary walls around graveyards, Rs 30,000 scholarship for any Muslim girl passing Class X, special privileges for madarsas, were among the several examples cited by BJP leaders as proof of the anti-Hindu policies of the governments headed first by Mulayam Singh Yadav and later by his son Akhilesh Yadav.

Like his tweets mentioned above, Yogi's anti-Muslim speeches and remarks have grabbed more headlines than the social or spiritual work done by him as MP and head priest of the Gorakhnath temple.

The chief minister sought to remove the tag of being anti-Muslim by insisting that more Muslims partake of food served at the Gorakhnath temple than Hindus, and more Muslims undergo treatment at the temple-run hospital. 'There is no discrimination on religious lines', he asserted in an interview to a TV channel.[8]

Muslims in Gorakhpur say, off the record, that members of their community working in commercial establishments in and around the Gorakhnath temple for their livelihood vouch for Yogi's impartiality towards them more out of compulsion or fear. They believe that Yogi's arrest in 2007 was an aberration: otherwise, he is law unto himself in Gorakhpur. That is why there is an apprehension in the minds of the minority community in general about their safety concerns.

As Urdu writer Shamsur Rahman Faruqi wrote in the *Indian Express*,

> For the price of being allowed to live in peace, the community will gladly suffer the names and achievements of the Muslim past blackened or excised from the national memory. Perhaps they'll be happy to end up as the Biblical "hewers of wood, drawers of water".[9]

Muslims recalled Yogi's speech at the VHP's Virat Hindu Sammelan in February 2015, in which he said, 'If given a chance, we will install statues of Goddess Gauri, Ganesh and Nandi in all the mosques' and 'if they kill one Hindu we will kill 100 of them'.[10] These are provocative statements that would never promote harmony, said a Muslim cleric in Lucknow.

Yogi Adityanath government's stand on madarsas—starting with the launch of a portal (Uttar Pradesh Madarsa Board) in August 2017 for online registration of 19,000 recognized and 560 aided madarsas—and making videography of flag hoisting and singing of national anthem on Republic Day and

Independence Day mandatory, made a section of Muslims apprehensive that the singing of national song Vande Mataram would next be made compulsory.

But so far there has been no such move on the part of the Yogi government, and the Muslims' fear on that count has so far remained unfounded. Yet, they continue to be apprehensive of the chief minister.

To avoid any trouble, madarsas in the state have on their own made Aadhar cards mandatory for admission-seekers lest they get implicated in false cases.

Just as it had happened after the announcement of closure of illegal abattoirs and the ban specifically on cow, and not buffalo, slaughter, the fear of attacks by vigilantes forced Lucknow's iconic kebab-seller Tunday to switch over to making chicken kebabs instead of its famous buffalo and mutton versions for several months. After some apprehension-filled months, business was back to normal in the state. Beef (of cow), in any case, was never sold openly in Uttar Pradesh markets like it is done in Kerala or the Northeastern states and that restriction continues.

Fasih Uddin Ahmed, a retired colonel whose father, Siraj Uddin Ahmed, was a DIG in Uttar Pradesh in 1947 when the state had only five DIGs, and whose father-in-law, Muzaffar Hasan, was a cabinet minister in Uttar Pradesh for 17 years, described his community's fears thus:

> The Muslim skepticism of the RSS dates back to the days of the Partition when, it is said, RSS cadres in Jammu region massacred migrating Muslims through deceit by making them believe that they would actually help them cross over to safety. Similar issues happened in undivided Bengal. History has counter narratives for both incidents but seems to have

settled in the minds of the first generation of Muslims who saw Partition. This skepticism has rubbed off on the second generation of Muslims [those born around Partition].

The political outfits fostered and even promoted this insecurity amongst largely uneducated Muslims masquerading as champions of their cause. The "secularists" instilled a fake sense of entitlement. It had three major effects on the Muslim masses: One, they did not invest in modern education and remained confined to madarsas giving rise to political aspirations of theologists who assumed the role of a bridge between the masses and the political class.

Two, a false sense of entitlement made them believe in persecution that was systematically magnified by the political class and the clergy to manage their intellectual captivity.

Three, due to lack of modern education gradually a mental delineation set in as a deprived class/ second rate citizens.

The critical mass was achieved with the destruction of Babri mosque where the traditionally tolerant Hindu mass went berserk and the Muslims relating to the methodical pogrom of Sikhs in 1984 were led to believe that their future and that of their faith was not secure in their own land. This collective fear was exploited to the hilt by the political class and the clergy of both communities—a watershed moment in polarization/divisiveness.

Around the same time the ugly face of Islamic terror started surfacing in a big way on world scene. The gruesome and brutal imagery demonized the Islamic faith, the political content of which was not easily understood by the Muslims of India. The clergy whipped up the emotions of common detached Muslims of India that the whole world was ganging up to wipe out their religion. The Hindu right wing clubbed the Indian Muslim as a tyrant/rogue/terror monger, which ghettoed the masses into believing all that they were not.

The next stage came up with the proliferation of social media and rapid opinion transfer amongst masses, further dividing and pushing the Muslims and Hindu masses apart.

Today, besides the common insecurities that afflict both Hindu and Muslim youth, the biggest insecurity is about their identity, endangered faith, their patriotism/ nationalism being questioned—all being viewed through pan Islamic prism.[11]

From Yogi's interview to India TV's Rajat Sharma it emerged that for him there is no virasat (read Moghul heritage) and (as mentioned earlier) even renaming Taj Mahal as Ram Mahal or Tejo Mahalay was not beyond him, though he would like the 'issue to be publicly debated.[12] In his opinion, Taj Mahal did not reflect Indian culture and he was opposed to giving a Taj replica as a gift to visiting foreign dignitaries. Instead, he advocates giving a copy of the Bhagavad Gita.[13]

In her article 'Taj and Bigotry' (*Indian Express*, 24 October 2017), Audrey Truschke (Assistant Professor of South Asian History at Rutgers University) writes,

Part of explaining the threat of the Taj, as seen by the BJP, lies in understanding the narrowness of the Hindu culture espoused by this political party and its cultural affiliates. Hindu nationalists often fancy themselves as belonging to a quintessentially Indian tradition that stretches back to time immemorial, but history tells a different story. Hindutva ideology is a political philosophy that dates to the late 19th

century. In other words, Hindu nationalists are not part of
an ancient tradition but rather practitioners of a new one.[14]

Yogi was forced to hum a different tune on the Taj Mahal after
an international outrage over BJP legislator Sangeet Som's
remark terming the Taj Mahal as a blot on India's history that
compelled the Centre to step in.

Taking a U-turn on 18 October 2017, Yogi said, 'The
fact of the matter is that Taj Mahal is the pride of India.
The sweat and blood of artisans and labourers in India went
into its making. It is a symbol of hard work which must be
respected.'[15] If this was not a complete turnaround then his
calling the monument 'a priceless jewel'[16] on 26 October
2017 certainly was, although in his entire speech Yogi did not
mention Shahjahan or Mumtaz even once or wonder who the
architect of the monument was.

The statement praising the Taj came as a relief but it also left
one wondering about which statement of Yogi could be taken
at its face value—the one made on India TV describing the
Moghul-era monument as a symbol of the culture of invaders or
the one calling it a priceless jewel made with the blood and toil
of Indian workmen.

Articles

For a better understanding of Yogi Adityanath's views on
Islam, Hinduism and Indian culture, one should go through
some of the 12 undated, unattributed opinion pieces written
over a period of time, and posted on his website http://www.
yogiadityanath.in/lekh.aspx. The articles/opinion pieces do
not carry the writers' names, but the fact that they are on his

personal website leads one to assume that they have Yogi's ideological approval.

In one of the articles titled, 'Saavdhan, Yeh Islami Aatankvad Hai' (Beware! This is Islamic Terrorism), the unknown writer asks, 'Kya hai ye aatankvad? Kya Islam hee aatankvad ka doosra roop hai (What is this terrorism? Is Islam the other face of terrorism)?'[17] The writer goes on to argue,

> Iss desh athva viswa ke kuchh kathit buddhijivi atankvaad ke saath Islam shabd jorey jaane ka virodh karte hain. Woh issey Islam ko badnaam karne ki saazish batate hain. Lekin aaj jise I.I.S. [*sic*] Al-Qaeda, SIMI, Lashkar-e-Tayyeba athva HuJI aadi dwara prayojit antakvaad kaha jaa raha hain, jissey gumraah berozgaaron ki kartoot kaha jaa raha hain, bharat sarkar inn atankvaadiyon ko bhaare ka sainik bana rahi hai va vasttav mein desh aur duniya ko nasht karne ka ek mazhabi junoon hain, jissey sirf Islam aur Islam ke naam par anjaam diya jaa raha hai.[18]

> [Some so-called intellectuals in this country and abroad object to linking Islam with terror. They call it a conspiracy to malign Islam. But what is being described as I.I.S., al-Qaeda, SIMI, Lashkar-e-Tayyeba and HuJI-sponsored terrorism, as misdeeds of misguided, jobless youth and the Government of India calls these terrorists mercenaries, is in reality an international religious fanaticism aimed at destroying the country and the world. It is being executed only in the name of Islam.]

The article concludes with a jingoistic prophecy of Hindu conquest of Afghanistan and Pakistan: 'If this nation and its ancient culture have to be safeguarded, then the larger Hindu society has to awaken.' It then says,

> Jab Bharat ka rashtratva jagega . . . tab jaagrat Hindu Mahakali kee tarah aatankvaadiyon ke narmundon kee maalaa pahan kar apne laplapaatee jivha se aatank ke paryaay nar pishachon ka raktpaan karega. Tab Panchnad (Afghanistan) aur Saptnad (Pakistan) me phir se bhagwa lahraayega.

> [When Bharat's nationalism awakens then the awakened Hindu, like the Goddess Kali, wearing a garland of terrorists' skulls, will drink the blood of these vampires who are synonymous with terror. Then the saffron pennant will again fly in Afghanistan and Pakistan.]

For the anonymous writer the 'so-called secularists' who are 'turning their face away from danger' are either 'ostrich like' or paurush heen (emasculated).

Similar rhetorical points are raised in another article titled 'Islam Aur Aatankvad', which was written after the 2008 serial blasts in Jaipur.

> Sawaal phir wahee ghoom-phir kar ki aakhir hatyaaon ka yeh silsila jo is dhartee se hinduon kaa safaya karne par tula hai, kab tak chalega? Kaun hain ye aatankee? Kya rishta hai inka is maatee se? Dher saare prashn aaj bhee anuttarit hain.[19]

> [Back to the same question of how long will the murders of Hindus, aimed at wiping them out of the face of this earth, continue? Who are these terrorists? What is their relation with this country? Lot of questions are unanswered even today.]

The article poses many more questions such as: Why have Hindus been completely wiped out in Afghanistan and Pakistan? Why is the cleansing of Hindus in Bangladesh in its last phase? Why have Muslim-dominated regions separated from Russia or want to part ways? Why has Yugoslavia splintered? Why do Muslims of the world want to obliterate Israel? Why every Muslim-dominated region does not hesitate in disrobing the country of which it is a part, its motherland? After all, why are Chechenya, Yugoslavia, Kosovo and Kashmir Valley in the same situation due only to one reason?

Jab tak 'jehad' aur 'jannat' ka vichaar iss dhartu par rahega antankvaad samapt nahi ho sakta. Aao sankalp karein jehad aur jannat ke vichaat ka samul naash karne ka. Tabhi dharm aur sanskriti bachegi aur hamari asmita bhi surakshit rahegi.[20]

[So long as the idea of 'jihad' and 'jannat' remains on this earth terrorism cannot be rooted out. Come take a pledge to root out the idea of 'jihad' and 'jannat'. Only then will our culture and our pride will be safe.]

Incidentally, views expressed in these articles find echo in former BBC journalist Tufail Ahmed's article on Indian Muslims in Firstpost.

The rising population changes the Muslim community's political and cultural behaviour. There are regions in India which are being proudly described as 'mini-Pakistan' by Muslims, not by Hindus. In the states of West Bengal, Bihar, Uttar Pradesh, Kerala and many other pockets, Muslims no longer behave as a minority community. In fact, this so-called minority community is electorally assertive and politically demanding, while forcing the majority Hindus to behave as a minority, notably at the election times by wearing caps and courting their minority votes.[21]

'Idiot Mujahideen', yet another article on Yogi's website dealing with the subject of Islam, terrorism and the threat to Hinduism, has this to say:

Islam ka anuyayee jahaan kahee bhee gayaa hai, kum athwaa zyada jo bhee uskee sankhyaa hai usne pooree duniya ko aatankit kiya hai.[22]

[Wherever has the follower of Islam gone, irrespective of whether their numbers were less or more, they have terrorized the entire world.]

The article concludes with the advice that Muslims should be treated as enemies and not friends. 'The only caution that we have to exercise is of treating the enemy like an enemy and not commit the mistake of making him a friend otherwise the consequence faced by Emperor Prithviraj Chauhan will be repeated.' Prithivraj Chauhan (reign 1178–1192) lost to Mohammad Ghori in 1192.

Creating Hype: Khatre Mein Hindu

Yogi is an unapologetic hardliner Hindu, wearing his religion literally on his sleeve. This is reflected in his Lok Sabha speech on communalism and the articles 'Khatre me Hindu' and 'Rashtreeyata ke Khilaaf hai Dharmantaran' (Conversion is against Nationalism), posted on his website, which are about his fear of Hindu culture being wiped out because of the rapid demographic changes in the country.

It is this perceived fear of demographic imbalance that feeds Adityanath's strident Hindutva, making him detest the idea of syncretic culture. The piece 'Conversion Is against Nationalism' says that on the one hand, demographic imbalance (due to conversion) has endangered social, cultural and political harmony and, on the other, it poses a constant challenge to national security because 'change of religion leads to change of nationality'.[23]

In 'Khatre Mein Hindu' (Hindu in Danger) Swami Vivekanand is quoted to underline, though not convincingly, the point that change of religion leads to change of nationality.

Jab pahlee baar Hindustan par Mughal aakraantaon ne hamlaa kiya thha tou us samay is desh me hinduon kee aabaadee 60 karod thhee. Lekin 1235 varshon ke baad yeh desh sun 1947 me aazaad hua tou hinduon kee kul aabaadee rah gayee maatr 30 karod. Arthaat 1235 varshon me hinduon kee aabaadee aadhee hona aakhir kya darshaataa hai? Yeh sach hai ki mazhab badalne par rashtriyta bhee badal jaatee hai.[24]

[When Muslim invaders attacked Hindustan for the first time the population of Hindus in the country was 60 crore. But when the country attained freedom in 1947 after 1235 years, the population of Hindus had dwindled to a mere 30 crores. What does this reduction of Hindu population by half show? It is true that change of religion leads to change of nationality.]

This claim defeats history and logic. Wikipedia shows India's population in the year 1500 as 1 crore. Therefore, Adityanath's claim that there were 60 crore Hindus at the time of Mughal invasion seems unconvincing. In fact, as per the official statistics, the entire population of undivided India in 1947 was 39 crores. After Partition, India's population was reduced to 33 crores. According to the 1951 Government of India census, the country's population was about 34 crores of which there were about 3.4 crores Muslims.[25]

Adityanath's argument nevertheless got a boost in January 2015 when the Narendra Modi government released religion-based census which said that the Muslim population in the country had grown by 24 per cent between 2001 and 2011, against the national average of 18 per cent.

On the contrary, interpreting the data on Population by Religious Communities of Census 2011, *The Hindu* pointed out that India's Muslim population was growing slower than it had in the previous decades, 'and its growth rate has slowed more sharply than that of the Hindus'.[26]

The RSS which has been organizing re-conversion of Muslims and Christians was clearly worried about the 'demographic disadvantage' that Hindus were placed at, vis-à-vis the Muslims. 'At a convention of newly married Hindu couples in Uttar Pradesh in August 2017, RSS worker Darpan said that to keep our culture and civilization alive we must seriously and responsibly think about our fertility rates,' reported *The Hindu*.[27]

The religion-based census triggered a race, with BJP leaders and a seer wanting Hindu women to become child-bearing machines. Party MP Sakshi Maharaj urged Hindu women to produce four children, while Shyamal Goswami, a BJP leader from Bengal, said that for Hinduism to survive all Hindu women should have at least five children. The Shankaracharya of Jyotirmath went a step further and advised Hindu women to have at least ten children 'to maintain their majority status'.[28]

This fear of losing demographic advantage was exacerbated by the release of population data in March 2017 by a US-based think tank, Pew Research Centre, which projected that the number of Muslims in India will rise to more than 300 million by 2050. 'But India is also expected to have 311 million Muslims in 2050 (11% of the global total), making it the country with the largest population of Muslims in the world. Currently, Indonesia has the world's largest number of Muslims,' the Pew report said.[29]

Commenting on the Pew data, Tufail Ahmed wrote in Firstpost,

> As per the research, the rise in Muslim population is high due to the young median age of 22 and high fertility rates, while 26 is the median age for Hindus in India. In India, Muslim women have 3.2 children per woman on average, while the figure for Hindu and Christian women is 2.5 and 2.3 children, respectively.[30]

Concurring with the unease these trends were causing in the BJP and RSS, Tufail Ahmed wrote,

> These population trends may cause anxiety among non-Muslims worldwide, who already appear to be affected by issues involving Islam. For example, the rise of Al-Qaeda and the Islamic State in the Middle East has caused migrations to Europe, while there are concerns on the nature of Islam itself,

as it affects communitarian relationships between Muslims
and non-Muslims in many parts of the world. In the streets
of London, groups of Islamist men stop non-Muslims from
holding hands in public, saying it is un-Islamic.[31]

Significantly, like Yogi, Tufail Ahmed, also blamed appeasement
by previous governments for the communal situation in India.

Largely due to the incompetence of Union Home Ministry,
whose job it is to shape the country's rule of law, the Indian
State too has learnt to bend its law enforcement to suit the
Muslims. For example, Hindus such as Kamlesh Tiwari [a
Hindu Mahasabha leader murdered by alleged Islamists in
Lucknow on 19 October 2019] can be arrested for criticising
the prophet of Islam, but the Indian State seems to be totally
powerless against Islamic clerics who publicly announce
rewards for anyone who criticizes Islam.[32]

But journalist Aarefa Johari disagrees. According to her,

The eagerness to produce more and more Hindu babies
stems from the unfounded paranoia about a growth in
India's Muslim population. Outfits like the Rashtriya
Swayam Sewak Sangh . . . have often peddled the theory
that Hindus in India are in danger of being outnumbered
by Muslims.[33]

Whether real or imaginary, the fear that Hindus would be
swamped by Muslims is being used by the BJP to exploit the
majority Hindu sentiments for politically consolidating its
position. Yogi is at the vanguard of the consolidation process

alongside Prime Minister Narendra Modi and Union Home Minister Amit Shah.

Yogi takes on Muslims and Christians, on the one hand, and the 'pseudo secularists' on the other. One line of his argument, as seen in his articles and speeches, accuses Muslims and Christians of converting Hindus to numerically gain an upper hand. The other part of his argument, as seen in his Lok Sabha speech on communalism, blames regional political outfits like the SP and the BSP for appeasing Muslims 'ignoring the grave threat they pose to Hindus per se and the country and its Hindu culture in general'.[34]

His vigorous denunciation of Islam for the threat it poses to Hinduism can be attributed to his spiritual lineage. It also reflects the influence of Samuel Huntington's theory as expounded in *The Clash of Civilizations* in which Islam has been shown to be in conflict with other religions in the world. The only difference here is that like Islam, Yogi's Hinduism is also in conflict with Christianity.

Whether or not Yogi read Huntington's book before forming his opinion is not known, but the events in Uttar Pradesh are playing out much on the lines of a civilizational clash in which 'as violence increases, the initial issues at stake tend to get redefined more exclusively as "us" against "them" and group cohesion and commitment are enhanced'.[35]

What will sound familiar to the Indian ear in the present context is this:

> Political leaders expand and deepen their appeals to ethnic and religious loyalties, and civilization consciousness strengthens in relation to other identities. A 'hate dynamic' emerges, compared to the 'security dilemma' in international relations,

in which mutual fears, distrust and hatred feed on each other.
Each side dramatizes and magnifies the distinction between
the forces of virtue and the forces of evil.[36]

In a more pointed reference to India, Huntington writes,

The conflict of civilizations is deeply rooted elsewhere in Asia.
The historic clash between Muslims and Hindus in the sub-
continent manifests itself now not only in the rivalry between
Pakistan and India but also in intensifying religious strife
within India between increasingly militant Hindu groups
and India's substantial Muslim minority. The destruction of
the Ayodhya mosque in December 1992 brought to the fore
the issue of whether India will remain a secular democratic
state or become a Hindu one.[37]

The overwhelming political dominance of the BJP in Uttar
Pradesh and the overt display of fervour by Hindu religionists
has Muslims apprehending whether India would shed its secular
tag if the BJP continues to gain in strength at the Centre and
in states.

Although the BJP does not have any credible opposition
in the north, it would still want to stamp its supremacy using
Hindutva and the social media trolls to bolster its chances. For
its Hindutva agenda the party and the RSS rely heavily on Yogi
Adityanath, after Prime Minister Narendra Modi and Amit
Shah. During the 2019 Lok Sabha elections the Uttar Pradesh
chief minister was especially sent to campaign in Gujarat,
Himachal Pradesh, the Northeast, Karnataka and Kerala.

Yogi was among those who, just before the March 2017
Assembly election, made a mountain out of a molehill in the

name of exodus of families from Kairana town in western Uttar Pradesh. It was the local BJP MP Hukum Singh, now deceased, who first raised an alarm over what he termed as 'exodus' of Hindus from this pocket of western Uttar Pradesh, widely referred to as Uttar Pradesh's 'wild west'.

The suspicion that this was yet another attempt to whip up Hindu passions came out to be true, with Hukum Singh going on the back foot shortly after a reality check was carried out, not only by the local administration but also by different media teams.

> Yes, this is more of a law and order problem and not a Hindu–Muslim issue,' Hukum Singh conceded three days after he had released a list of 346 persons who, he alleged, were compelled to flee from their homes in Kairana by the dominant local Muslims. This was in sharp contrast to what he had said initially, when he went to the extent of equating Kairana with the exodus of Pandits from Kashmir. In a subsequent interview, Singh 'claimed that he never raised the issue of exodus of any particular community'.[38]

Even as Prime Minister Narendra Modi focused only on 'development'—a card that gave him an unprecedented surge in the 2014 Lok Sabha poll, Yogi left no stone unturned to whip up the Kairana issue to an extent that it even prompted the National Human Rights Commission (NHRC) to issue notice to then Akhilesh Yadav government.

On the flip side, the nudge by the NHRC got an otherwise lax Uttar Pradesh administration to get down to brass tacks and do a door-to-door reality check. This opened a pandora's box of falsehoods packed in Hukum Singh's initial allegations.

A report on 118 names submitted by the Uttar Pradesh police and Shamli district administration found that 5 of them were dead for several years, while 55 had moved out of Kairana 6 to 11 years ago and 46 had left in 2011. A dozen of the names mentioned in the list were very much there in Kairana.

While backtracking on the issue, Hukum Singh promptly sought to clarify that 'by mistake someone in my team mentioned Hindu families. I asked them to change that. I am convinced that this is not a Hindu–Muslim issue. This is just a list of people who have left Kairana under duress', he confessed before media persons in Kairana.[39]

Another reality check by a media team revealed that most of the people who left Kairana had their own personal reasons— economic or social. If one left in search of better prospects in Haryana or in Delhi, then another went away to provide better education to his children, since Kairana has no educational institution of repute. However, there was no denying that some of the persons mentioned had fled the town because of unabated extortion by local criminal gangs, enjoying the patronage of successive political regimes. Even Hukum Singh conceded that, but he went on to insist that, 'gangsters active in this area all happen to be Muslims and those who have fled on their account were Hindus', which was factually correct.

Even after the record was set straight, Yogi continued to rake up the Kairana issue whenever it suited him to arouse Hindu passions. Even when it came to campaigning for elections to the local bodies, he did not hesitate to claim credit for preventing 'Kairana type of incidents' from happening.

Reiterating his old allegation that Hindus were compelled to march out of Kairana town because of harassment by powerful Muslim goons enjoying patronage of the earlier government, he claimed, 'restoration of the rule of law now has brought an end to such exodus.'

Divisive Utterances

Here are a few samples from Yogi Adityanath's speeches which contributed to polarization and, many believe, led to voting on communal lines:

June 2015: In Varanasi, the Prime Minister's constituency, Adityanath said: 'Those opposing yoga and Surya Namaskar should either leave India or drown themselves in the ocean.'[40]

November 2015:

These people speak the language of terrorists. There is no difference between the language of Shah Rukh Khan and Hafiz Saeed. He should remember that if a huge mass of people boycotts his films, he will have to wander on the streets like a normal Muslim.[41]

The remark was in response to Shah Rukh Khan's comment on growing intolerance. 'There is nothing worse than religious intolerance and that it would take India to Dark Ages,' the superstar had said.[42]

June 2016: While the world hailed Mother Teresa for her work among lepers and the poor, Adityanath saw her as a conspirator and spreader of Christianity: 'Teresa was part of a conspiracy to convert Hindus to Christianity. Large-scale conversions to Christianity in the Northeast had led to a separatist movement in Arunachal Pradesh, Tripura, Meghalaya, and Nagaland.'[43]

February 2017: A month before the Assembly elections, Adityanath talked about the exodus of Hindus from Kairana and prepared the pitch for votes to swing the BJP way.

> Issues like exodus of Hindus from Kairana, love jihad and women's safety will dominate the poll scene. Yogi is not talking about today. Yogi is talking about the future. The BJP will not let Western Uttar Pradesh turn into another Kashmir. Political leaders in this country speak against the majority community in the name of secularism. Governments in UP give land for *kabristan* but not for *shamshanghat*.[44]

He had earlier blamed pseudo-secularism and appeasement policies of Uttar Pradesh governments for the exodus because of which the population of Hindus in Kairana 'has come down from 68 per cent to 8 per cent'.

Love Jihad: Christophe Jaffrelot wrote in the *Indian Express* about Adityanath's definition of love jihad, his 'pet theme' during the 2014 election campaign. The definition as culled out from his website states that it is

> a system where a girl surrounded with fragrance is enticed into a stinking world; where the girl leaves her civilised parents for parents who might have been siblings in the past; where purity is replaced with ugliness; where relationships have no meaning; where a woman is supposed to give birth every nine months; where the girl is not free to practice her religion; and if the girl realises her mistakes and wants to be freed, she is sold off.[45]

Opening the Door, Just a Bit

Political compulsions seem to have forced Yogi to stop looking at Muslims as his bête noire, at least for the time being. He appeared to have mellowed somewhat after becoming chief minister as he did not lash out at the minorities—read Muslims and Christians—the way he did during election campaigns and as five-time MP. At least not until the protests over the anti-Citizenship Amendment Act when he came down on the protesters with a heavy hand, even at the expense of law.

He may not have compromised on strident Hindutva as proven by his order on slaughterhouses banning sale of beef (cow meat) and putting up hoardings with photos and addresses of anti-CAA protesters on Lucknow's main roads. Because of the office he now holds, Yogi seems to have realized he cannot be a stormy petrel which he earlier was.

One does not expect Yogi Adityanath, chief minister of India's largest state, to go around spewing venom against minorities like he used to do as mahant-cum-MP. So, while we hear statements like 'sabka saath, sabka vikas' and 'no appeasement' of any community, he continues to propagate that doing Surya Namaskar was similar to offering namaz. 'Those opposing the yogic exercise wanted to divide the society on religious lines,' he said on Yoga Day in March 2017.

Similarly, he has stuck to his view that all Muslim kings were 'invaders' and the monuments built by them are an eyesore to him.

As chief minister, Yogi's immediate task is to ensure the state's development and fulfil the promises which his party made to the electorate before the 2017 Assembly elections. Given his image, it was hard to imagine that as chief minister of Uttar

Pradesh Yogi would be able to take everyone along and ensure development of all (sabka saath, sabka vikas) as promised by Prime Minister Modi in his election speeches. But contrary to his earlier utterances, Adityanath now also assures the minorities that there will not be any discrimination whether one wears a 'tilak' or 'topee' while asserting that there will not be any more appeasement either.

To prove his genuineness, his government announced that every year it will provide funds for the marriage of 100 poor Muslim girls in a common ceremony. That a change towards Muslims would be visible so early in Yogi Adityanath's tenure was hard to imagine, and Muslims, who find the sword of National Register of Citizens (NRC) hanging over them, would hardly be sanguine about him.

Call it political opportunism or compulsion, the party—which did not field a single Muslim candidate in the Lok Sabha elections of 2014 and the Uttar Pradesh Assembly elections in 2017—opened its doors, however narrowly, to Muslims in the local body polls in 2017. Four Muslims, including the son of former SP MLC Bukkal Nawab, who vacated his seat to facilitate Uttar Pradesh Deputy Chief Minister Keshav Prasad Maurya's entry into the Upper House, were given tickets for corporators. The party also went soft on Nawab who faced charges of illegally amassing property after he 'sacrificed' his seat for Maurya.

In some of the nagar panchayats where Muslim presence is strong, the party found it fit to give tickets to members of the community. In places like Unnao, Shahjahanpur, Bijnor, Meerut, Kanpur, Amethi and many other districts, Muslims figured in BJP's list of candidates.

Giving credit to Prime Minister Narendra Modi and Yogi Adityanath, party spokesman Harish Srivastava said that it was because of their development model that people from all sections and categories were applying for tickets. It is a proof of the BJP being an inclusive party as 'we have reaffirmed time and again our commitment to development of all and appeasement of none'.

'We are not an anti-Muslim party. When it comes to ticket distribution all parties look at winnability of candidates, irrespective of their caste and creed. That is why Muslims, who were missing in the assembly poll list, now find a place in the list for elections to local bodies. It had nothing to do with religion,' Srivastava told the authors in an interview.[46]

The local bodies' elections being all about grassroots politics, the BJP could ill-afford to exclude Muslims, and fielding members of the community out of political compulsion goes to show that the party was taking these elections seriously.

In the 2012 local bodies elections, the BJP fielded only 842 candidates in 5,148 wards. While it had no candidate in Muslim-dominated panchayats, against 980 posts of corporators the party fielded only 844 candidates. For the Varanasi Municipal Corporation election, the party fielded only 78 candidates against 90 seats because it did not have candidates for Muslim-dominated localities.

With Muslims accounting for 50 to 70 per cent of voters in Aligarh, Shamli, Moradabad, Firozabad and Sambhal nagar panchayats, the BJP had little choice other than giving tickets to Muslims as it wanted to expand its base.

In the last panchayat elections held between May and July 2021, the same problem cropped up once again, compelling the BJP leadership to include a few Muslims in the party's list of nominees. The idea behind holding such elections was to empower people's representatives at the grassroots level through establishment of local self-government in all villages.

However, the manner in which the elections process has been carried out through the years speaks volumes of how all players in the system have systematically defeated the very fundamentals of the Mahatma's dream of ushering in 'panchayati raj' in the country.

What appears to have punctured the whole concept behind the process is the inclusion of the element of indirect election at one level. It is this indirect election of heads of zila panchayats and development blocks that has given rise to play of money power, muscle power as also blatant misuse of government authority, leading to altering the original mandate of the common masses. Crossing all limits in June–July 2021, was the visibly biased role of government and police officials, thereby giving rise to yet another controversy.

In Etawah on 10 July 2021, an SP-rank officer was thrashed by BJP goons in full public view. In Unnao district, a photojournalist trying to capture alleged irregularities by BJP activists was beaten up by the district chief development officer—a young IAS officer—who behaved like a ruling party worker.

While the four-tier election is largely direct, and all adults in the village elect gram pradhans and gram panchayat members, the election of zila panchayat chairpersons and block pramukhs is indirect—by the directly elected members. That is where all hell breaks loose, but no meaningful voice is raised against the malpractices simply because successive political parties in power manage to reap their own harvest out of the irregularities that have prevailed and grown with the passage of time.

It was, therefore, no surprise for the ruling BJP to be revelling in the glory of its resounding victory in these elections over the months of June and July 2021. BJP won on 66 of the state's 75 seats of zila panchayat chiefs and, likewise, 649 of the 825 posts of block pramukh. Nearly 40 per cent of these were bagged unopposed by the ruling party.

Chief Minister Yogi Adityanath and his team instantly got down to blowing their own trumpet for this victory.

On their part, both Prime Minister Modi as well as Union Home Minister Amit Shah promptly hailed the Uttar Pradesh chief minister for the 'big win'.

No one, however, has cared to explain the magic behind the overnight conversion of a humiliating defeat in the direct election of zila panchayat members into a resounding victory at the subsequent indirect election of zila panchayat and block chiefs.

In all, election was held for 3,051 members of zila panchayats in April–May 2021. While the nominations were not done on party lines, all mainstream political parties openly declared their support for different candidates. The results showed that SP led with as many as 853 winners, followed by BJP's 732 and BSP's 321. The remaining winners were independents.

However, the numbers won by opposition parties were rendered meaningless by the party in power, which managed to twist and turn the people's mandate. For instance, in Bijnor district in western Uttar Pradesh, BJP-supported candidates won only five seats of members. But when it came to electing the local zila panchayat chief, this figure swelled to 20, which makes it obvious that 15 members were won over by the ruling

party by whatever means—money power, muscle power or
official intimidation.

Ideally, such a roaring victory in a rural election barely
seven months before the Assembly poll would be considered a
precursor to the eventual battle of the ballot in March 2022.
However, the manner in which all democratic norms were
bruised and battered in the zila panchayat chairperson and
block pramukh polls raises serious doubts about the same trend
playing out in the Assembly election.

Going by the past experience of BJP's arch political rivals, it
can be stated that the picture has not been as rosy for the ruling
parties when they went for Assembly elections, after registering
resounding victories in panchayat polls.

Take for instance Akhilesh Yadav's SP which bagged almost
as many seats in the previous panchayat polls in 2015 as BJP
won in 2021. As many as 80 per cent of the zila panchayat
chairpersons carried the SP flag. Yet the party lost miserably
in the 2017 Assembly elections with a score of just 47 in the
403-member Uttar Pradesh assembly, with BJP winning a
record 312 seats.

Likewise, Mayawati's BSP managed its supremacy on 85
per cent seats of zila panchayat chiefs in 2010, while she was
in power. However, the Assembly poll that followed in 2012
brought the party's graph down to 80, while Akhilesh pedalled
his way to power with 224 seats.

Yet, it goes without saying that with its panchayat-level
chieftains in place now, the ruling party is surely better equipped
to counter the misgivings of the people, who faced unprecedented
challenges on account of the gross mismanagement of the
COVID-19 second wave, which caused untold misery at the
grassroots level. That the Yogi Adityanath government has

moved heaven and earth to cover up its failures in providing adequate medical care during the pandemic through a blitzkrieg of publicity campaigns is an open secret. But whether this will pay the desired political dividends in the much-awaited Assembly election in March 2022 remains a million-dollar question.

10

YOGI

THE PEOPLE'S REPRESENTATIVE

As a student Ajay Singh Bisht may have dabbled in college politics, but it was only as Yogi Adityanath that he tasted his first electoral victory.

In college one of his brothers-in-law wanted him to join the Student's Federation of India—Communist Party of India's student wing—for his foray into student union elections. But according to his friends, an acquaintance, Pramod Rawat alias Tunna, persuaded him to join the ABVP, the student wing of the BJP, which also has its roots in the RSS.

Ajay Bisht began to actively participate in ABVP's activities, but despite all his efforts he was denied a ticket to contest the college election, following which he chose to jump into the fray as an independent. Even though Ajay lost the election, he came into the spotlight, thereby marking his first step into public life.

Once Ajay joined the Gorakhnath temple as the principal disciple of Mahant Avaidyanath and became Yogi Adityanath, he not only became his spiritual successor but also his political heir. After all, Avaidyanath had trained his disciple not only for serving the larger cause of Hindu religion but also of religion-driven politics.

Avaidyanath represented Gorakhpur's Maniram constituency in the Uttar Pradesh Assembly as an independent for five consecutive terms: 1962, 1967, 1969, 1974 and 1977.

As Avaidyanath was ageing, it was time for him to pass on his political mantle to his favourite shishya (disciple). Thus, began Adityanath's initiation into national politics in 1996 when Mahant Avaidyanath entrusted him with the responsibility of managing his Lok Sabha poll campaign.

On his retirement from active politics in 1998, Avaidyanath declared Adityanath as his political heir and nominated him for the Lok Sabha seat vacated by him. Following in his guru's footsteps, Adityanath successfully contested his first parliamentary election in 1998, and he became the youngest member of the 12th Lok Sabha at age 26. He subsequently went on to win four successive parliamentary elections from Gorakhpur—in 1999, 2004, 2009 and 2014, becoming a five-time MP.

Adityanath won his first election by 26,000 votes, but the victory margin plunged in 1999 to only 7,339 votes. The reduced victory margin came as a jolt for the young MP who then raised the HYV to boost his tally in subsequent elections.

Stint in Parliament

As the youngest parliamentarian, Adityanath's first stint in the Lok Sabha in 1998 was largely spent in learning the ropes. He was member of the Parliamentary Committee on Food, Civil

Supplies and Public Distribution and its subcommittee on
department of sugar and edible oils. He also was a member of
the Consultative Committee of the Home Ministry.

After his re-election to the House in 1999, he retained his
membership of the two panels. During his third term as MP,
he was part of the Committee on Government Assurances and
member of the panel on external affairs while retaining his place
on the Home Ministry's Consultative Committee.

From 2009 to 2014, he was member of the Panel on
Transport, Tourism and Culture. From September 2014 he was
Chairperson of the Joint Committee on Salaries and Allowances
of Members of Parliament. Under his leadership, the committee
proposed to double the salary of MPs from Rs 50,000 per
month to Rs 100,000 per month. The daily allowance of
Rs 2,000 (when Parliament is session) was also proposed to be
raised to Rs 4,000. A hike in MPs pension from the present
Rs 20,000 per month to Rs 35,000 per month was also
suggested.[1] So much for all his loud talk on austerity.

The membership of the various committees would have
given the Gorakhpur MP an idea of issues pertaining to the
departments as he matured into a seasoned parliamentarian.

He was an active participant in debates between 2009 and
2014 and asked more questions than an average MP, although
his 72 per cent attendance in the House was below the 79 per
cent averaged by other MPs from Uttar Pradesh, and the 76 per
cent average attendance of other MPs.

As per the PRS Legislative Research data, 11 per cent of
debates in which Adityanath took part in the 15th Lok Sabha
were about issues of concern to Hindus.[2] These included
reorganization of Amarnath Shrine Board and facilities for
Amarnath pilgrims, lifting the ban on Kailash Mansarovar
Yatra via Nepal and developing Mithilanchal—a proposed

state comprising Mithila and extending up to Nepal, which has Ramayan-era significance.

The debates in which he participated in this term before being appointed the chief minister of Uttar Pradesh were about a nationwide ban on cow slaughter, safety of Hindu pilgrims and, more significantly, Uniform Civil Code.[3]

The Gorakhpur MP participated in a few debates on issues related to river pollution, budget, central status for Gorakhpur University and creation of Poorvanchal as a separate state.

In the sixteenth Lok Sabha, Adityanath's participation in parliamentary debates pertaining to the Uniform Civil Code, national ban on cow slaughter and Enemy Property Bill[4] created much discussion. In the debate on Enemy Property (Amendment and Validation) Bill, 2016, Adityanath argued,

> If a government really fulfils this order allowing properties to be returned to owners, half the cities of this country will be destroyed . . . a new class struggle will be created inside the country and . . . all the citizens of Pakistan will start making backdated ration cards together with those few vote bank merchants within India, and will start saying 'we have been living in India since 1947'. Under this guise an attempt is being made to bring those people inside India.[5]

On cow slaughter and the Uniform Civil Code, Adityanath moved bills to amend the Constitution.

Private Member's Bills

In July 2014 Adityanath moved a private member's bill seeking 'to prohibit the slaughter of cow and its progeny' across the country.[6]

Those 'contravening the provisions' of the Bill were liable to 'be punished with imprisonment which may extend to 10 years or with fine which may extend to rupees one lakh or both'.

Apparently influenced by the chief minister's view, the state law commission made a similar recommendation in its draft bill on the ban on cow slaughter in Uttar Pradesh.[7]

In the same month, July 2014, Adityanath moved another bill for introducing the Uniform Civil Code in the country. Called the Constitution (Amendment) Bill 2014 (Omission of Article 44, etc.), the bill sought removal of Article 44 of the Constitution which states that 'The State shall endeavour to secure for the citizens a uniform civil code throughout the territory of India'. As it is a directive principle this provision is not legally enforceable. Adityanath's Bill sought to amend the Constitution to insert Article 51C and part IV B to read, 'The State shall secure for the citizen a uniform civil code.'

The third constitutional amendment, also in 2014, sought by Adityanath was for changing the name of the country. The Constitution (Amendment) Bill (Amendment of Article 1 etc.) seeks to change the country's name from 'India that is Bharat' to 'Bharat that is Hindustan'.[8]

His fourth and fifth private member's Bills were moved in 2015.[9] Through the Constitution (Amendment) Bill, 2015 (Insertion of new Article 25A) Adityanath wanted a ban on religious conversions in the country.

His last Bill—High Court at Allahabad (Establishment of a Permanent Bench at Gorakhpur)—was for the setting up of a permanent Bench of the Allahabad High Court in his parliamentary constituency.

All the five bills were awaiting Lok Sabha's approval at the time Adityanath[10] resigned from Parliament to become the chief

minister of Uttar Pradesh in 2017. Four of these Bills are in sync
with the RSS agenda of declaring India a Hindu Rashtra and
checking the growth of Muslim population.

Cow slaughter ban has already become a big issue with
vigilante groups, who have been taking the law in their hands.
Kerala and the Northeastern states have rebuffed the idea
because beef consumption is part of the common diet in these
states. While BJP has made political inroads in Kerala and has
succeeded in riding on to power in the Northeast, the party
leadership skilfully skirts the cow-slaughter issue in these regions.

Taking on Adityanath's detractors, the then Union
Urban Development Minister M. Venkaiah Naidu, now
the vice president of India, wrote on his Facebook page on
19 March 2017: 'It is unfortunate that some opponents,
communalists are trying to portray him as a rabble-rouser and
fringe personality. They should go through his parliamentary
debates. Those reveal his seasoned thinking on various issues
of governance.'

In the wake of the death of 64 children in three days—
9, 10 and 11 August 2017—at the BRD Medical College in
Gorakhpur, former Union Health Minister Ghulam Nabi Azad
accused Adityanath of not having done enough to get Central
aid to improve facilities at the medical college despite having
been a five-time MP of Gorakhpur.[11]

Adityanath was under attack not only because he had
represented Gorakhpur in Parliament but also because the
tragedy occurred just two days after he had inspected the
hospital.

Quoting PRS Legislative Research, Firstpost news portal
wrote on 15 August that out of the 57 Lok Sabha debates in
which Adityanath had taken part, three were on encephalitis.

The first time he raised the issue was in 2011. Adityanath was 'critical' of the UPA government for taking the scourge of encephalitis lightly. 'I have been raising this issue many times but the government has done little. Don't the innocent people of eastern Uttar Pradesh have the right to live a healthy life?' he had then asked.

In his farewell speech in Lok Sabha, after taking over as chief minister of Uttar Pradesh, he again raised the issue of encephalitis. 'Several times I had drawn the attention of the House to the 34 encephalitis-affected districts of Eastern Uttar Pradesh and the loss of lives of innocent children because of the disease,' he pointed out.

Attacking 'those who talk about minorities, lower castes and disadvantaged communities', Adityanath said that more than 90 per cent of children who die due to encephalitis every year belong to the minority community and lower castes, yet 'nobody has tried to reach out to them'.

In 2010 Adityanath embarrassed his party by refusing to support the women's reservation bill and stating that he would defy the whip if it was issued. 'There is no question of a whip in favour of the Bill; we are public representatives and not bonded labour,' he told the *Hindustan Times*.[12] It was not his opposition to the women's quota bill per se that raised eyebrows but his chauvinistic views on women and their role in society. A defiant Adityanath told the newspaper,

> We will push for a discussion in the party with all MPs on the women's quota issue, as was decided during a meeting at Advaniji's (Lal Krishna Advani) residence. This must happen, or I will resign as MP. Air-conditioned room people in Delhi cannot decide public policy.

He then came up with a quote (to the same newspaper) which has been used to brand him as a misogynist, and shocked even his classmate. 'If men develop feminine traits, they become gods, but if women develop masculine traits they become demons. Western ideas of women's liberation should be properly analysed in the Indian context,' said Adityanath who wanted women to focus more on household chores and rearing children.

In this context, he wanted an analysis to be done to see how quota for women in panchayat and local bodies had influenced their role as mothers and wives.

After being elected member of the Uttar Pradesh Legislative Council, Yogi Adityanath resigned from the membership of the Lok Sabha on 21 September 2017. With Yogi out of the way, the BJP may find it easy to move the women's quota bill once again. As of now, the bill has lapsed.

Speech on Communalism

In his 13 August 2014 speech, delivered in the Lok Sabha in his usual combative style, the Gorakhpur MP castigated the Congress and the Communists for their politics of appeasement which had led to Hindus 'closing their ranks' and voting for the BJP.

Participating in the debate on communalism, Adityanath took a light-hearted jibe against Leader of Opposition Mallikarjun Kharge for quoting different figures of communal riots in the country. 'I was surprised that when he was reading from his written statement he said 113 (communal) incidents took place but when he was speaking he said there were over 600 incidents. The whole country, I suppose, knows what the truth is,' Adityanath said.[13]

Unsparing, he said he would take Kharge beyond these figures and also accused the Congress for making communally-biased announcements. He even sought an apology from Kharge. He went on to add, 'Sir, 580 incidents occurred in the country in which 91 people were killed and 1899 were injured in incidents of communal violence across non-BJP ruled states in 2011, when BJP was not in power at the centre.'

Although Maharashtra was ahead in terms of number of communal incidents (88) and casualties (15), Adityanath chose to accord Uttar Pradesh the dubious distinction of being the state where maximum communal incidents (84) and casualties (12) took place. The number of injured in Uttar Pradesh was given as 347. At the third place was Karnataka where 70 communal incidents took place in 2011. Both Maharashtra and Karnataka, he did not forget to mention, were ruled by the Congress Party.

Adityanath then rattled off figures of communal incidents in 2012 and 2013. While 668 incidents took place in 2012, in which 94 died and 2117 were injured, 823 incidents were reported in 2013.

While acknowledging that the law and order was a state subject and the administration in states worked according to the political will of the party in power, he accused the Congress Party of not paying honest attention to the communal agenda of their governments/allies to go into the genesis of polarization.

'Why is polarisation happening? What are the factors responsible for polarisation?' Adityanath asked before answering the questions himself.[14]

On the one hand, he said, they claim to be secular and on the other, the agenda they implement is based on communal lines. 'In a one-sided action these people announce salaries for imams but ignore over 12 lakh sadhus and pujaris living in the country. Is this a secular agenda?' he tossed the question at the Opposition amidst cries of 'shame, shame' from his fellow BJP MPs. 'Delhi government did it and so did the governments of West Bengal and Maharashtra . . . They divide the society on communal lines,' Yogi asserted.[15]

In his Lok Sabha speech, he termed certain decisions of Akhilesh Yadav's government as proof of his policy of appeasement. Among these, he cited the allocation of 20 per cent of the development funds for Muslim-dominated localities and a budgetary provision of Rs 300 crores for construction of boundary walls around graveyards.

'The Supreme Court says that squatting should not be allowed in public places in the name of mandir, masjid, madarsa, mazar or any religious faith but in Uttar Pradesh this is being done unhindered using the boundary wall as façade,' Adityanath said. 'The administration does not intervene because of the government's intent. Won't this lead to communal polarisation,' he asked.[16]

'The Samajwadi Party made a dirty attempt to withdraw cases against those who are a threat to the nation's security and who challenge Bharat's integrity and promote violence in the country,' he said accusing the Akhilesh Yadav government in Uttar Pradesh of playing communal vote bank politics. 'Had it not been for the judiciary those terrorists would have been out creating havoc in the country,' he said in the same speech.

In its 2012 election manifesto, the SP tried to please its Muslim vote bank by promising in its manifesto that if voted to power it would withdraw terror cases against 'innocent Muslim youths' lodged in various jails of Uttar Pradesh. After coming to power, Chief Minister Akhilesh Yadav ordered the release of 19 terror accused. They included those allegedly involved in Varanasi serial blasts and the serial bomb blasts in Faizabad and Lucknow courts. Two of the accused were convicted by the trial court in August 2018. Earlier, in June 2013, the Allahabad High Court had stayed the government's order to withdraw the cases.

Addressing the Chair, he said that it is very important to have a discussion on who is communal, a tag used to brand the BJP. Answering the question himself, Adityanath said that according to 'what we have known and what we have understood, communal is one who thinks that his god, deity or prophet is the best. And only those who follow him have the right to live, others don't. I feel he is communal'.[17]

He went on to add, 'Hindu life philosophy does not allow this. We gave the message of sarve bhavantu sukhinah (may all be happy). Live and let live is what our philosophy believes in. Has this country ever denied any race of religion shelter or opportunity to flourish?'[18]

In his opinion, 'When a conspiracy is being hatched against the Hindu philosophy, then Hindus must close ranks.' He felt that it was the result of their (Opposition's) prejudiced actions against the Hindus that the community was compelled to react.

> When a Muslim from Bharat goes for Haj pilgrimage he is not identified as an Indian, Pakistani or Bangladeshi but as a Hindu. However, they feel offended when we apply the same Hindu identity on them here. Hindu is not communalism, Hindu is a symbol of nationalism. And if they defame Hindutva, the symbol of India's nationalism, then these people will have to pay the price.[19]

Adityanath quoted Rabindranath Tagore as saying that in order to understand India's identity, one must understand Swami Vivekanand, who said, '[S]ay with pride that we are Hindus.' Adityanath added that Swami Vivekanand, who represented India in the World's Parliament of Religions, was neither communal, nor did he belong to any political party.[20]

Adityanath glaringly ignored that part of Swami Vivekanand's Chicago address in which he said,

> Sectarianism, bigotry and its horrible descendant, fanaticism, have long possessed this beautiful Earth. They have filled the earth with violence, drenched it often with human blood, destroyed civilisation and sent whole nations to despair.[21]

Adityanath asked,

> What kind of treatment is being meted out to the Hindu who was known in the country and the whole world for his tolerance? He was displaced from Kashmir and this House did not discuss it even once. The secularists remained mum when 3.5 lakh Kashmiri Pandits were forced out of the state.[22]

Discussing the Northeast and the role of the 'secularists', Adityanath said:

> In 2012, for three months Bodo tribals were being killed in riots in Assam but nobody said a word. No discussion was initiated in the House even as Assam was aflame. What has happened there? Bangladeshi infiltrators have become their

own and those living there for ages and are this country's citizens became strangers.[23]

He added:

These people are responsible for the changed demographic profile of North-East. The districts of Kokrajhar, Dhubri, Chirang and Barpeta have faced the worst riots because the Bangladeshi infiltrators there are grabbing land. These people have given them work permits along with ration cards.

When Hindus were forced to flee Kashmir, not once did they feel anguished. It was a rare case in the world when people of a country were displaced and forced to lead the life of a nomad in their own country. These politicians did not even express concern over riots which happened in Mumbai, Jamshedpur and Bhagalpur under the Congress rule.

In 1984, they did not feel ashamed even at the massacre of Sikhs, whose gurus had laid their lives for the country. They who have blood of communal violence on their hands talk of communal harmony.[24]

Lambasting the Congress for the August 2012 riots at Mumbai's Azad Maidan over persecution of Rohingyas in Myanmar, Adityanath said that a martyr's memorial was vandalized, policemen and media persons were assaulted, but they remained silent. There were clashes in Pune, Bareilly, Allahabad, Lucknow and Kanpur too, but the Congress and SP turned a blind eye.

Posing the questions, who is spreading communal violence in the country and who is trying to divide the country in the name of Sachar Committee, Adityanath said, 'They were responsible for the division of the country on communal lines in

1947 and are working on a Pakistani agenda to again divide the country on communal lines . . .'[25]

'These people have a communal agenda, not us,'[26] he asserted as he trained his guns once again on Uttar Pradesh where 118 communal incidents had taken place in 2012, 247 in 2013 and 65 from March to May 2014. Clashes in Saharanpur took place as the state government and the district administration refused to follow the High Court's order permitting the construction of a gurudwara.

'In Kaanth village of Moradabad, clashes occurred over use of loudspeaker by a temple. The village has three mosques which were allowed to retain their loudspeakers while the one at the temple was pulled down. Is this secularism, a secular agenda?' Yogi asked angrily. After becoming chief minister, he went on to declare that the 'word secularism is the biggest lie told since independence'.[27]

Farewell Speech in the Lok Sabha

Two days after assuming office as chief minister of Uttar Pradesh, Adityanath went to attend the Lok Sabha on 21 March 2017. In his farewell speech, he praised the BJP government at the Centre and assured the House that his government will work for all sections of society without discrimination. His main focus, Adityanath said, was on development, and not on castes.

Adityanath repeated the promises made during election campaign. 'The BJP government in Uttar Pradesh will ensure a goondagardi mukt (crime free) and bhrashtachar mukt (corruption free) society,'[28] he said.

Needless to say, that in his first six months as chief minister his government grappled to contain both crime and corruption.

His anti-Romeo squads proved ineffective in checking crime against women even as he shuffled and reshuffled senior- and junior-level police officers.

Adityanath began his speech by praising Narendra Modi for the high economic growth rate, firmly establishing a welfare government and good governance in the last three years. 'The country today has become an ideal for democracy in the world and democratically governed countries. That is why wherever elections are being held Prime Minister Narendra Modi is regarded as an icon. People want to see and learn about our development model.'

Recalling the poor economy inherited by the Narendra Modi government, Adityanath said,

> The government was faced with adverse circumstances in 2014 when the budgetary deficit stood at 8.9 per cent of the GDP, revenue deficit touched 2.8 per cent of the GDP and the rate of inflation was 11.2 per cent and current account deficit was 4.6 per cent.

In the previous three years, he said, 'the government has been able to increase the growth rate from 8 to 8.5 per cent, astonishing the world.' He added, 'The world wanted to see the impact of demonetisation on the economy. Yet despite demonetisation in November 2016, the country's growth rate stood at 7.9 per cent.'

He then went on to explain how various welfare schemes like Jan-Dhan, Ujjwala Yojana, Make in India, Digital India and so on, were aimed at empowering the poorest member of the society which, according to him, 'no previous government had done.'

Adityanath said he had repeatedly raised the issue of encephalitis in the House, highlighting how the menace had gripped 34 districts of eastern Uttar Pradesh. 'Innocent children were dying. What surprised me was that those who talked of Dalits and minorities did not show any sympathy even though 90 per cent of victims were from these categories,' he pointed out.

There is, however, no caste and community-wise break-up of encephalitis deaths available. In an article in the *WHO South-East Asia Journal of Public Health 2012*, Roop Kumari and Pyare L. Joshi provide an insight into the reasons why Japanese encephalitis continues to play havoc in eastern Uttar Pradesh.[29]

Gorakhpur's BRD Hospital—which witnessed a spike in encephalitis deaths in August 2017—and some of its adjoining areas are infested with pigs. When Adityanath's attention was drawn by the authors (in the interview mentioned earlier) to the root of the menace which lies in gross insanitation, mushrooming growth of the pig population in and around BRD Medical College and large parts of Gorakhpur, and other eastern Uttar Pradesh districts, he found it convenient to blame it on the media.

He shot back,

Don't forget that when we started *swachhata abhiyan* (cleanliness drive) by providing soap to poor people, the media tore us apart by terming our effort as an insult to the downtrodden. Our idea was to inculcate the spirit of cleanliness among those sections where hygiene standards are low. But you people did not let us do that. And now you are criticizing us for insanitation.

The aggression with which Yogi seeks to defend every act of omission or commission of his government reflects—rightly or wrongly—that there is little room for admitting faults or shortcomings. Perhaps old habits die hard. As a spiritual head of a temple trust that enjoys a following of millions of people, it is perhaps quite natural for him to feel offended when anyone raises a question. In a religious order, the head often has the last word and seldom anyone questions him. His word is law for all those who pay obeisance to him and his temple. No wonder, therefore, once officially gathered statistics are furnished before him by his bureaucracy, which he regards as the last word, he sees no reason for anyone else to question those numbers.

Taking recourse to citing statistics to prove that the number of deaths in Gorakhpur was blown out of proportion, he went on to argue, as told to the authors,

> If you go by sheer statistics there were fewer encephalitis deaths in Gorakhpur during the month of August this year [2017] as compared to the two preceding years. As many as 668 children died during the corresponding month in 2015 and 587 in 2016, but this year the figure has dropped to 325, yet you all gave me a bad name. There has been a definite fall in Japanese Encephalitis from 6 per cent to 2 per cent—all because of measures initiated by me.

According to Adityanath, even as the encephalitis menace has been rampant in the region since 1977, no concrete measures were taken prior to 1998 when he first raised the issue in Parliament. He asserted that it was due to his efforts that dedicated encephalitis wards were created in the Gorakhpur medical college, and pediatric ICUs were set up in government hospitals in at least 20 districts of eastern Uttar Pradesh.

He claimed in an interview with the authors,

> It was due to my initiative that a Virology Research Centre has been created in Gorakhpur. Let me also tell you that this is for the first time that as many as 92 lakh children have been immunized for encephalitis after I managed to get the much-needed vaccine for the dreaded epidemic.

Countering Adityanath's claim on a viral research centre, a former professor of the BRD Medical College said that the order to set up the centre was issued by the Allahabad High Court in 2007.[30] 'Well, this is now a full-fledged regional centre of the Pune based National Institute of Virology under the aegis of Indian Council of Medical Research but what it still lacks is the desired number of scientists', the professor closely associated with the Japanese Encephalitis (JE) eradication campaign, told the author.

On 22 June 2019, Yogi Adityanath claimed that his state was successful in controlling the spread of JE and Acute Encephalitis Syndrome (AES).[31] His remarks came at a time when 128 children died of encephalitis in Bihar. Yogi Adityanath made the statement at a review meeting held at Gorakhpur's BRD Medical College.

And exactly two days later, the Supreme Court issued notices to the Uttar Pradesh and Bihar governments to provide details of the steps taken to combat and contain the dreaded disease.[32]

On 30 August 2020, the Uttar Pradesh chief minister asserted that the fight against encephalitis was in its last phase in Gorakhpur and its surrounding areas, and that the disease would be eradicated in the region in two years.

Adityanath told reporters in Gorakhpur,

> The region is in the last phase of its fight against encephalitis and in two years, the disease, which was the cause of death of a huge number of people for the last 40 years, will be eradicated from the Gorakhpur-Basti commissionary (divisions), if efforts undertaken in the last three years continue.

He even went to the extent of claiming that it was his successful handling of the menace of encephalitis in Gorakhpur and adjoining areas of eastern Uttar Pradesh that made it possible for him to tackle COVID-19 equally well. And if official statistics are to be believed, there is a remarkable fall in the number of cases of both AES as well as JE that was responsible for taking the lives of hundreds of children in successive years until 2018. Uttar Pradesh's Health Minister Siddharth Nath Singh claimed a 66 per cent fall in the killer disease.[33]

11

THE NEPAL CONNECTION

In a dissertation on Nepal, Yogi narrates how the country got its name from Pal, which in Tibetan means wool. A community residing in the area from Bichli Patti to Tibet and northern parts of Himalayas called the territory Pal because of the abundant availability of wool. 'Nay', a term used by Tibetan Bhutiyas for caves, was prefixed to give the country its name.

At Gorkha in western Nepal is a cave temple of Gorakhnath, described as the 'sacred hearth of Gorkha race'. It is to this race the Nepalese royal family belongs, making the country an important pilgrimage centre for Nath yogis.

The name Kathmandu means Kath Mandir (Temple of Wood), which is said to have been built around AD 1600 in honour of Gorakhnath, the founder of the Shaivite monastic tradition. Gorakhnath was named Goraksha by his Guru Matsyendranath, the yogi who started the Nath sampradaya (sect). Hatha yoga, which the Nath yogis practice, is believed to have been started by Guru Gorakhnath.

There is another temple at Bagmati, one of 14 zones of Nepal, about 5 km from Kathmandu. Guru Matsyendranath is the presiding deity at this temple as it is widely believed that Matsyendranath, to whom the Nath panth owes its origin, was born in the village of Bungamati. Another temple dedicated to him is located in Patan.

Nepal has had a long association with sadhus of the Nath order, such as Gorakhnath, right from the beginning of the Shah dynasty.[1]

According to C. Marrewa-Karwoski of Columbia University,

Prithvi Narayan Shah of Nepal and Man Singh of Jodhpur were also devotees of Nath yogis and their powers. Both men had particularly close relationship with the community during their battles of succession and credited Naths for their rule. As a result they repaid the community handsomely with both material wealth and loyalty . . . Shah also accorded them with political cache.[2]

'Guru Gorakhnath, believed to be Shiva's incarnation in human form, is the presiding deity of Nepal's royal dynasty. Legend has it that as a seven-year-old child Prithvi Narayan Shah, who ruled Nepal in the 18th century, was blessed by Gorakhnath . . .'[3] Folklore also says that 'Guru Gorakhnath, a patron "saint" and guardian to the Shahs' was enraged when, as a child, Prithvi Narayan threw the prasad offered by the great yogi. The ascetic then cursed that Prithvi Narayan's dynasty would end with the tenth king.[4] The mythical anecdote came to be recalled after the massacre of Nepal's royal family in June 2001.

Nepalese writer Prakash Raj traced the influence of the Nath sect on Nepal's politics to Yogi Narharinath, who supported 'not a ceremonial but an active monarchy', much the same way as Adityanath has been doing so ardently.

Parallels are drawn between Yogi Narharinath, who died in 2002, and Yogi Adityanath—both born in the Himalayan region, the former in Nepal's Karnali zone and the latter in India's Garhwal. Yogi Adityanath is a Kshatriya and so was Narharinath.[5] That is where the similarity ends because while Adityanath made strides in politics, Narharinath remained relatively unknown in Nepal politics. He formed a political party—Karmabir Mahamandal—during Nepal's first parliamentary elections in 1959 but not much is known about him as a politician. Adityanath's political star, meanwhile, continues to be in ascendance.

The Gorakhpur temple had a historical relationship with the Shah dynasty. The presiding deity of the House of Shahs was Guru Gorakhnath and French social anthropologist Veronique Bouillier explains why:

> To place his kingdom under some god's patronage and to portray himself as this god's instrument, is a common way for a king to legitimate his power. In many legends concerning the foundation of the small western Nepalese kingdoms, this divine protection is secured through the medium of holy persons, Nath Siddhas or Yogis, whose magical exploits give the king conquering power or steadfastness . . . So it is written in the *Gorkha Vamsavali* (The Chronicle of Gorkha) that Prithvi Narayan succeeds in his enterprise through the favour of Gorakhnath.[6]

Because of Nepal's long association with Nath yogis, Adityanath is not seen as an outsider by a large section of Nepalese as he represents both Hindutva as well as a strong monastic tradition. His outpourings of nationalist and Hindutva sentiment on Nepal have strong relevance for India as he is unequivocal in his views on the two subjects. His concerns over Nepal being weaned away from India seem to be coming true as Communist China has gained greater influence in the neighbouring country under the government of Prime Minister K.P. Sharma Oli. However, Yogi's fears of Christianity and Islam gaining a strong foothold and threatening its Hindu character have been belied by the recent political developments in Nepal.

Yogi's views on royalty and a Hindu state have been Nepal specific, though some of them could be interpreted in the Indian context as well. He is apprehensive of the spread of Islam and Christianity in the Himalayan kingdom, and the Leftists and Maoists gaining control over government to alter Nepal's Hindu character. He apprehends that if Maoists, Christian and Islamic forces continue to rise in Nepal they will pose a serious challenge also to India's unity and integrity. All that is happening in Nepal in the name of secularism is a deception, according to him.

He has reciprocated the sentiments of his followers in Nepal by voicing concern over political developments in that country since 2001 when King Birendra Shah and members of his family were massacred at the Narayanhiti Royal Palace.

When an interim Constitution in 2006 declared Nepal a secular state, and monarchy was abolished in 2008, Yogi was upset.

'Yogi Adityanath wasn't happy when Nepal was declared a "secular state" without the mandate of the people. It remains to be seen if he will try to make Nepal a Hindu state again,' Prakash Raj wrote in his piece in the *Kathmandu Post*.[7]

With Yogi being the tallest of Nath sect priests in India, the impact of this spiritual connect is visible in his wholehearted support for a constitutional monarchy and opposition to the idea of a secular Nepal. Hindu Rashtra is how he would like to see Nepal and has stoutly championed that cause.

Having assimilated aggressive Hindutva as the guiding principle of his religious and political philosophy, it was natural for Yogi to propagate the hardline, militant form of Hindutva vis-à-vis Islam and Christianity along with the idea of Bharat. The same refrain dominated his election speeches in the run-up to the 2017 Assembly elections in Gujarat, Himachal Pradesh, Karnataka, and even in Kerala, where he was sent in October to take on the Marxists and Islamists. It was his combative style which is believed to have led the RSS and BJP to use Yogi as a star campaigner in poll-bound states.

Apart from his speeches, nothing illustrates Yogi's views on Hindutva and Nepal better than his 52-page dissertation on the neighbouring country available on his website. 'Hindu Rashtra Nepal: Ateet Aur Vartmaan'[8] (Hindu Nation Nepal: Past and Present) traces the Himalayan state's religious and cultural past to establish the strong affinity which it shares with India. The essay also helps understand why Yogi perhaps enjoys greater trust of the RSS than of the BJP.

Written in 2006, when Nepal was in the grip of people's movement against the 'undemocratic' rule of King Gyanendra, the essay underlines the bond he enjoys with the Hindu-majority state and its erstwhile royal family.

Stronger views against secularism in Nepal appear after the 'Upsanhaar' (Epilogue) of the dissertation. Titled 'Antar-raashtreey saazishon ke jaal me phansta Himalayee Rashtra Nepal' (Nepal getting caught in international conspiracies),

Yogi makes it abundantly clear that '18th May, 2006 was a black chapter in the history of Nepal', a constitutional Hindu state, when its 'kangaroo parliament, in an unprecedented and unfortunate' decision, passed a resolution to make the Hindu Rashtra a secular state.[9] In 2015 too he criticized the Nepal government's move to declare it a 'secular state' and demanded that the decision be scrapped.[10]

Although Yogi forcefully denied that his views on Nepal have any underlying meaning for India, he has been relentlessly pursuing his dream of making India Bharat—a Hindu state. His worry, as expressed in the essay, is that 'the forces which carried out conversions in Nepal were also behind changing its character from Hindu to secular', and asserts, 'After Nepal they would begin targeting India to make it *Mughalistan* or *Maoland*.'[11]

For Yogi there are obvious similarities between Nepal and India, and this is how he explains it in his dissertation: 'Nepal chirkaal se Hindu dharm, sanskriti aur sabhyataa ka Bharatvarsh kee hee tarah ek pramukh kendra rahaa hai' (Since time immemorial Nepal, like India, has been an important centre of Hindu religion, culture and civilization).

He expresses relief over Hindus and Buddhists being in majority in Nepal, which has helped retain the Himalayan state's Hindu character, despite an increase in the population of Muslims and Christians.

Yogi's dissertation also examines in detail Nepal's ancient, medieval, modern history, Puranic and mythological references, culture and tribes, and establishes linkages to substantiate the argument that the neighbouring country has been like India's 'sahodar', younger brother.

Yogi analyses the situation in Nepal after the failure of democratically elected governments in preventing the resurgence of Maoists, the massacre of the royal family and their role in amending the Constitution under pressure from a miniscule minority of Christians and Muslims.

In the context of Nepal, he posed a set of questions for Indians who were opposed to monarchy and favoured democracy:

> Bharat ke andar jo log raja ka virodh kar rahe hain ve chaahe saamyavaadi hon ya anya log, unse poochha jaanaa chahiye kya Maovaadiyon kaa loktantra me vishwas hai? Kya Nepal mein bahudaleey loktantra kee sthaapna ke pashchaat chunee gayee sarkaaron ne desh mein shanti aur vyavastha banaane mein apekshit safaltaa praapt kee? Itnahee nahee, hamey inse ye bhee poochhna chaahiye ki kya Pakistan mein loktantra hai? Kya Cheen mein athwa Vatican me loktantra hai? Yadi nahee hai toh ye log wahaan loktantra kee bahaalee ke liye kyon anurodh nahee kar rahe hain?[12]

> [Those in India, whether communists or others, who are opposing the king, should be asked if Maoists believe in democracy? Did the elected governments in Nepal succeed in maintaining peace and order after the establishment of multi-party democracy? We must also ask them if there is democracy in Pakistan. Is there democracy in China or the Vatican? If not, then why don't these people seek restoration of democracy there?]

Does Adityanath's strong defence of Nepal's constitutional monarchy and derision of those supporting a democratically elected government give a clue to the future of secularism and democracy in India, just in case he manages his way to the prime minister's office?

When the authors drew Yogi's attention to his article wherein he expressed his displeasure about the new Nepali dispensation favouring secular and democratic values, Adityanath alleged that his views had been twisted. He asserted

> Please view it in the context in which I wrote that. But what the media does is to skip the context and give out half-truths in order to project me in poor light. If you make it a point to view my remarks in a particular context, you will always find me wrong.

Asked to comment on his widely perceived 'communal' agenda and the tendency to give everything a Hindu–Muslim colour, he did not mince words in pointedly accusing the media of painting him black. 'The media has its own bias and mindset against me,' he charged, while posing counter-questions: 'I would like to know what you understand of secularism? Can there be a more secular nation than India, where people of all castes, creed or faith have lived together for centuries?'

Yogi expressed the same sentiment when he was asked by the authors whether he had altered the philosophy of Gorakhnath, who did not believe in sanatan dharma, a practice now being aggressively advocated by him.

He later reverted to his familiar territory of minority bashing, accusing them of being responsible for India—a 'Sanatanee' Hindu state since times immemorial—not becoming a Hindu Rashtra. 'But for the "scheming" Muslims and Christians, India would have become a Hindu state,' was his prognosis.

Yogi uses Nepal to voice his aversion for 'so-called secularism' in India. He wants that the concept of secularism be given a serious rethinking. His reason: Hindu minority and the Muslim majority lived in harmony for so long as there was a Hindu king in Kashmir but as soon as the 'fever' of secularism gripped the state 'the heaven on earth turned into hell'. The situation in the Northeast is almost similar, he said to buttress his point that India has been 'a big victim of secularism'.[13]

Citing attacks on the Indian Parliament, Akshardham, Raghunath temple in Jammu and on the three-most revered Hindu shrines at Ayodhya, Varanasi and Mathura, during Mughal rule, Yogi asked whether the minorities would have got away with such acts in any other country.

Faizan Mustafa, vice chancellor of NALSAR University of Law, Hyderabad, countered Yogi in an article in the *Indian Express* of 27 November 2017, which he begins by quoting Friedrich Nietzsche:

'God is dead. God remains dead. And we have killed him. Yet his shadow still looms.' India is a secular country where religion still occupies the centre-stage. It is often said that the political structure of secularism is irrelevant and out of place in societies like India where religions are totalising in nature . . . India's failure in erecting a wall of separation between religion and state—like in the US—was the first blunder of our republic . . .The narrative of secularisation is typically recounted as a story of progress and the gradual emancipation from religion through the exercise of reason.[14]

A mahant becoming a chief minister proves the failure of secularism in India, argues Mustafa.

Referring to the Constituent Assembly, Mustafa said that some members wanted the Constitution's Preamble to begin with the phrase 'In the name of God'. 'The Uttar Pradesh chief minister should read the Constituent Assembly debates. He would be shocked to know that when the matter was put to a vote, God lost,' Mustafa wrote.[15]

Sanjeev Sabhlok, leader of the little-known Swarna Bharat Party, attacked Yogi for his decision to build a Ram statue in Ayodhya in his article in the *Times of India*:

> There was a time when we thought BJP knew the meaning of secularism. When it said that the Haj subsidy amounts to appeasement, we agreed . . . But BJP's intent was different— to impose Hindutva, a collectivist political ideology derived from a distorted understanding of Hinduism. Instead of separating the state from religion, BJP has been stoking the Ram temple issue and imposing ban on cow slaughter. Even if it were true that Hindus don't eat beef, BJP's imposition of its belief wouldn't pass muster as an example of 'genuine' secularism.[16]

Building his case for the separation of state from religion, Sabhlok wrote,

> The idea of divine right of kings ended in England with the 1688 Glorious Revolution. As a corollary, in 1689, John Locke set out the principle of separation of state and religion—that God 'prescribed unto His followers no new form of government, nor put He the sword into any magistrate's hand.'[17]

The Western concept of secularism was sought to be grafted onto our Constitution but 'our founding fathers . . . mangled it up', added Sabhlok. He called the government's decision to build a statue of Ram, as 'taking a huge step backward'. According to him, 'But we must note that some of the taxes used in this statue would amount to forcible extraction from those who do not believe in Ram. It is hard to work out the difference between such taxes and the much hated "jizya" that BJP founders railed against.' (At its meeting on 1 November 2019, the chief minister's cabinet cleared a budget of Rs 447.46 crore for complete development of Ayodhya including a 221m tall statue of Ram.)

The Swarna Bharat Party, Sabhlok wrote in the same piece, would have no objection to Adityanath pursuing 'his faith in his private capacity even as he serves as chief minister'. 'All our party is saying is that he can't use the machine of the government to promote his faith. He can build a huge Ram statue if he likes, but at his own expense on his own private land.'

But with Yogi calling secularism the biggest lie, the interpretation of the term now needs to be looked at strictly through the prism of Hindutva.

The logic for making Nepal, and India, Hindu states as explained by Yogi is simple.

> If Nepal with only 5 per cent of non-Hindus (Muslims and Christians) has to be a secular state then Bangladesh, which had 30 per cent Hindus at the time of its creation, Malaysia, which has 20 per cent Hindus and 20 per cent Chinese, should also be declared secular states.[18]

Yogi puts the blame for the rise in conversions to Christianity on America and Pope John Paul II's India visit in 1999. During his visit the Pope 'affirmed people's rights to change their religion', and him asking Asian bishops to 'evangelise the region

in the coming millennium'[19] has been picked up to infer that the
pontiff was aware where in Asia conversions were going to take
place. 'Pope knows that conversion is not possible in China,
Afghanistan, Pakistan, Bangladesh and Arab countries as it is
unlawful and punishable with death penalty.' Therefore, Yogi
deduced, 'the Pope's targets are the Hindu nation Nepal' and
the 'Hindu-majority country Bharat.'

Yet another worry of Yogi is that the people and the
governments in Nepal and India have closed their eyes to the
'unholy intentions' of these forces which, according to him, 'are
operating from behind Maoists, pseudo-secularists and multi-
party democratic system.' In his opinion, they were succeeding
in their goals.

After the dissolution of Nepal's Parliament, Yogi gave a
memorandum signed by 120 MPs to then Prime Minister
Manmohan Singh but rued that under pressure from the
communist parties, the latter did not act on it.

Yogi's spiritual and political guru Mahant Avaidyanath
had met the then King of Nepal (Gyanendra Bir Bikram Shah)
to appeal for maintaining the country's Hindu character. An
agreement was reached between the two on four points, the main
being that Nepal was to remain a Hindu nation with a Hindu
king as its constitutional head. The other points of agreement
included ban on conversions and cow slaughter.

The appointment as chief minister of someone holding
views cited above, 'triggered speculation' in the neighbouring
country. Given the fact that he represents the seat of Nepal's
presiding deity, Yogi is not considered an outsider in Nepal
in religious and cultural terms. Wrote Yubaraj Ghimire in the
Indian Express after Yogi's appointment as chief minister in
March 2017, that his appointment as chief minister generated

some apprehension both in India and Nepal about his future role because

> Adityanath, during his visits to Nepal during the past four years, and the interactions with people going to see him from Nepal, has rarely concealed his views and anger that the country's journey to a 'secular republic' was something imposed by the Maoists under the influence of external 'money and design'.[20]

Ghimire also wrote that Yogi 'clearly discouraged the UPA government from legitimizing "red terror" asking instead that India encourage Nepal to make their multi-party democracy "vibrant" and let the monarchy continue as a "symbol of Nepal's identity and sovereignty"'.[21]

Yogi's dissertation appeared around the same time as the World Hindu Conference at which the Nepalese King's ADC Bharat Kesar Singh—who was also the president of the World Hindu Federation—alleged that large-scale conversions were being carried out under the Maoist-supported government and gave a call 'to defend Hindu culture worldwide'.

'Cows are being slaughtered on a large scale and Hindus are facing threats from several quarters. Sanskrit is no longer being taught in Nepali schools and the government of Nepal has stopped financing Sanskrit institutions,' he lamented.[22] Speakers at this conference (in 2006) included both Mahant Avaidyanath and Yogi Adityanath.

In his book on Nepal, *Battles of the New Republic*, Prashant Jha writes:

> News reports suggested that the monarchy's allies in Nepal and India had begun a campaign, final effort, to protect

the Shah dynasty. Earlier in the year, when the Madhes
movement had sprung up, there had been dark references to
how it was a 'regressive' movement backed by 'reactionaries'
from across the border.[23]

He adds, 'Common to these plots to destabilise the peace
process was the figure of Yogi Adityanath, the acting head of the
Gorakhnath Math, and a leader of the Bharatiya Janata Party
(BJP).'[24]

Suggesting that Yogi played a direct role in inciting Nepal's
Madhesis, Jha says: 'And right before the Madhesi movement for
rights had broken out in Nepal's southern plains in January 2007 . . .
he had hosted a meeting of Madhesi leaders, including Upendra
Yadav, to encourage them to start an anti-Maoist agitation.'[25]

An article titled 'Khatre mein Hindu' (Hindus in Danger)
on Yogi's website reads:

> Vishwa kaa ek maatr Hindu rashtra Nepal pichhle ek dashak
> se adhik samay se Maovaadi hinsa se itna pust hua ki aaj uske
> astitva par hee khatre ke baadal mandraa rahe hain . . . Nepal
> ke astitva par aayaa khatraa maatr ek rashtra kaa khatra nahee
> hai, yeh ek sanskriti ko vinasht karne kee saazish hai.[26]

> [Nepal, the world's only Hindu nation has been so devastated
> by Maoist-related violence for more than a decade that today
> its existence is in danger. The danger hovering over Nepal is
> not merely a danger to a country but it is a conspiracy to wipe
> out a culture.]

It will be interesting to reproduce Jha's brief encounter with the
Gorakhpur mahant in August 2007. Here's how he describes it:

I waited. After ten minutes, Adityanath pointed to me and said, 'Speak'.

I introduced myself and asked him what he thought of the situation in Nepal.

He said, 'All of you have spoilt a paradise. There is anarchy. The Maoists haven't given up arms and want to grab power through goonda raj. They want to extend their influence from Pashupati to Tirupati. Nepal might disintegrate. The unifying force in Nepal, like the soul that unites the body, is the Hindu king and Hindu culture. *Yeh secularism kyon laad diya waha pe* (why was secularism imposed there?)'.[27]

Yogi's reasons for the Nepal king's failure, provide a telling insight into his mind.

The problem was that raja was not aggressive enough. His mistake was he was too soft. I have not met him since 2004 but my assessment is he gave up too easily. He should have gone after everyone who opposed him. The king should not be silent and must take matters in his hand. He has our support. Hindu monarchy and Hindu state cannot be divorced from each other.[28]

As chief minister, is Yogi exhibiting qualities the 'raja' lacked? Did Yogi expect the Nepal king to be aggressive and go after his critics the way he is doing?

Yogi is further quoted as emphasizing, 'Who is the king is not important. What is essential is that he should be a Hindu. It is the soul that unites that body . . .'

Such is Adityanath's obsession with Nepal that his government decided to invite a representative of the Nepalese government for the investors' summit held in Lucknow in February 2018. This was the first time that Nepal, which itself needs big foreign investments, was invited for an investment meet in any Indian state.

12

WHEN ADITYANATH BROKE DOWN

On 28 January 2007, Yogi Adityanath was arrested for making a communally charged speech to incite a mob in Gorakhpur. He was released after 11 days, when a court granted him bail on 7 February 2007.

On 12 March 2007, a month after his release, when Yogi went to the Lok Sabha, he was still unnerved by his incarceration. The moment he stood up to speak in the House, Yogi's sobs drowned his words.[1]

While describing his ordeal, the then third-time MP broke down repeatedly. He pleaded his innocence and sought protection of the House. Referring to Sunil Mahato, a Jharkhand Mukti Morcha (JMM) MP who was assassinated near Jamshedpur on 4 March 2007, Yogi asked the Speaker, 'Will we get protection or will our condition be the same as that of Sunil Mahato?'

Accusing the Mulayam Singh Yadav government of maligning and tormenting him, he said he was a victim of 'political conspiracy' and that he never treated politics as a profession. He said he had given up his family for the sake of sanyas.

For the first 15 seconds or so he could not speak as tears choked his voice. After comforting words from Speaker Somnath Chatterjee, Yogi regained some composure and said,

> I have been elected MP from Gorakhpur for the third time. The first time I won by 25,000 votes, second time by 50,000 [Election Commission records, however, show a victory margin of 7,000 votes] and third time by about 1.5 lakh votes. But for some time now I am being made a victim of political vendetta. I only want to know if I am a member of this House or not? Will this House provide protection or not? If it cannot give protection then I would like to resign from this House.
>
> This [House membership] holds no significance for me . . . no significance at all. I have taken *sanyas* from life to serve the society. I have left my family, my parents but today I am being branded a criminal only out of political bias because I had exposed corruption, because I had raised my voice against ISI and anti-national activities on Indo-Nepal border and had been regularly drawing the attention of the House towards the problem. I have been raising the issue of starvation deaths due to administrative corruption. That is why all kinds of charges against me are being cooked up.[2]

In his book *Yogi Adityanath and the Hindu Yuva Vahini,* Dhirendra K. Jha writes:

> The sight of Yogi shedding tears shocked his Thakur supporters. It was seen as a sign of weakness unbecoming of a male belonging to a martial caste. Soon, however, his subordinates in the Hindu Yuva Vahini (HYV) started

rebuilding his image, arguing that he was a sensitive man full of emotions even as many locals called him a coward capable only of spreading mob violence.[3]

Jha further says,

> Nevertheless, as Adityanath's image of a firebrand leader took a serious hit, so did his outfit's activities in eastern UP. For some time the HYV appeared to be in a shambles and Adityanath refrained from leading the mob and participating in attacks on Muslims as he was earlier wont to. Later, even as the HYV revived its organizational activities, his re-activation was restricted to making inflammatory speeches and participating in token actions.[4]

In Jha's assessment, in his speeches, Yogi 'still followed the same old extremist politics. But in action, he appeared to have become cautious even if he claimed to be the same old Yogi'.

Here is what led to Adityanath's arrest in 2007:

> On 26 January 2007, one Raj Kumar Agrahari was injured in a group clash following an altercation during a Muharram procession in Gorakhpur. To avoid escalation of tension the district magistrate (DM) barred Adityanath from visiting the site. Adityanath also agreed to abide by the instruction.

Subsequently, Agrahari died of grievous injuries. Adityanath allegedly used his death as a reason to violate prohibitory orders. According to reports, Adityanath started a non-violent dharna at the site where he and his supporters allegedly made inflammatory speeches. Soon there was arson in which a Muslim shrine was set afire.

With the situation worsening, curfew was clamped. Adityanath defied the curfew restrictions and was arrested on charges of disturbing peace. After his arrest, arson and violence by HYV members escalated.

The Hate Speech

In his alleged highly inflammatory speech delivered outside the Gorakhpur railway station in violation of Section 144, Adityanath purportedly told his followers:

> Agar ek hindu ka khoon bahega toh ek hindu ke khoon ke badle hum aane waale samay mein prashashan se FIR darj nahi karayenge, balki kum se kum das aise logon kee hatya usse karawayenge. Agar Hindu gharon aur dukanon mein aag lagaata hai to main yeh nahi manata hun ki aapko in sab krityon ko karne se koi rok sakta hai.

> [If the blood of one Hindu is spilled, then to avenge the murder of one Hindu, we will not file FIRs but will get at least ten people killed . . . If homes and shops of Hindus are burnt then I do not think anyone can stop you from carrying out such retaliatory acts . . .]

He allegedly went on to add, 'Anything can be done to defend the Hindu honour. Be prepared to fight for yourself.'[5]

Continuing in the same vein, Adityanath is alleged to have said,

> Because it is a Hindu who has been killed, a Hindu trader robbed, Hindu traders' houses and vehicles were torched,

Hindu shops vandalized, the administration has not taken it seriously. If the administration does not avenge the killing of the trader then we will take revenge. All that has been happening in Gorakhpur since January 4 is state-sponsored terrorism. Only the people can end this state-sponsored terrorism and you should come forward to do so. If we don't act now for the welfare of the Hindus our future generations will never forgive us. Prepare for the final battle. If you stand up just once you will see that Gorakhpur will be peaceful for years to come.[6]

He charged the police for insulting Agrahari's body by dragging it like an animal. He also allegedly told the crowd not to allow any Muharram procession, as the Islamic month of mourning was on.

Criminal Cases against Yogi

This incident led to the filing of two separate cases against Yogi, both of which have since been dismissed after the authenticity of the video was challenged.

One case was filed by a Gorakhpur resident Rasheed Khan and the other by a local advocate Parvez Parvaz, who is languishing in jail on alleged charges of rape, and Asad Hayat.

Rasheed Khan's petition was against an order of the Gorakhpur Sessions Judge overturning a judicial magistrate's decision to take cognizance of Yogi's prosecution sanction allowed by the government. Parvaz, whose persistent requests for registering a case against Adityanath were ignored by the district administration, moved the Allahabad High Court which, in turn, asked him to approach the court of Chief Judicial Magistrate.

Rasheed Khan's Petition

For the case against Yogi, the Uttar Pradesh government's sanction was required and, interestingly, it was granted in 2009 by the then Mayawati government. The trial court took cognizance of the sanction. But things took a different turn when in 2014 Manoj Khemka, another accused, moved the Sessions court which overturned the trial court's order.[7]

Rasheed Khan challenged this order in the Allahabad High Court, which dismissed the case in February 2018 but directed the Chief Judicial Magistrate (CJM) to decide the matter afresh.[8]

Dismissing Khan's petition on 1 February 2018, Justice B.K. Narayana said,

> No interference with the impugned order is warranted. This application lacks merit and is accordingly dismissed. However, by way of abundant caution, C.J.M, Gorakhpur, is directed to decide the matter afresh pursuant to the impugned order of remand strictly in accordance with law and in the exercise of his unfettered independent discretion, without being influenced by observations, if any, made by the revisional court in the impugned order.[9]

The High Court asked the Gorakhpur lower court to also consider Rasheed Khan's plea to argue against the rejection of sanction.

Claiming partial victory, Farman Naqvi, who represented Rasheed Khan, said,

> Our application has been dismissed only partially. The order has gone in our favour because it gives scope for

re-examination of the merits of the case by the judicial magistrate and a chance to put forward our arguments, something we were denied last time. We might also move the Supreme Court.

Additional Advocate-General Manish Goel, who represented the state, said, 'Cognizance of prosecution sanction was taken by the judicial magistrate. But that cognizance order was set aside by a sessions judge on behalf of the accused last year on the ground that it was not applicable in the eyes of law.'

Parvez Parvaz's Case

Parvaz, an activist, filed an application on 16 November 2007 under Section 156 (3) CrPC before the CJM, Gorakhpur, alleging that Mahant Yogi Adityanath had been spreading hatred among Hindus and Muslims. The application was registered, but in his order dated 29 July 2008, the CJM rejected the application on the ground that another FIR about the same incident was lodged by a person named Hazrat at the Cantonment police station. Parvaz challenged this order.[10]

On 26 September 2008, a single-judge bench of the High Court set aside the CJM's order and directed him to pass fresh order on Parvaz's application and also ensure that proper investigation is carried out after the registration of FIR.[11]

Claiming to be a witness to the 27 January rally, Parvaz wrote to the Gorakhpur police chief on 28 January 2007 describing in detail what he had seen and heard, and asked for action to be taken against Yogi. The same day the latter was arrested, only to be released on bail 11 days later.

Yogi's arrest, however, had nothing to do with Parvaz's complaint. So, he wrote another letter on 29 January emphasizing that it was Yogi's speech that led to violence in which bogies of a train were torched, an imam (Muslim clergy) was set ablaze, mosques were vandalized and even the DM's office ransacked. This letter, too, drew no response.

Parvaz said he subsequently wrote four more letters to the senior superintendent of police, but each of these met the same fate.

Mulayam Singh Yadav, who had ordered firing on kar sevaks attempting to storm the Babri Masjid in Ayodhya in 1990, was again the chief minister in 2007 when the local Muslim community felt that netaji would live up to the epithet of 'Maulana' Mulayam and come out in their support. But he did not.

For reasons political or administrative, Parvaz's attempts to get an FIR registered were stonewalled.

Following the High Court's directive, a case under sections 153, 153 A, 153 B, 295, 295 B, 147, 143, 395, 436, 435, 302, 427, 452 of the IPC, read with Section 7 of the Criminal Law Amendment Act was registered against Adityanath and others at Gorakhpur's Cantonment police station on 2 November 2008. Subsequently, on 3 November 2008 the state government ordered an inquiry by the Crime Branch, Criminal Investigation Department (CB-CID).[12]

The single judge's order said,

It is very unfortunate that due to lack of adequate legal knowledge, without going in the allegations made in that application, the learned CJM has rejected the application merely on the ground that in view of the FIR registered at case Crime No. 145 of 2007 at P.S. Cantt., there is no justification to get the second FIR registered. This view of the learned CJM is wholly erroneous.[13]

The police had earlier refuted Parvaz's allegations and gave Adityanath a clean chit. Dismissing Parvaz's allegations as baseless, the police report described Yogi as highly respected and Gorakhpur's renowned MP. The report highlighted the actions police had taken to control the situation, citing imposition of curfew and Yogi's arrest.

The police, who had earlier arrested Yogi for his inflammatory speech, now denied that any anti-Muslim slogans were raised and refused to register an FIR. They contended that the matter was 'too old', and as several FIRs had already been lodged, there was no justification to register yet another one.

As Mulayam's SP had lost the April 2007 election and BSP was in power, Parvaz wrote to Chief Minister Mayawati seeking her help in the matter. Even she turned a deaf ear to Parvaz's plea.

Interestingly, the police used Mayawati's silence on Parvaz's request to argue that the complainant was not speaking the truth. The police labelled Parvaz's allegations against Yogi as 'politically motivated' and 'exaggerated'.

Making matters worse, the police went a step further and accused Parvaz of 'indulging in communal politics' and described him as a 'controversial political person.'

For four months the case kept getting adjourned in the CJM's court. An article in The Wire by Ajit Sahi stated,

The CJM then asked for another police report. This second police report, filed on April 16, 2008, made a U-turn.

Whereas the first report claimed there was no ground to register a case against Adityanath and that the allegations against him were politically motivated, the second report said the police had already registered an FIR in the matter and that it would be illegal to register a second FIR over it.[14]

Parvaz also submitted a compact disc containing Yogi's speech and challenged the second report of the police. The CJM, however, accepted the second police report and dismissed Parvaz's plea for an FIR.

Five persons, including Adityanath, were named in the FIR eventually registered by Parvaz. Among others was Gorakhpur Mayor Anju Chaudhary.

Charges against the accused under various sections of the IPC pertained to murder, attempt to murder, criminal conspiracy, unlawful assembly, rioting, dacoity, destruction of property, assault, wrongful assault and giving provocation to cause riots.

The charges also included promoting enmity on grounds of religion, demanding abrogation of citizenship rights of a group of people and hurting religious sentiments.

In the meantime, Anju Chaudhary moved the Supreme Court which granted a stay against proceedings in the matter. Four years later, in December 2012, the apex court rejected Chaudhary's petition and the CB-CID was entrusted with the inquiry.[15]

Since the CB-CID is under the state government's control, the complainants did not expect a fair investigation. Parvaz, who had been dogged in his 'fight for justice' all these years, was aware of this. He said he approached the High Court with the request that the case should be investigated by a central agency with the court monitoring its progress.

In 2014 Yogi was re-elected to Parliament for the fifth time and with other co-accused also being elected representatives, the government's sanction was needed to prosecute them. Sanction, however, was sought only for the prosecution of Yogi.

Accordingly, the CB-CID, which found sufficient evidence to prosecute the accused, made a formal request for the government's nod in 2015.

Although the SP was in power and Akhilesh Yadav was at the helm, the government sat over the CB-CID request.

The agency needed sanction to prosecute the accused for, among other things,

1. promoting enmity between different groups on grounds of religion and doing acts prejudicial to maintenance of harmony;
2. deliberate and malicious acts, intended to outrage religious feeling of any class by insulting its religion or religious beliefs; and
3. imputations, assertions prejudicial to national integration.[16]

For reasons known only to Akhilesh Yadav, he neither gave permission to prosecute nor did he offer any explanation for dragging his feet. If he thought that by denying sanction, he would be able to win Hindu votes in the 2017 election, the results proved how immature his political calculations were.

With the 'accused' Yogi becoming chief minister on 19 March 2017, the chances of getting the government's nod for prosecution completely receded.

The new government joined the legal battle and contended that the petitioner had a vested interest to seek prosecution

of the accused. One of the reasons for revival of the case was
the petitioner's 'political opposition' to Yogi. The government
argued that Parvaz began pursuing the case only after Yogi
became chief minister, when the fact of the matter was that
Parvaz had been pursuing the case for ten long years.

The state also disputed the authenticity of the compact
disc (CD) submitted by Parvaz in the court of the CJM. The
CB-CID claimed that the forensic test of the CD containing
the video recording of Adityanath's purported hate speech of
27 January 2007 showed that it was 'edited and tampered' with.

The court was also informed by the chief secretary, who
appeared in person, that forensic tests indicated the CD was
doctored. The original CD, Parvaz countered, had not even
been sent to the forensic lab.

Though considered supportive evidence, the CD is a crucial
part of the case. Parvaz alleged that what the CB-CID sent to
the Central Forensic Science Laboratory (CFSL) on 14 August
2014—six years after he gave it to the CJM's court—was not
the original CD.

Parvaz claimed that the CFSL's report mentioned that
the CD was wrapped in a sheet of the *City Focus* newspaper of
5 June 2014, whereas he had submitted it in April 2008. And
he asserted that he had not wrapped it in any newspaper.

Ajit Sahi wrote in the Wire,

There is even more glaring dissonance between the forensic
report and the CD's provenance. The CFSL report said it
found two folders in the CD, one of which contained a film
named *Saffron War. Saffron War* is a documentary critical
of Adityanath's communal activities, made in 2011 by two
Lucknow-based civil liberty activists Rajeev Yadav and

Shahnawaz Alam. How could that film be on CD/DVD Parvaz submitted in 2008?[17]

Parvaz also denied submitting a damaged CD as claimed in the CFSL report. The forensic lab's report stated that the CD which it received had a crack.

Suspecting foul play, Parvaz uploaded the CD on YouTube.

The controversial CD was shown to Yogi during an interview by a news channel. He did not deny making the speech but the government in its affidavit said the TV programme was 'not admissible as evidence and hence there was no justification for the investigation officer to probe the same'.

Demolishing the government's defence, Ajit Sahi wrote:

But the most significant part of the CD lies outside its examination. Since May 11, 2017 the state government has repeatedly told the high court that it refused sanction for Yogi's prosecution on the basis of CD's forensic report.

But the CFSL sent the report in October 2014, whereas the CB-CID decided in April 2015 that it had enough evidence to prosecute Adityanath.

Surely then, the CB-CID—a competent and independent agency in the state's own estimation—was confident that it had enough evidence to override the negative forensic report.

It appears that Akhilesh Yadav, on the one hand, sat over Parvaz's request for sanction of prosecution proceedings and, on the other, gave a free hand to CB-CID conducting the probe.

Justices Krishna Murari and Akhilesh Chandra Sharma of the Allahabad High Court relied on the forensic laboratory's report which said that the CD sent by Parvaz was tampered. On that basis, the court refused to order investigation by an agency other than the CB-CID.[18]

On 31 July, the court allowed Parvaz's plea challenging the state home department's decision to deny sanction to prosecute Yogi, but the division bench of Justice Murari and Justice Sharma in a detailed order dated February 2018 said that the 'order cannot be held illegal or without jurisdiction'.[19]

The case dragged on until 22 February 2018 when the Allahabad High Court dismissed Parvaz's petition challenging the Uttar Pradesh government's refusal to allow the chief minister's prosecution. The court also dismissed his demand for a CBI probe into the hate speech case.[20]

On the petitioners' plea for a probe by an independent agency 'as the state police's CB-CID was deliberately delaying and impeding investigation', Justices Krishna Murari and Akhilesh Chandra said, 'We see no good ground to transfer the investigation to some other agency.'[21] The judges also did not find any wrong in 'the refusal to grant sanction or any other illegality in the order, which may require any interference by this court'.

Petitioner's counsel S. Farman Naqvi said,

> The CD we had submitted to the Gorakhpur court in 2008 was received in November 2017 by the high court along with the records of the Gorakhpur CJM's court, it was opened in the presence of both judges and found in a sealed cover. When a CD is found intact by the HC then it should have asked which CD was examined by the forensic lab in 2014.

Naqvi described the verdict as 'hopelessly disappointing' and the findings 'illegal and contrary to facts'.

The government and its investigating agency may have raised doubts about the authenticity of the CD but Adityanath himself did not deny making the controversial speech. In August 2014, Adityanath was interviewed by Rajat Sharma on *Aapkee Adalat*. Sharma ran the clip to ascertain if the Gorakhpur mahant had actually made the speech. Instead of denying, Adityanath justified the alleged speech:

> Dekhiye mainey uss baat ko conditional kaha hai. Agar koi aapko maarega to mujhe lagta hai ki saamne koi manav hoga to uss manav ko aap maan sakte hain ki aapne thappad maara aap doosra thappad bhi sehan kar sakte hain, lekin agar danav hai to ek haath se maarta hai toh doosre haath se jawab deejiye. Main ek sanyasi hoon. Agar hame shaastra ka prashikshan diya gaya to shaastra ke saath saath shastra ka bhi. Agar humare ek haath mein maala hai toh doosre haath mein bhaala bhi le kar chalte hain. Usse samaj ko shisht bhi kiyajaa sake aur dushton ko unke kritya ki sazaa bhi di jaa sake . . .[22]

> [Look I had made a qualified statement. If a human being hits you, then it is understandable that you will offer him the second cheek, but if a demon hits you, you should give it back. I am a monk. If I have been trained in scriptures, then along with that I have also been trained in arms. If I have a rosary in one hand, I also carry a spear in the other so that right conduct can be instilled in society, and rascals can also be punished for their misdeeds . . .]

The Maharajganj Case

After the dismissal of the two petitions against him for inciting communal violence, Adityanath had just one more case, a more serious one, to contend with. Even this was dismissed by the trial court on 5 April 2018. A year later in July 2019 the Allahabad High Court's special court for MPs and MLAs also dismissed the case of murder of head constable Satya Prakash Yadav, against the chief minister.[23]

In 1999, the station house officer of Kotwali police station of Maharajganj district bordering Nepal, lodged an FIR against Adityanath, who was then a BJP MP, and 24 other named accused under various sections of the IPC including murder.[24]

The IPC sections under which the case was registered included criminal intimidation (506), promoting communal disharmony (153A), trespassing on burial spaces (297), defiling/ destroying/ damaging any place of worship with the intention of insulting the religion of any class, besides Section 302 (murder).

According to the FIR number 43/99 lodged by SHO V.K. Srivastava, armed with guns and rifles, Yogi and his supporters reached Pachrukhia village in 14–15 vehicles and started making provocative speeches and then reached a graveyard, raising slogans. They started vandalizing graves and planting peepal saplings. 'When we policemen opposed this, Yogi began to threaten us and began making provocative speeches to incite communal passion,' the SHO stated in his FIR.

The police FIR said that 13 persons were arrested on the spot but 'Adityanath fled with his supporters towards Maharajganj'. They reached a place where SP leader Talat Aziz was addressing her party workers. 'On being exhorted by Yogi, his supporters began firing at the SP workers while fleeing towards Maharajganj. Talat Aziz's security guard, Head Constable Satya Prakash Yadav, was grievously injured. Three others, Afaq Ali, Najmulla and Ishrat, were injured in the firing,' the FIR stated.

Despite the FIR being filed by the police, the case dragged on until Adityanath became the chief minister. Although Yogi was the main accused, he did not appear even once before the lower court where the case was being heard, said Talat Aziz.

Based on a cross-FIR lodged by Yogi against Talat Aziz on the day the police registered a case against the Gorakhnath temple head, the trial court concluded that Aziz had concealed some facts. Yogi's FIR claimed that his supporters too suffered injuries in retaliatory action from Aziz's side. The trial court said that Talat Aziz had not mentioned retaliation from her side.

Yogi Adityanath's tribulations ended with the dismissal of the case.

13

ACTIONS, RESTRAINTS, OBSESSIONS AND FAILURES

When 44-year-old Yogi Adityanath assumed office as the chief minister of Uttar Pradesh, he was the first saffron-clad person in the country to don the mantle—the only other example being that of Uma Bharti, who did a brief stint as the chief minister of Madhya Pradesh.

According to his election affidavit[1] filed in 2014, the Uttar Pradesh chief minister had been charged based on a long list of criminal offences under the Indian Penal Code's Section 435 (mischief by fire or explosive substance), Section 506 (criminal intimidation), Section 307 (attempt to murder), three charges related to punishment for rioting under Section 147, Section 148 (rioting, armed with deadly weapon) and two charges under Section 297 (trespassing on burial places).[2]

Amidst all kinds of doubts and suspicions, he sprang many surprises and wittingly or unwittingly, he seemed to be all set to prove his critics wrong.

The signs of change began to show right from the time he assumed office. Sure enough, it was no mean task for any hardcore communally-charged rabble-rouser to turn into an objective and balanced statesman. But he was clearly trying to do his best to make it loud and clear that his new focus would remain on ensuring good governance—something the country's most populous state had not seen in several decades.

After playing years of communal politics, when Yogi Adityanath took off under his new avatar with the much-hyped 'discrimination with none and appeasement of none' slogan, he was not taken seriously. Rather, the utterance was taken with a heavy pinch of salt. Evidently, the message was directed towards Muslims, who had naturally become very apprehensive about his attitude towards them.

What seemed to support his assurance were certain lesser-known facts about the head of the Gorakhnath temple. Who would imagine that Yogi not only preferred to entrust his temple accounts to a Muslim but had given the charge of his gaushala (cow shed), too, to a member of the minority community?

Would he follow the same objectivity in governance? That was the million-dollar question doing the rounds in the corridors of power at that time. Surprisingly, his style of governance was a welcome departure from the past—particularly, the multiple regimes headed by Mulayam Singh Yadav, Mayawati or even Akhilesh Yadav.

Yogi refrained from going in for a drastic administrative overhaul soon after taking charge. Perhaps, he took the cue from his role model, Prime Minister Narendra Modi—who instead of judging top bureaucrats by their association with the previous Manmohan Singh government, gave them a chance to prove themselves. Only those who failed to live up to the raised standards of the new government were shown the door. Already many lethargic officials were busy pulling up their socks while the corrupt and tainted were looking for cover as the message being sent out was loud and clear—'mend your ways or face the music.'

Unlike his predecessors Akhilesh or Mayawati who preferred to function from their official residence and avoided the chief minister's office, Yogi proved to be different in many ways. He set a new precedent by transacting business from his office invariably well beyond midnight—literally giving sleepless nights to the big 'babus'. The practice of official meetings routinely continuing till late in the night was stopped after some time. Ashok Kumar Shukla, an officer of the Provincial Civil Services, was sacked for tweeting against one such meeting of which he was a part. A report in the *Times of India* (dated 23 November 2019), said, 'On February 5, 2018 when Shukla was SDM Amethi, he reportedly wrote on his Facebook wall: In the name of a meeting yesterday, I sat from 2 pm to 12.40 am. Most of your officers are falling sick Yogiji.'[3] The government denied that Shukla had to sit in the meeting that long and disputed the time mentioned by him. The other charge that led to Shukla's dismissal was of illegal allocation of government land to a person in Hardoi.

In order to make the chief minister accessible to the common man, Yogi changed the rules of the game. Unlike Mayawati who kept herself completely insulated and did not even like movement of people on the road outside her official residence, or an Akhilesh who began well by holding a regular janata darbar (people's court) in the beginning but finally adopted the Mayawati line, Yogi chose to once again throw open the doors of the chief minister residence to the common man. And among the relief seekers seen at the janata darbar were the poor, cutting across caste, creed and religious lines. Giving daily audience to the public was also stopped after some time, and janata darbar have been few and far between in the last few years of Adityanath's tenure.

When Akhilesh Yadav initially started the durbar, it was a welcome change for thousands of poverty-ridden people who did not have any other means to take their grievance to the portals of power. However, what began as a five-day affair every week, gradually tapered off to four days, three days and eventually to once a week. With the passage of time even that was given a go-by and towards the end of his term it was back to Mayawati days, when a common man could not dream of having an audience with the chief minister.

After resuming the practice, Yogi Adityanath was out to prove that he was the people's man and would not shirk from letting himself be accessible to common people. Even more significantly, there was hardly a day when a couple of Muslim women were not visible in the janata darbar.

Quite strategically, the chief minister's PR officials ensured that the name and other particulars of such burqa-clad women or Muslim men found prominent mention in the routine press releases issued by them. Obviously, the idea was to prove that this Hindutva icon chief minister does not believe in any kind of discrimination on religious lines. The department of information and public relations made it a point to publicize how Muslim women going to Yogi Adityanath's durbar had a common complaint about talaq (divorce) at the drop of the hat. Evidently, the idea was to build opinion in favour of Prime Minister Narendra Modi's decision to do away with the practice of triple talaq.

As time went by, Yogi too chose to say goodbye to the 'janata durbars', for them to be only resumed intermittently whenever any election was to be held. But most of the times, such 'durbars' were attended by one of his nominee ministers, who would provide succor to the crowd on his behalf. Now closer to the March 2022 elections, it is back to the daily durbar, but usually sans the chief minister himself.

Despite being a novice in governance, Adityanath's biggest strength was his integrity—something terribly lacking in many of his predecessors. Even after more than four years, while fingers are pointed at some of his cabinet colleagues and his team of bureaucrats, Adityanath's financial and moral integrity remains spotless. Government officials who had observed him from close quarters during their postings in Gorakhpur were ready to vouch for the man's moral fibre, even as many of them felt he was despotic at times. But that was how he could make the most meaningful difference to Uttar Pradesh's rampantly corrupt and grossly lethargic system of governance. Officials right from top to bottom were strictly warned to furnish details of their moveable and immoveable assets—believed to be a precursor to identifying those living beyond their means. That warning proved good only for newspaper headlines.

Although drastic measures against big defaulters were still awaited, Adityanath seemed to impress many with the kind of start he made. Knowing that well begun is half done, everyone looked at him with awe and hope. But, as time went by, his actions began to show that his earlier priorities were being given a 'go-bye', and it seemed that he was not willing to look beyond his HYV agenda—that begins and ends with aggressive Hindutva. Getting entrapped in three of his core issues—cow protection, love jihad and ghar wapsi—Adityanath was unable to look beyond them in his first year.

It was only after a push from the Centre that things began to move in terms of development of the state. With the Prime Minister Narendra Modi stressing that to make India a USD5 trillion economy by 2025, Uttar Pradesh needed to grow into a trillion-dollar economy. That for a laggard state is a tall order.

Even after the state's gross domestic product (GDP) grew at a rate higher than the national average, the Finance Commission led by its Chairman N.K. Singh said during a visit to Lucknow on 22 October 2019 that the state's growth rate would have to accelerate to its full capacity.

Not satisfied with the progress until then, Singh said, as reported by the *Economic Times*

> For India to become a USD 5 trillion economy, UP has to become a USD 1 trillion economy. For development of UP a new growth rate is needed. If UP continues to move at this (current) rate, then it will not be able to become a USD 1 trillion economy.[4]

Cynicism over the state's economy reaching USD 1 trillion persisted even as the buzz around the upcoming defence corridor neared a crescendo.

In its presentation before the Finance Commission, the government explained just how big the economic challenges confronting the state were. The per capita income of the state was down to nearly half of the national average. While the national per capita income in 2018–19 was Rs 1,26,406, in Uttar Pradesh it was only Rs 64,330. For its people-centric schemes the state asked for Rs 1.02 lakh crore from the Centre.

With a sharp slowdown in the economy due to the pandemic the Centre has even refused to give the states their share of the Goods and Services Tax (GST).

Yogi Adityanath started off very well. His first 53 days went off smoothly as he did his every bit to prove that here was a 'chief minister with a difference'. But what he did quite blatantly on the 54th day in office took away, in one stroke, all the sheen from the image that he was trying to cast for himself. At the end of the day, he could not resist the temptation of following the old beaten track—at least as far as acknowledging his own fault was concerned.

The government headed by the 44-year-old sadhu-turned politician flatly denied permission to its own police to prosecute him for allegedly making hate speeches for which he was charged in 2007.

The issue was raised through a Public Interest Litigation (PIL) before the Allahabad High Court. The IPC sections sought to be invoked against Yogi necessitated the state government's permission to initiate prosecution proceedings against him. The sanction had been pending even with the Akhilesh Yadav government. But apparently the old dictum—I scratch your back, you scratch mine—was what led Akhilesh to sleep over it.

Eventually, when the High Court issued a reminder and the state chief secretary was summoned by the court, the Uttar Pradesh government filed an affidavit denying permission to prosecute its chief minister.

Interestingly, the permission was denied on the plea that preliminary investigations by the police had termed the recordings as 'morphed'. It came as no surprise as that is the tactic often adopted by politicians to get themselves a clean chit, particularly from charges of making hate speeches or indulging in corrupt activities. Cops, too, find it convenient to build an alibi on those very lines whenever their investigations are 'predetermined'.

There have been several cases in which politicians have got away with murder by establishing anyhow that the evidence against them is 'fabricated' in one form or the other.

SP chief Mulayam Singh Yadav managed to prove that the CD carrying his audio clips, issuing threats to senior IPS officer Amitabh Thakur, was 'doctored'.

Last year, a sting operation exposed the then Uttarakhand Chief Minister Harish Rawat offering money to buy off some legislators to save his government. But when the matter was taken to court, Rawat managed to get away by skillfully building the benefit of doubt on the simple plea that the recordings were 'doctored'. With change in power at the Centre and in the hill state the case was handed over to the CBI, which booked Rawat for horse-trading to save his government.

The infamous CD of late Amar Singh in conversation with some Uttar Pradesh bureaucrats, industrialists and Bollywood actresses had also put him to much embarrassment. But eventually, he moved the apex court to get the contents of the CD banned from public broadcast on the same plea that the CDs were 'morphed'.

One-time BJP National President Bangaru Laxman, who was caught on camera accepting money, too, pleaded innocent and eventually got away by proving that the CDs in question were 'altered'.

A few years back, BJP MP Varun Gandhi, too, got reprieve from the courts, even as video clips purportedly showed him making highly provocative and inflammatory speeches in Pilibhit, his parliamentary constituency. Varun succeeded in creating doubts about the authenticity of the recordings on the usual plea that the CDs were 'doctored'.

More recently, BSP supremo Mayawati termed as 'fake', her purported voice recording exposing her underhand demand for money from her now-expelled party leader Nasimuddin Siddiqui.

What is strange is that most Indian politicians allegedly involved in all such dishonest acts invariably get away in judicial scrutiny—thanks to the unaccounted wealth at their command with which they can engage the top-of-the-line exorbitantly expensive lawyers, who use their legal acumen to create an escape route for their political clients.

So, it was no surprise when Yogi Adityanath, too, was exonerated from the charge of making inflammatory speeches which incited communal passions and sparked violent Hindu–Muslim clashes in his hometown, Gorakhpur, way back in 2007. Interestingly, it was none other than CBI's own forensic laboratory that found his recordings 'doctored'. It was another matter that the CBI forensic lab report was issued towards the end of 2014.

It was easy for the then chief secretary, Rahul Bhatnagar, to stand up in court to give a 'convincing' reason to ensure a clean chit for the chief minister. And the official plea that none of the other BJP leaders facing similar accusations as Adityanath had been prosecuted, also came in handy to get him off the hook.

Yogi Adityanath's first cabinet meeting on 5 April 2017 turned out to be a damp squib. Other than one significant decision— waiver of farm loans up to Rs 1 lakh—the two-hour-long maiden cabinet meeting concluded without any substantial outcome.

As the much-awaited cabinet meeting happened only after a 16-day long wait, the expectations were naturally high. And the longer the meeting went, expectations too soared. At the end of a long day, it turned out that the day-long exercise was much ado about nothing.

There could be no denying that the new chief minister tried to keep the promise of farm loan waiver made by Prime Minister Narendra Modi in one of his poll rallies in Uttar Pradesh.

While the loan waiver was widely welcomed by various kisan unions, everyone felt that it was nowhere close to a solution to the farming community's perennial problem of loans. Exploitation at the hands of local moneylenders charging astronomical rates of interest continues to be one of the reasons for farmers' suicides. Shockingly, not much has changed for the poor farmer who continues to remain at the receiving end, as was portrayed in India's classic film *Mother India* way back in the late 1950s. Other than superficial cosmetics, successive governments since Independence have failed to get to the root of the plight of poor farmers.

Evidently, the cabinet did not go deeper into the problem which springs largely on account of the farmer being denied remunerative price for his produce by ignoring the cost input. On the other hand, BJP leaders see the loan waiver as a political tool to garner votes quite in line with what the Congress did until some years ago for its own survival.

The government's move to issue Kisan Rahat Bonds (farmer relief bonds) to offset the total burden of Rs 36,000 crore on account of the waiver to about 2.13 crore small and marginal farmers also appeared to have been a hasty and half-baked decision. Conceived soon after the Yogi government was formed, the decision was aborted about three months later as the Centre refused to support its proposal.

Dropping the plan, the then Uttar Pradesh Finance Minister Rajesh Agarwal told the *Economic Times* in July 2017, 'We are not floating any bonds. Not even a rupee would be sought as loan from any financial institution.'[5] The decision to drop the idea of raising funds from the market was necessitated after the then Union Finance Minister Arun Jaitely flatly refused to contribute even a penny towards the loan waiver. Relief for farmers came much later not from the state but the Centre which announced several schemes to bail out the farming community.

In the 2017 Assembly elections, the BJP made Yogi Adityanath a star campaigner, especially during the last two phases involving 89 seats in eastern Uttar Pradesh. The party had won only 11 of these seats in 2012. In a series of election meetings, Adityanath attacked the SP government's 'appeasement' policy and warned the Hindus that money meant for development of the state would be used in the development of 'kabristan'—graveyards.

Trust on Yogi's polarization skills paid off as the BJP swept the region. The rise in his stature from 2012 to 2017 was incredible. Acknowledging his contribution in its stupendous victory in Uttar Pradesh, the BJP made him a star campaigner in the Gujarat Assembly election the same year.

Major Decisions in Early Days as Chief Minister

With regard to the ban on illegal slaughterhouses or constitution of anti-Romeo squads, these were put on board. It was another matter that the manner in which both the issues were being tackled seemed quite lackadaisical.

On the anti-Romeo squads, all that the new cabinet chose to do was to pat its own back for launching the much-hyped move, supposedly aimed at ensuring safety of young girls against sexual harassment in public. Rather late in the day, the chief minister did take serious note of the excesses on young boys and girls seen sitting or walking together in public places, but no action was taken against a single cop guilty of harassing innocent couples.

Worse, no cognizance was taken of incidents of actual sexual harassment in public spaces. And this nuisance grew manifold. It was noticed only when it blew out of proportion on the Banaras Hindu University (BHU) campus in September 2017, when Yogi was completing six months in office. The 'anti-Romeo squads' came to be questioned because they did nothing to check rampant harassment and molestation of girls that had become the order of the day on the prestigious BHU campus.

On the 'love jihad' front too, the chief minister drew much flak as the cases that were brought to the fore by the administration turned out to be blatant examples of undue harassment of couples going ahead with mixed-religion marriages. The government's focus was particularly against Muslim boys marrying Hindu girls. Significantly, most of the cases highlighted by the police happened to be of 'willing partners'. It was rare to find a case of 'enticement' with the intent of carrying out forced conversion—as was alleged by Adityanath and his men.

As if good sense prevailed, Yogi's tirade against 'love jihad' dropped to a low key for some time. But targeting youngsters in the name of 'love jihad' was renewed in 2020, when the chief minister once again began building a fresh narrative around it.

In the state's old industrial hub of Kanpur, the local police got down to virtually joining hands with the VHP, which seemed to be hell bent on labelling all inter-religion marriages as 'love jihad'—essentially to serve their long-standing political agenda of religious polarization.

What reinforced VHP's campaign was a strong word from Chief Minister Yogi Adityanath, who on 28 August 2020 directed the home department to prepare an action plan 'to bring an end to love jihad'. And once such a directive was in place from the chief minister, 'love jihad' was blown into a serious menace, far beyond all proportions. However, a close study of the state's crime records gave a completely different picture. In all, there were less than a dozen reported cases of such marriages between a Hindu girl and Muslim boy. And these, too, were limited to just five of Uttar Pradesh's 75 districts—Kanpur, Meerut, Aligarh, Lakhimpur-Kheri and Ghaziabad.

Significantly, in five of these cases, the Hindu girls openly refuted the accusations of 'love jihad' levelled by the police, on the basis of complaints made by their parents.

What turned up during the course of the investigations was that the complaints were usually made by angry parents, for whom the idea of inter-religion marriage was outrageous and thoroughly unacceptable. So, they found it convenient to come up with stories alleging enticement of their daughters by Muslim boys.

According to a statement issued by the state police headquarters, there were only two cases in 2020 where the girls stood by the allegations of 'cheating, enticement and harassment', made by their parents.

The most glaring such case was registered at Kanpur's Kidwai Nagar police station, where a woman Satrupa Yadav had lodged a complaint alleging kidnapping of her 22-year-old daughter Shalini by a Muslim neighbour, Faisal. The complainant had even accused Faisal of looting Rs 10 lakhs from the girl's parents, who alleged that the Muslim boy took away their daughter at gunpoint.

A police team was dutifully sent on a manhunt. They discovered Shalini in a house in a locality under Chandni Mahal police station in Delhi, where she was found living happily with Faisal. The Kanpur police took them into custody. But, Shalini managed to move a petition before the Delhi High Court, which directed the concerned police station to have her statement recorded before a magistrate. Shalini flatly refuted the allegations made by her parents, making it loud and clear that she had married Faisal entirely out of her own choice and that she wanted to live only with him. She stated that all the allegations made by her parents were false and concocted. Yet, the Kanpur police refused to close the case.

However, there can be no denying that isolated incidents in which Muslim boys actually indulged in what is officially conceived as 'love jihad' have occurred. Take the case of a Ghaziabad-based Muslim boy Shamshad, who enticed a young Hindu widow, Priya, into marriage by falsely projecting himself as a Hindu. Priya also took her minor daughter Kashish with her to Shamshad's home in his village under Partapur police station in Ghaziabad district in January 2020. After getting her converted to Islam and performing a proper nikah with Priya, he murdered both mother and daughter and buried them in his own house. The case was taken up by Priya's friend, who took it to its logical conclusion and got Shamshad convicted and sent to jail.

There were two other cases of duping of young girls by Muslim youth in Meerut district, and the accused were brought to book. However, what is strange is that even in cases where the girls had deposed before the magistrate that they wanted to live with the Muslim man of their choice with whom they had chosen to get married, the police were not ready to give them clearance.

One such notable case was in Kanpur where the matter went up to the Zonal Inspector General of Police Mohit Agarwal. And far from settling the issue on the basis of facts, Agarwal constituted a nine-member team under a deputy superintendent of police (SP) to investigate all cases of Hindu–Muslim marriages over the past two years.

'The probe would find out if there was any inter-connection between different Muslim youth who have entered into wedlock with Hindu girls', he told local mediapersons in Kanpur. And went on to add, 'the special police team would also see if such youth were being funded from abroad; we will go into their call log records.'[6]

Deputy SP Vikas Kumar Pandey, who heads the special police team, went to the extent of asserting that he would even try to find out whether any middleman was involved in fixing the Hindu–Muslim marriages in question. Even others involved in the probe seemed to be bent upon somehow finding fault with the Muslim youth so that they could be booked and punished.

Even the ghar wapsi card played by Adityanath very vocally, turned out to be largely exaggerated. Neither he nor his band of HYV men could bring out a single person who claimed to have undergone a coercive conversion and was now keen on returning to his original Hindu faith. Such incidents made it increasingly evident that HYV was out to whip up Hindu passions by raising the bogey of forced conversions, with the obvious intent of forging a communal divide that would eventually help to polarize voters.

Yogi Adityanath's yet another major decision to purchase 80 lakh tons of wheat at a minimum support price was also not without glaring inconsistencies. It neither made financial sense nor did it match with the existing infrastructure. Even as the target was just about one-fourth of Uttar Pradesh's total wheat production of about 300 lakh tons, the state's wheat storage capacity was just about 36 lakh tons. And according to official figures, some 23 lakh tons of wheat was already stocked in warehouses, which left space for only about 13 lakh tons additionally. Where would the state government store such a huge stock of wheat had apparently not been looked into. To top it all, past records showed that in the best of times the Uttar Pradesh government could not procure more than 45 lakh tons of wheat.

Illegal mining was rampant across the state during the rule of Akhilesh Yadav and Mayawati. With the Allahabad High Court's order for a CBI inquiry already in place, Yogi government pursued the case with vigour. The CBI and the Enforcement Directorate carried out raids against some IAS officers. When the DMs of Gonda and Fatehpur were suspended, a message was sought to be sent to bureaucrats that Yogi's government was unlike the previous ones. Yet, it would be wrong to say that illegal mining activity has been completely stopped. In Banda, where this author went just before the 2019 Lok Sabha elections, illegal mining of red sand from Ken River was going on unabated. In fact, as time lapsed the government suffered memory loss about the whole issue. Nobody knows what happened to the IAS and other officers named in the case. Was it all an eyewash to gain publicity?

The new cabinet's decision to constitute a group of ministers to travel across the country and abroad to prepare a new industrial policy for the state was like putting old wine into new bottles. Such exercises have been undertaken umpteen times by successive governments over the past, only to end up as free junkets for the political class. The best of industrial policies prepared over the past have only gathered dust in the labyrinths of the Uttar Pradesh secretariat.

As investors have always preferred other states, Adityanath government decided to hold an investors summit in 2018. It was claimed to be a huge success with investment proposals worth Rs 4.68 lakh crore coming in, after the Prime Minister Narendra Modi himself made a strong pitch for the state. Modi exhorted the state to compete with Maharashtra in becoming a trillion-dollar economy. Buoyed by the 'success' of its first investors meet, the government planned to host a global investors summit in October–November 2020 but the COVID-19 pandemic dashed all possibilities.

Those familiar with the investors summit in Uttar Pradesh know that only a fraction of the MoUs signed actually materialized. However, in September 2020, Alok Kumar (Uttar Pradesh government's additional chief secretary, industrial development) claimed that out of the 150 MoUs signed during the UP Investors Summit 2018, 18 MoUs worth Rs 4,095.96 crore have commenced commercial operations, while another 31 worth Rs 12,858.34 crore are in project implementation stage.[7]

Illegal Slaughterhouses and Cow Obsession

While action against illegal slaughterhouses was welcome, it was only slaughterhouse owners who had to bear the brunt. No action was initiated against those without whose patronage and active protection the slaughterhouses could not have thrived. And these patrons were none other than officials of municipalities and the Uttar Pradesh State Pollution Control Board, besides, of course, the police.

What came as a surprise was that only 26 illegal slaughterhouses had been shut by the government and that it was not averse to the idea of renewing their licences through the due process of law. There was no talk of bringing to book such officials who had turned a blind eye to allow operation of illegal slaughterhouses or to those functioning long after expiry of their licences.

Significantly, it was also discovered that the state government–run slaughterhouses had not been operational for at least three years. This naturally led to sprouting of illegal abattoirs which were systematically allowed to carry on their business by corrupt officials.

The sufferers were not only ordinary meat-shop owners but also the large non-vegetarian population of the state. For nearly three months, meat became scarce in Lucknow. What was sold clandestinely—under the patronage of the police—was priced very high. The famous Tunday Kababs was left with no option but to switch to chicken kababs. Their delicacies—buffalo or mutton kababs—were completely unavailable. With the term, 'beef' being used for both cow and buffalo, it was difficult to distinguish between the banned cow's meat and the legal buffalo meat. The government seemed least interested in resolving the issue by demarcating between the legal and the illegal meat. And Yogi Adityanath's spokespersons did not hesitate to go on the record to say: 'Why should people be just dying for non-vegetarian food at all.' Surely a solution to the problem created by the new government was not on its list of priorities.

Widespread criticism, however, compelled the government to gradually go soft on the issue, but no concrete steps were taken to resolve the issue of cow versus buffalo. Issuance of licence to meat shops remained a distant cry. This naturally gave convenient opportunity to cops and other enforcement agencies to make a fast buck by turning a blind eye to 'under the table' sales. The following headline from 2019—Yogi's third year in office— summed up the situation: 'Moradabad: 14 cops suspended, inquiry initiated for failure to prevent animal slaughter'.[8]

Meat sellers confided that they had to shell out anything between Rs 300 and Rs 500 per day to policemen and civic officials for looking the other way. No one knew why proper licences were not being issued by the administration. The common complaint of meat sellers was that even when they filed their applications after fulfilling all laid-down conditions, their applications were left to gather dust. Thus, if slaughterhouses and meat shops were running, it was obviously in the knowledge of authorities concerned. They remained vulnerable as those very officials could haul them up anytime for carrying out their business 'illegally' even as they denied them a legitimate permit for which they had applied.

The Uttar Pradesh government's double standards were out in the open when Urban Development Minister Suresh Khanna plainly told a delegation of meat exporters that the government was in no mood to invest crores in upgrading the dormant state-owned slaughterhouses.

While children might have been dying due to want of oxygen in the Gorakhpur Medical College and filth and squalor might have been at the root of the perennial menace of killer encephalitis in large parts of eastern Uttar Pradesh, Yogi's focus remained on the cow.

The most shocking example of this was his delayed and insensitive response to the killing of Police Inspector Subodh Kumar Singh by a frenzied Hindu mob in Bulandshahr over alleged cow slaughter in December 2018. Singh was shot in the head on 3 December. The incident sent shock waves across the state, but the chief minister spoke about the incident four days later, on 7 December. Instead of expressing outrage over the senseless murder of a police officer, Yogi called it 'an accident'. He called a meeting to review the mob lynching only after he had addressed election rallies in Telangana and Rajasthan and attended a laser show in Gorakhpur.[9] The chief minister had clearly underlined his priorities.

Blow by blow, as the mystery behind the sudden rampage was unfolding itself, it became increasingly evident that that there was some kind of a vicious design to incite communal frenzy in Bulandshahr in December 2018 on the lines of the infamous Muzaffarnagar riots of 2013.

If it was a simple incident of eve-teasing that snowballed into the Muzaffarnagar riots, it was the story of an alleged cow-slaughter that gave rise to the violence in Bulandshahr, which is as communally volatile as its neighbouring Muzaffarnagar.

If the two sides involved in the Muzaffarnagar incident were Hindus and Muslims, the mischief-mongers in Bulandshahr were leaving no stone unturned to blame it all on Muslims who had gathered in one corner of the village to participate in a three-day religious event (Ijtima). 'Lakhs of Muslims had gathered in the village, where the local Hindu temple offered space to them to take the spill over; but they went to the extent of indulging in cow slaughter and thereafter gunning down the local police inspector', roared Ajay Gautam, a spokesman of 'Hum Hindu', a self-styled Hindutva organization, on the TV18 network on 4 December 2018. That the Yogi Adityanath government chose to apparently play ball became quite evident when a senior police official told a press conference in Lucknow the same evening that the Muslim gathering drew a crowd of 15 lakhs.

The figure looked quite exaggerated as the entire village is stated to be not big enough to accommodate such a mammoth number.

Local VHP and Bajrang Dal leaders were the first ones to go to the police station with their complaint against what they perceived as 'cow-slaughter'. While the cops, led by the now-slain SHO Subodh Kumar Singh, were in the process of registering the necessary FIR, a few Bajrang Dal activists brought the remains of some cow carcasses in a tractor-trolley, which was placed in the middle of the Bulandshahr–Delhi highway. They also began to pelt stones at the police station. The cops were caught off guard and the SHO was hit by a stone on his head, leaving him bleeding profusely. Since the crowds were swelling, the cops thought it best to rush their SHO for treatment; so, they somehow managed to get into their jeep and drive away amidst the heavy stone-pelting. They could barely cover a short distance when they were intercepted by the crowds once again. The barrage of stones on the police vehicle continued, followed by gunshots, leaving the cops completely cornered. Soon a bullet, fired from a close range, pierced the police inspector's head, while the other cops ran for their lives.

It was only after reinforcements arrived that the violent mobs dispersed. Meanwhile, they ransacked the police station and caused irreparable damage to police vehicles and property. Top cops who were initially going soft on the Bajrang Dal or VHP finally decided to book some of the local leaders, including the Bulandshahr district Bajrang Dal chief Yogesh Raj, as among the key accused when they realized that the frenzied mob led by them had taken the life of a man in khaki.

The local police said that they were under pressure to register a 'weak' case against the senior Bajrang Dal and VHP leaders accused of the violence. However, there was much resistance from the police ranks, where anger was brewing against the killing of a member of the 'khaki' the fraternity.

Perhaps that is what prompted the chief minister to assuage the feelings of the victim's family by offering an enhanced monetary compensation of Rs 50 lakhs (Rs 40 lakhs to Subodh Kumar Singh's wife and Rs 10 lakhs to his parents).

In keeping with the chief minister's stand on cows, the Uttar Pradesh government decided that the upkeep of cattle in the state would henceforth also be the responsibility of private- and public-sector enterprises which would be required to spend part of their corporate social responsibility (CSR) fund for better care of cows and bulls.

'It is not mandatory but they will be persuaded to chip in by setting up cow dung based gas plants or units that can utilize cow's urine etc for making products of domestic use', said Rajiv Gupta (who was the then chairman of the Uttar Pradesh Gau Seva Aayog).[10]

A meeting chaired by the chief minister on 30 August 2017 said that companies should be involved through CSR to take up the responsibility of promoting panchgavya (products based on cow dung, cow urine, milk, curd and ghee). The meeting decided that the Central government be requested to give tax relief to companies, institutions and organizations giving aid for the upkeep of cattle.

The Jhansi division commissioner was specifically asked to get in touch with Ayurvedic pharma company Baidyanath regarding uses of cow urine.

Rajiv Gupta said a Kanpur-based company was utilizing 120 tons of cow dung daily to produce CNG and supply it to different units. The revenue generated is used for maintaining gaushalas. It not only helps animals but also provides livelihood and helps development of local areas, he felt. He added that some of India's big corporate houses have already made contributions to gaushalas as part of their CSR initiatives. These included the Tatas and pharma biggie Alembic.

With bovines being central to the RSS and BJP's political agenda, the Uttar Pradesh government seemed to have copied the template prepared by the Gujarat and Rajasthan governments. Rajasthan, too, has made upkeep of cow and its family part of CSR.

It is not that cow upkeep was being left to the private sector alone. The Uttar Pradesh government also earmarked Rs 2,000 crore for the purpose. The 30 August meeting decided that cow protection committees headed by DMs be set up at the district level. These committees will work under the supervision of Gau Seva Aayog.

These committees would be required to ensure smooth functioning of gaushalas at the district level and help them achieve self-reliance by assisting them in promoting cow-based products like compost, biogas, mosquito repellant coils, soap, incense sticks, gonyl (phenyl made from cow urine).

It was decided that a beginning be made by establishing govansh van vihar (cattle forest area) in every district of Bundelkhand, each capable of providing feed for about a thousand stray cattle. The divisional commissioner of Bundelkhand was expected to ensure sheds, godowns for fodder and drinking water points in gaushalas falling under each district.

To raise funds for stray-cow shelters in the state, the government decided to impose an additional fee of Re 0.50 to Rs 2.00 on every bottle of beer and Indian Made Foreign Liquor, besides a special fee of Rs 10 per bottle consumed in bars. Announced in January 2019, the government expected to raise Rs 155 crore annually from this cess.

The 2012 census of livestock population put the total bovine population in Uttar Pradesh at 50,18,240, out of which the number of stray cattle was 10,09,436.[11] In the 20th livestock survey the number of stray cattle is missing.

Describing the menace of stray cattle in the districts of Bundelkhand, R.K. Yadav (professor in the department of genetics and plant breeding at the prestigious Chandra Shekhar Azad University of Agriculture and Technology, Kanpur) said that rampaging herds of abandoned and unproductive cattle are creating havoc in the fields. 'Moving from one field to the other, they are virtually running over standing crops causing huge loss to farmers.'[12]

The situation was aggravated particularly after some outfits started a violent movement against slaughterhouses and killing of cattle. Consequently, there has been a marked increase in the number of stray cattle. On the other hand, the leather industry has been facing shortage of raw material.

According to Sushil Kumar, programme coordinator at the Krishi Vigyan Kendra, Mahoba, 'There are 200–400 such animals in a herd, wherever they go they bring destruction.' Mahoba's chief veterinary officer conceded that there were no official figures on stray cattle but 'locals put it at over 50,000 in Mahoba alone'.[13]

Spread across 13 districts of Uttar Pradesh and Madhya Pradesh, the Bundelkhand region accounts for 19 per cent of the total production of lentils. Apart from damage to crops, the increasing number of stray cattle is becoming a big nuisance for motorists on the roads and often causing accidents. Night journey by road in Bundelkhand is not considered safe as stray cattle can appear on the highways from nowhere and cause a mishap.

A report in the *Sunday Express* (6 January 2019) stated that as per the 2012 census the cattle population in Uttar Pradesh was at 1.9 crore, of which 10 lakh were being rendered surplus annually. The report also said that the existing and proposed cow shelters can take in only 6–7 lakh cattle and that the cost of feeding them would come to around Rs 2,190 crore per year. Until then, the state had 514 cow shelters and 104 were proposed to be constructed.[14]

A *Hindustan Times* report put the number of stray cattle in Uttar Pradesh at 'around 10 lakh' of which 'about 4 lakh are living in 4000 temporary shelters'.[15]

The marginal and submarginal farmers are largely dependent on milch cattle for livelihood as their small land holdings are economically unviable. However, they are not keen to maintain the unproductive cattle. They mostly abandon animals as soon as they stop giving milk, and as a result more and more livestock end up as stray cattle.

Earlier, there was a tradition of Annapratha, very popular in the entire Bundelkhand region, under which farmers left their animals at specifically earmarked fields close to natural sources of water like rivers and ponds. The villagers collectively fulfilled their requirement of fodder, and they also intentionally kept their fields fallow during 'zaid' cropping season during summer in the area.

However, this tradition is no longer being followed and nobody is bothered about herds of unproductive animals. There is no fodder for them, and if there is a drought, heat wave or other unfavourable weather conditions many of the animals, particularly calves, die. And the fear of cow vigilantes has also led the scavenging communities to shun their jobs or else they could be accused of killing or smuggling cows.

Although to stop the harassment or killing of innocent people in the name of cow smuggling/slaughter for beef, the chief minister ordered Gau Seva Aayog to issue certificates to those ferrying cattle for bona fide reasons. It did not stop vigilante groups from taking the law into their hands. The murder of police inspector Subodh Kumar Singh was one such glaring example.

The state government also decided that MPs and MLAs be requested to visit govansh van vihars and gaushalas, and contribute towards their maintenance from their local area development funds.

Ironically, even as stray cattle rule the roads and fields in Uttar Pradesh, the latest livestock census shows the state's cattle population at about 18.8 million—a decline of 3.93 per cent over the previous count taken in 2012, when the cattle population was 19.6 million. The decline must be even more worrisome for Adityanath whose primary concern is cows.

The euphoria created by the rise of a saffron-clad sadhu to the position of Uttar Pradesh chief minister began to fade in barely four months of his ascendency to the political throne. His stock started falling faster than that of his SP predecessor Akhilesh Yadav, whose graph had begun to decline only after a good 24 months, manifesting in a virtual wash out of his party in 2014, when Narendra Modi led the BJP to an unprecedented win of 73 of the state's 80 Lok Sabha seats. By any standards, Adityanath's falling graph so early in the day was a sad commentary on his quality of governance.

What left everyone stupefied was non-governance in a regime which is ironically led by a well-meaning, forthright and committed man of integrity. But what was going wrong was apparently even beyond his own comprehension. Whether it was on account of a closed mind or undue pressures from within his party is not known. And those who were supposed to be his mentors obviously did not have their head above their shoulders. It was common knowledge that they were having a field day in poking their noses in anything and everything to take advantage of his inexperience in running a government.

The only exception was the posting of IAS officers, where the chief minister rightly and largely preferred to go by the advice of an upright chief secretary, Rajiv Kumar, who had come back to the state after doing a stint in the cabinet secretariat and later as the Union Shipping Secretary. Several controversial bureaucrats, who called the shots in successive regimes and had even managed to retain lucrative jobs in the beginning of this new dispensation too, were eventually shunted out after Rajiv Kumar's intervention.

Tragic Deaths in Gorakhpur Medical College

What came as a devastating blow to the government, particularly the chief minister, was the spate of deaths of children, 63 in all, in Yogi's religious and political fiefdom, Gorakhpur, in a matter of just five days, simply because the government failed to ensure uninterrupted supply of oxygen to the city's most important Baba Raghav Das Medical College hospital. The supply was cut because the oxygen supplier had not been paid his long-pending dues of Rs 68 lakh.

Significantly, the chief minister, who had himself visited the hospital barely three days earlier, was kept in the dark about children dying even while he was taking rounds of the hospital, which is the main referral medical centre in the region. The local officials including the DM, who accompanied him, did not care to apprise him of the acute shortage of oxygen.

With his past experience limited only to the Gorakhnath temple trust, Yogi was at his wit's end when he heard the tragic news through the media, while he was busy attending a function under the auspices of the Swachh Bharat Mission in Allahabad.

Not used to be being questioned in his capacity as supremo of a religious math, he chose to promptly go into denial mode, without realizing that his own local administrative machinery led by the DM had already spilled the beans by admitting that suspension of oxygen supply had led to the deaths.

Oxygen supply to the medical college was disrupted because of non-payment of long-pending dues to the supplier, who had been running from pillar to post for the past few months only to be told that the college had yet to receive the funds from the government. The medical college principal Dr Rajiv Misra, too, had shot off several letters to the medical education department in Lucknow, but those responsible were said to have remained unresponsive. Apparently, the oxygen supplier was left with no choice but to stop the supply as he claimed to have been left with no funds to pay the parent supplier.

The inordinate delay in payment of bills finally resulted in the death of 63 children but it failed to wake up the official machinery from their slumber until these deaths hit the headlines. That left the chief minister completely rattled and, therefore, vulnerable to blindly believing whatever his officials wanted him to believe. He shut his eyes and ears to reality. Little could he fathom that running the state was not as simple as calling the shots in a religious math, where his word is law.

The entire administrative machinery of the medical education department as well as in the chief minister's secretariat danced to the chief minister's tune. Everyone including Health Minister Siddharth Nath Singh, who was sent to Gorakhpur, remained focused only on establishing that the deaths were not caused on account of shortage of oxygen.

What the chief minister and others failed to understand and explain was the simple question: if their contention was correct, then why action was taken against the medical college principal who was suspended for failing to ensure oxygen supply; and why an FIR was lodged against the oxygen supplier? On the other hand, no action was ordered against principal secretary (medical education) or director-general (medical education), who are alleged to have sat over the payment file for months.

An inquiry ordered by the government into the role of Dr Kafeel Khan, who was arrested in the case, established that shortage of oxygen indeed was responsible for the tragedy.

> The report was submitted on April 18, 2019 by investigating officer Himanshu Kumar, principal secretary (stamps & registration department), to the medical education department of the UP government. The 15-page report, a copy of which is with TOI, states that Kafeel was not guilty of medical negligence on his part and that he had made all efforts to control the situation on the night of August 10–11, 2017, when for 54 hours, the hospital was dealing with oxygen shortage.[16]

The inquiry corroborated that Dr Khan rushed to the hospital and made arrangements for jumbo oxygen cylinders given the 'sudden shortage of liquid oxygen'. While it became evident that Dr Khan's act of procuring oxygen cylinders through his personal contacts saved some lives, it did in the bargain also establish the acute shortage of oxygen.

No wonder action against Dr Khan was taken allegedly for doing private practice while his more important role in trying to save lives was overlooked. The travails of Dr Kafeel Khan had only just begun with handmaiden-like bureaucrats dancing to the tune of their masters who only know how to be vindictive. Dr Khan spent seven months in jail after his first arrest on 2 September before the Allahabad High Court granted him bail. Soon after his bail was allowed, he was again hauled up for creating a 'ruckus' at the Bahraich district hospital. He managed to get bail on the same day, but within 24 hours he was back in jail for allegedly having submitted fake documents to open a bank account in 2009. That Dr Khan was a victim of vendetta became clear when the Special Task Force of Uttar Pradesh Police arrested him on 29 January 2020 for allegedly making a provocative speech at an anti-CAA protest at Aligarh Muslim University in December 2019.

Subsequently, the draconian National Security Act (NSA) was invoked against Dr Khan. After the first three months of detention ended in May, his arrest was extended till August. He was finally granted bail by the Allahabad High Court which found his arrest 'bad in law'. It also refuted the government's charge that Khan's speech was aimed at spreading hatred. In the court's view, the speech gave 'a call for national integrity and unity among the citizens'. So vindictive is the government that Dr Khan's release is no guarantee he won't be implicated in another case. The *Times of India* said in an editorial, 'Khan's case shocks for another reason: His detention under NSA began two months after the speech, just when he secured bail in a related criminal case. There was no proximate or live cause at that time to necessitate detention.'[17] The *Times of India* editorial also cautioned governments coming under the influence of *Singham*, a Bollywood movie in which a valiant and honest policeman fights injustice and decides to teach a lesson to a corrupt politician. The epithet of *Singham* aptly describes the Yogi Adityanath government.

What is more shocking is that despite the High Court's strongly worded order, no action has been taken against the police and bureaucrats who caused immense mental trauma to Dr Khan and his family.

More than anybody else, Yogi Adityanath had always known it first-hand how Gorakhpur and some adjoining districts were highly prone to fatal diseases like JE. In fact, during his visit to Gorakhpur a day after the tragedy was discovered, the chief minister admitted, 'Who knows the pain of JE deaths more than me; I am the one who has raised the issue from the streets to parliament.' He went on to further blow his own trumpet to claim his role in getting the Central government to sanction an AIIMS in Gorakhpur. 'But what this city also needs is full-fledged research centre for vector borne diseases and I am going to appeal to the prime minister for setting up one', he asserted.[18] He also made it a point to profusely thank Prime Minister Modi for sending Union Health Minister J.P. Nadda, Union Minister of State for Health Anupriya Patel and Union Health Secretary C.K. Misra to personally take stock of the situation in Gorakhpur.

If his previous day's press conference on 12 August 2017 in Lucknow focused heavily on self-praise about all that he had done to improve health facilities in and around Gorakhpur, the following day's press conference (on 13 August 2017) in Gorakhpur was loaded with praise for the prime minister. The only thing he avoided mentioning was the reason for the prolonged delay in payment of oxygen bills. Instead, he sought to give sermons to the media for what he alleged as publication of 'false news' about deaths occurring due to lack of oxygen.

Both press conferences remained typical monologues, leaving very little room for questions. It simply reflected Adityanath's old habit of addressing a captive media in his math.

On taking over as chief minister, Adityanath made tall promises about special arrangements to combat the menace of JE but he did not hesitate to cut down the allocation for health in his first budget of the state. The health and family welfare sector accounted for a mere 5 per cent of the proposed outlay in the 2017–18 revised estimates.[19] In the 2019–20 budget the allocation for health sector was increased by 15 per cent.

Adityanath's oft-repeated assertion about zero tolerance for corruption also proved to be hollow as oxygen bills remained unpaid because of the rampant malpractice of kickbacks and commissions for which the medical education department is particularly notorious. It was all on record that repeated letters were sent by the oxygen supplier to the medical college principal, who in turn went about shooting requests to the medical education department without eliciting any response.

People's experience suggests—rightly or wrongly— that anybody dealing with the medical education or health department or for that matter any other wing of the government knows how difficult it is to get any bills cleared without fulfilling the demands of certain officials—from the lowest to the top. The 'cuts', according to many, were often heavy and 'unreasonable', leading to prolonged bargaining, which more often than not cause inordinate delay in payments. 'Your payment can get stuck at any level, so it does not suffice if you have shelled out big money to the person sitting at the top; without satisfying each one at every level, you cannot get away,' confessed a supplier of medicines to the authors.

Asked how he made up for these 'extra payments', the supplier shot back, 'What else can you do other than include that component in our invoices.' Sure enough, that affects the price, which naturally gets inflated. But who cares? Those in a position to question are themselves the underhand beneficiaries. Trouble arises and payments are held back on one pretext or the other only when somebody in the official hierarchy does not receive what is 'unlawfully' due to him.

The biggest exposure about large-scale kickbacks and commissions in the health sector of Uttar Pradesh came in the form of the Rs 8,000 crore National Rural Health Mission (NRHM) scam during the Mayawati regime. Even though many heads including that of the then mission director Pradeep Shukla (IAS) rolled in that scam, the action has not deterred the corrupt. Shukla did spend a few months behind bars, but at the end of the day political masters in subsequent governments came to his rescue.

But Adityanath, as it appears, did not seem to care to fix prima facie responsibility for the Gorakhpur tragedy. What became glaringly visible in his actions was a streak of double standards. His attention seemed to be focused only towards proving his point right. Action against the medical college principal Dr Rajiv Misra may be fair if it were for his incompetence or for his blatant indulgence in irregular practice like letting his wife (a homoeopathic doctor in the Ayush wing) to function as de facto principal. Even though his incompetence was widely known at all levels, he enjoyed the patronage of his superiors in the secretariat so he could get away with murder. It was the then principal secretary (health) who was alleged to have sat over the file for release of funds to pay the oxygen bills. The medical college principal came under the axe only when it became necessary for the chief minister to fix the responsibility on someone.

It was an open secret that Dr Rajiv Misra's wife was calling the shots in the medical college. Adityanath, however, was unaware of it even when nothing moves without the mahant's knowledge in Gorakhpur. Interestingly, Director-General (Medical Education) Dr K.K. Gupta went on record to describe the medical college principal as 'corrupt'. He also alleged that the principal's wife, Dr Purnima Misra, functioned as a de facto principal and openly sought bribes from suppliers and contractors.

Funds were finally released by the then Principal Secretary (Medical Education) Anita Bhatnagar Jain only after she was told by the medical college principal that suspension of oxygen supply had left two children dead. It was only after the number of casualties rose that the spate of deaths could no longer be kept under the wraps.

Gorakhpur DM Rajiv Singh Rautela, who was the first to attribute the deaths to lack of oxygen, would have also been in the firing line, if it were not for his proximity to the chief minister who had handpicked him for the key job. In fact, sources confirmed that Rautela was the first IAS officer to be posted by the chief minister. Adityanath did not spare anybody who dared to speak the truth.

Take the case of Dr Kafeel Ahmad, encephalitis ward in-charge, who was fired after being initially praised for the yeoman service he did by running around to personally arrange for oxygen cylinders which saved some lives. His act of procuring oxygen cylinders was viewed as circumstantial evidence that oxygen was indeed in short supply in the medical college—which clearly contradicted the chief minister's claim.

Adityanath was widely believed to have not come out of the Gorakhnath-math frame which allowed him totalitarian authority to showcase whatever suited his whims. It was an irony of fate that Gorakhpur, which gave him name, fame and ultimately the dream chair of chief minister, now gave him the first pangs of governance. Apparently, he was shaken by the news and could not figure out how to react. After all, until then, it had been all smooth sailing. So, he chose to bide his time and finally made up his mind to visit Gorakhpur after a good 36 hours.

Even after spending hours in the fateful wards and meeting the families of those who were still battling with their lives, he did not show the desired sensitivity to announce any kind of ex-gratia relief, which is a done practice, as the state and its representatives were responsible for the loss of lives. On the contrary, taking advantage of the situation and to score a few brownie points, former Chief Minister Akhilesh Yadav, who visited Gorakhpur on 14 August, announced a cash relief of Rs 2 lakh for each of the victims' families.

Perhaps, Adityanath is yet to realize that running the state in a democratic set-up is a different ballgame from running a religious trust. Questions were bound to be raised and an elected representative of the people—particularly the head of government—is constitutionally answerable to the common man. Sadly, in Gorakhpur, that very common man was being made to pay with the lives of his children simply because their own Yogi 'Maharaj' government had failed to ensure payment of bills to the oxygen supplier.

Another major embarrassment during his initial days was the much-hyped 'recovery' of a lethal explosive from the precincts of the state Vidhan Sabha in June 2017. Evidently, the administration made a mountain out of a mole hill thinking that the terror angle would boost the government's pro-Hindutva image.

The Uttar Pradesh government, which went the whole hog to term the incident as a conspiracy to blow up the Vidhan

Sabha, had to eventually go on the backfoot after it was revealed that the white powder recovered from under the seat of an SP MLA was not lethal explosive, as initially claimed by the local police.

The state-government's Lucknow-based forensic laboratory too described the 150 gm powder wrapped in a piece of paper as the extremely lethal PETN, which even sniffer dogs cannot detect. Apparently, the lab officials and the police jumped to the conclusion without even carrying out the necessary tests.

What followed was a high drama with Chief Minister Yogi Adityanath going to the extent of making a statement in the state Assembly and terming the incident as some kind of a conspiracy against the state's 22 crore people. His supporters hyped it as a plot against the chief minister.

'One conspirator tried to compromise the security of more than 500 law-makers and other employees and this cannot be allowed,' the chief minister said.[20] He chose to refer the matter to the National Investigation Agency (NIA), which he rightly thought was appropriate to get to the bottom of the alleged 'conspiracy'.

The powder was sent to the Central Forensic Laboratory at Agra for further tests. Four days after it was sent to the Agra lab, the state government went into a denial mode. 'The forensic lab in Lucknow had confirmed that the powder was the lethal PETN so we did not consider the need to send it to any other place,' an official spokesman told media persons. 'It requires two more tests—gas chromatography mass spectrum and Infrared spectrum test,' the spokesman added.[21] He declined to comment where these two tests were going to be carried out since the poorly equipped Lucknow laboratory did not have the capability to perform the tests.

Why the state government chose to deny having sent the powder to the central lab in Agra was baffling. Even until a day earlier, a top police officer of the state had himself told this author that 'the Agra lab has yet to send its findings'.

Insiders claimed that the denial came following instructions from the 'top', after NIA refused to register the case. After all, NIA sleuths had discovered that the entire premise of the complaint was misconceived. Since the Agra central lab's refusal to confirm the findings of the Lucknow lab was bound to cause much embarrassment to the chief minister, the government went into damage control. A diktat was therefore issued to the state officials to flatly deny that the powder was ever sent to Agra.

Experts in the Army maintained that even an explosive powder kept in a packet is harmless until it is converted into a device together with a detonator. In case of the Uttar Pradesh Vidhan Sabha incident, some powder was simply found wrapped in a piece of paper.

A senior police official told this author on the condition of anonymity that the entire faux pas took place because of a half-baked report by the Lucknow lab. He also alleged that the lab director had a track record of 'cooking up' a fake report in the past for which he had received serious reprimand. Yet, he did not wish to miss the opportunity to be more loyal than the king.

The lab director was suspended two months later.

14

SAFETY OF WOMEN?

UNBRIDLED POLICE

The Uttar Pradesh government under Yogi Adityanath has laid much emphasis on the safety of women, with a series of measures being announced from time to time to build confidence among women about their security.

However, despite such loud announcements like the launch of 'mission shakti', in October 2020, women have remained on the edge in the state. The 'Women Power Helpline 1090', started by the preceding Akhilesh Yadav government, was diluted after Yogi Adityanath decided to merge it with 'Dial 100', which is meant for other emergencies. But even 'Dial 100' was subsequently re-christened '112', apparently because that too was initiated by his main political adversary and bête noire Akhilesh Yadav.

'Mission Shakti' was launched from Balrampur, about 150 kilometres from the state capital, as a homage to a young Dalit girl who was brutally raped there. The chief minister made it a point to mention the rape incident while kicking off the programme from the town. He added that Mission Shakti was started with the hope of guaranteeing respect and safety for every woman in Uttar Pradesh.[1]

Yogi Adityanath tweeted that 'women are the symbol of strength', and 'they are sacred as per the traditions of the "Sanatan Dharm"'. The festival of Navratri is the proof of that, he said. Yogi also stated that there is a need to inculcate within the new generation, the carriers of our culture, a feeling of respect towards women; on the other hand, there was a need to develop self-reliance among women.[2] Referring to incorrigible young men who would not mend their ways, the chief minister sought to make it very clear that, 'they will be ostracized and their photographs will be displayed at road-crossings'. However, fact remains that such culprits were never shamed in this manner.[3]

The Balrampur rape incident was preceded by equally or perhaps even more heinous incidents of rapes and gang rapes in Unnao, Shahjahanpur and Hathras, the news of which rocked the entire nation. And in each of these cases, the perpetrators of the crime happened to be prominent BJP leaders or those allegedly enjoying the patronage of the ruling party. Kuldeep Singh Sengar, for example, the accused in the Unnao rape case, was a BJP MLA. He was later expelled from the party following his conviction in the case. Significantly, according to the National Crime Record Bureau's annual report 'Crime in India' in 2019, India reported 4,05,861 cases of crimes against women in 2019. Uttar Pradesh topped the list with 59,853 such incidents.[4]

Unnao Rape Case

On the 4 June 2017, a 17-year-old minor girl was kidnapped from her village, Mankhi, in Uttar Pradesh and raped by BJP

MLA Kuldeep Singh Sengar, his brother Jaideep alias Atul Singh and others. Seventeen days later, on 21 June 2017, the girl was found in Auraiya—116 kilometres away from her village.[5]

The next day, on 22 June 2017, an FIR was lodged, although the police officers were reluctant in doing so. Even after the victim's heart-rending appeals, the legislator was not named in the FIR. In fact, it was alleged that the cops went to the extent of pushing the victim's family out of the police station when they insisted on Sengar being named in the report. As if to add insult to injury, the case was registered only under Section 363 (kidnapping) and Section 366 (kidnapping a woman to compel her for marriage) of the Indian Penal Code. Yet, no action was taken, and the victim's voice fell on deaf ears.

While the family went about raising their voice again and again, the father of the victim was beaten black and blue by the legislator's brother and co-accused Jaideep alias Atul Sengar and his henchmen on 4 April 2018. Their insolence became visible when they themselves allegedly put up a video of the father being thrashed on social media. When the victim's father went to the police station to lodge a report, he was booked on trumped-up charges, put in the lock-up and sent to jail.

Four days later, on 8 April 2018, in an obviously desperate attempt to make herself heard, the victim tried to immolate herself in front of Chief Minister Yogi Adityanath's residence in Lucknow.

Barely 24 hours ahead, the victim's father succumbed to his injuries. The post-mortem report mentioned the cause of his death to be 'blood poisoning', along with injuries on his body.

No sooner than the incident hit the headlines, eminent senior advocate Gopal Swarup Chaturvedi moved a petition before the Allahabad High Court to take up the case. Not only was his request for a court-monitored investigation conceded by the High Court, but he was also appointed as the amicus curie.

Thanks to the court's intervention, the Uttar Pradesh government rose out of its deep slumber. What followed was the instant handing over of the case to the CBI on 12 April 2018. The agency ordered the arrest of Kuldeep Singh Sengar and all his cohorts involved in the rape as also in the alleged murder of the victim's father. Following this, as the social media was flooded with posts lambasting the ruling dispensation, Chief Minister Yogi Adityanath refuted the echoing charge that there was a definite attempt by the official machinery to shield Sengar. On the contrary, he went about claiming that he had in reality dealt very firmly with the matter. The next day, CBI arrested the woman who had earlier taken the poor victim to Sengar under the pretext of getting her a job.[6]

Meanwhile, the victim's trauma continued for more than a year. And when the case started proceeding, a 20-year-old case was dug out against the uncle of the victim, and he was awarded 10-year imprisonment by a trial court on 2 July 2019.

In an even more dramatic development a few days later, the victim and her advocate were both grievously injured when a truck hit their car on a highway while they were en route to the Rae Bareli District Court for the hearing that had been shifted to the neighbouring district. The paternal and the maternal aunts of the victim succumbed to their injuries in the crash. Shortly thereafter, Sengar was not only relieved from his duties in the party, but also formally expelled from the BJP.[7]

Responding to a request made on behalf of the victim's family, the Supreme Court, on 2 August 2019 transferred five ongoing cases from the Lucknow CBI Court to the Delhi CBI Court. These cases included the death of the victim's father in police custody while he was booked under the Arms Act, besides the two gang rapes that the victim was subjected to over a week's span. Meanwhile, the Supreme Court, directed the Uttar Pradesh government to pay an interim compensation of Rs 25 lakhs to the victim.

A few days later, on 18 August 2019, Yunus, a key witness in the case, died under mysterious circumstances.[8] No post-mortem was done by the police.

Even while MLA Sengar was in Sitapur jail under the charges brought against him, the BJP leadership did not let his past criminal acts come in the way of their overt bonhomie. On the 6 June 2019, BJP's Unnao MP Sachchidanand Sakshi alias Sakshi Maharaj, who himself has a controversial track record, met Sengar after the general election to express his gratitude for his win to him. The saffron-clad Sakshi attributed his victory to Sengar's blessings.

Finally, on the fateful day of 20 December 2019, Sengar was convicted of charges under Section 376(2) of the IPC and the special court in Delhi awarded him a sentence of incarceration for life. Sengar was sentenced for his remaining biological life, while six others were awarded 10-year imprisonments in two cases linked to the death of the victim's father. Even though this sentence was welcome, the delayed and often denied justice by the police and other law enforcement agencies caused significant damage to the reputation of Yogi Adityanath and his government in Uttar Pradesh.

Earlier, much drama was witnessed over the 'arrest' of Sengar, who was spotted roaming around the streets of Lucknow even as the police described him as an 'absconder'. Sengar went to the extent of releasing his own video from outside the residence of Lucknow Senior Superintendent of Police, declaring, 'I have come here to tell the media that I am not an "absconder", as the media is projecting me to be.'

What became pretty evident was that the state government and the police were dragging their feet in the case and action was initiated only after the Allahabad High Court's intervention. The dubious role of the men in khaki was amply visible in the utterances of the then Director General of Police O.P. Singh, who has since retired. During his interaction with the media, when he was asked why he was going about referring to Sengar as 'maan-neeya Vidhayak ji' (honourable MLA), he sheepishly pleaded, 'Well, by virtue of being a member of the state assembly, he will have to be referred to as honourable MLA until he is convicted by court.'[9]

Considering all that, it was surely not inappropriate to assume that the ground reality in Sengar's case actually diluted the chief minister's claim that even the high and mighty would not be spared for indulging in unlawful acts. It also put a question mark on his tall claims that criminals had abandoned the state and taken refuge elsewhere as a result of the spree of police encounters that have taken place. The prevailing ground reality seemed no different from the days of the previous regime under Samajwadi Party's Akhilesh Yadav, when outlaws connected with the then ruling party were allegedly allowed to have a free run.

It was widely felt that the Yogi Adityanath government would have not initiated any meaningful action in the case had the matter not been taken up by the Allahabad High Court.

Even as it was hotly debated whether Sengar indeed enjoyed the patronage of the state government, the Allahabad High Court came down heavily on the Uttar Pradesh government, clearly indicating that the then one-year-old dispensation left no stone unturned to protect the party MLA, who was finally arrested after the CBI took over the case.[10]

The High Court bench comprising Chief Justice D.B. Bhonsale and Justice Sumeet Kumar, which had taken suo motu cognizance of the sensational case, did not mince words in castigating the state advocate general Raghvendra Singh, who clearly went out of his way to extend all help to the accused. 'The approach of the learned Advocate General is not only appalling but shocks the conscience of the Court in the backdrop of the instant case', the court observed in its 20-page landmark order. The order points out,

> The disturbing feature of the case is that the law and order machinery and the government officials were directly in league and under the influence of Kuldeep Singh Sengar. The Doctor did not examine the prosecutrix, nor did the Circle Officer, Shafipur, register the crime, though hand written complaint of the prosecutrix was sent from the office of the Chief Minister. On petty offence, father of prosecutrix was beaten up by the brother, and the goons of Kuldeep Singh and was arrested and in the custody was beaten mercilessly. It further appears that false cases were lodged against the family members. Finally, father of the prosecutrix succumbed to injuries. The prosecutrix unable to face the pressures exercised upon her by Kuldeep Singh, who was having the backing of the law and order machinery of district Unnao, attempted to immolate herself to draw the attention of the society that she needs help and protection of the custodians of law, which was put to the winds at the behest of the accused Kuldeep Singh.[11]

Taking strong exception to the Advocate General's soft attitude towards the accused, the court said,

> We are constrained to record the approach and attitude of the learned Advocate General, during the course of hearing, in contending that no accused person, including Kuldeep Singh, can be arrested without the Investigating Officer following the procedure prescribed under CrPC and collecting evidence in support of the allegation of rape.[12]

Taking serious note of the administration's obvious collusion, the court pointed out,

> The prosecutrix and her family members have been running from post to pillar but her complaint was not registered, despite approaching the Chief Minister. The influence of the accused Kuldeep Singh in the district police administration is such that the Circle Officer also declined to lodge the report on the complaint duly forwarded by the office of the Chief Minister. The Medical Officer declined to examine the prosecutrix, mandatorily required, where a woman alleges rape. Even the procedure for taking down the FIR/Crime 0316 dated 20.06.2017 under the provisions of CrPC was not followed. The complaint was not reduced to writing by a female police personnel and video graphed. False cases were lodged against the Chacha of the prosecutrix and on petty offence father was arrested and brutally assaulted. The Chief Medical Officer furnished fitness certificate and sent the father to jail where he succumbed to injuries.

It added,

> The accused Kuldeep Singh from the narration of facts in the
> report of ADG dated 11 April 2018, taken on face value, clearly
> reflects that the accused has been using his office and influence
> with impunity to tamper evidence and witnesses, further, has
> exercised undue influence with law and order machinery to
> manipulate and coerce the family members of the prosecutrix
> and brutally assaulted her father. This is a classic case where
> we find that the accused persons have not kept a single stone
> unturned to terrorize not only victim/prosecutrix but her family
> members and other witnesses. The victim has lost her father
> merely because cognizance was not taken of her complaint
> made in August 2017. Had the police taken cognizance of the
> complaint to the Chief Minister and forwarded to the concerned
> police station at that stage, perhaps, further damage, including
> the death of prosecutrix's father would not have taken place.

Lamenting over the advocate general's repeated plea for not
arresting the accused MLA, the court held, 'In the backdrop of
the facts noted by the Special Investigation Team (SIT), learned
Advocate General on repeated query vehemently and categorically
stated that the Investigating Officer will not arrest the accused
Kuldeep Singh until statements under Section 161/164 CrPC
are recorded and in the opinion of the Investigating Officer the
accused is, prima facie, involved in the commission of the crime.'

It went on to add,

> The approach of the learned Advocate General not only
> exudes an unpleasant flavour, but raises doubts about the

> bona fides of the police authorities at the highest level.
> We are unable to persuade ourselves in accepting the
> contention of learned Advocate General that the accused
> in the circumstances cannot be arrested. In our opinion,
> arrest of the accused in the present case is necessarily
> required to safeguard the majesty of law and the dignity
> of the prosecutrix and to instill confidence that free and
> fair investigation shall be undertaken by the Investigating
> agency.[13]

Casting further aspersions on the advocate general, the bench
headed by the chief justice said,

> The purpose of CrPC is to facilitate the enquiry and
> investigation into the commission/omission of the crimes.
> No person or State officer can take technical pleas which does
> not sub-serve the interest of investigation or fails to protect
> the victim of heinous crime. If the argument and the stand
> of learned Advocate General is to be accepted, it will send
> a wrong and devastating message in the society and would
> directly facilitate the cause of the accused in the instant case
> and the inaction of the Investigating Agency in bringing the
> culprit to the book.

Reacting sharply to the advocate general's consistent plea that
the MLA could not be arrested unless the investigation officer
found sufficient evidence to establish the charges levelled against
the accused MLA, the court said, 'We specifically asked learned
Advocate General as to whether such procedure is being followed
by the Investigating Agency in the State of Uttar Pradesh in all
such cases, he could not reply our query.'

Top legal luminaries of the state were of the view that it was rare for the High Court to be castigating the advocate general in such severe terms. They also felt that but for the High Court's intervention, perhaps the all-powerful MLA would have gone scot-free, especially since he enjoyed such blatant patronage of the state.

Chinmayanand Case

The ink of the Unnao rape case verdict had barely dried when another case of alleged rape came to light from a Shahjahanpur-based college run by the saffron-clad Swami-turned-politician and former Union minister Chinmayanand.[14]

A 23-year-old law student from the Swami's college accused him of sexually exploiting her over a period of time. According to her complaint, the Swami had allegedly got videos shot of her in her bathroom and had been blackmailing her on the basis of those. She also released some secretly made videos of certain sleazy acts of the Swami, who could be seen enjoying massages by young inmates of the college hostel.[15]

Chinmayanand is the president of the managing committee of Shahjahanpur's Swami Shukdevanand Postgraduate College, where the girl was a student. The Swami had been a Union minister in the Atal Bihari Vajpayee government's third stint between 1999 and 2004. He was a member of the Lok Sabha from Jaunpur constituency in Uttar Pradesh during the period.

As soon as her exposé of a self-made video went viral on the social media, Swami Chinmayanand moved a counter-complaint against the girl, accusing her and some of her friends of making an effort to extort Rs 5 crores from him. While the police arrested the Swami after much dilly-dallying over the girl's complaint, it went on an overdrive based on the Swami's counter-complaint and arrested the girl in just a matter of five days, on 25 September 2019.[16]

The Swami pleaded being 'unwell' and so managed to get himself hospitalized under police watch.

Meanwhile, the girl moved the apex court, which directed the state government to constitute an SIT to probe the case. The SIT swooped in on the young girl one early morning while she was still in bed at her home in Shahjahanpur. She was taken to the local hospital in for a medical examination, after which she was rushed to the Kotwali police station and put under arrest.

According to the victim's family members, the cops darted into their home and literally pulled the poor girl out of her bedroom, dragging her into a police vehicle. She was forced to sign some documents in Kotwali after which she was sent to jail, they said. A local court later remanded her to judicial custody for 14 days. Significantly, the cops got into action barely a few hours before the girl's plea for anticipatory bail was to be heard by a local court, where the case was listed.

'We have enough evidence to prove that the girl was involved in the bid [to] extort money from Swami Chinmayanand', SIT chief Naveen Arora told media persons in Shahjahanpur. He, however, failed to explain why the saffron-clad Swami was allowed to cool his heels in a hospital even after the doctors had declared him 'fit' and 'fine'. Hospital records described him as being kept 'under observation'. What was even more glaring is that Arora, an inspector general of police, told the media that Chinmayanand had admitted to all the accusations against him and that he felt 'ashamed' about everything.[17] 'The Swami has confessed that he did get himself massaged from the woman', said Arora.[18] Swami Chinmayanand expressed remorse after his arrest. "'Main apne kiye kritya se sharminda hun (I am ashamed of my deeds)", Swami Chinmayanand said when we asked him about the allegations made by the young woman against him', Arora told reporters.

Arora added that the woman and Chinmayanand had also exchanged phone calls and spoken around 200 times since 1 January 2019. 'We have sent Swami's mobile phone to the Forensic Science Laboratory (FSL) to recover data from it', said Arora. He however, admitted that key pieces of evidence against Chinmayanand in the sexual abuse case were missing—for instance, the pair of spectacles with hidden camera worn by the woman had not been recovered by the SIT and the state forensic science laboratory could not recover data deleted by Chinmayanand on his mobile phone.

It was strange that the same officer preferred to book Chinmayanand only under the 'softer' provisions of the rape law. He was charged of 'misusing authority for sexual intercourse' or 'sexual intercourse not amounting to the offence of rape'.[19] Significantly, unlike rape, this offence is punishable with fine and imprisonment up to a maximum of 10 years. The offence of 'rape' invites imprisonment of seven years, which could extendable up to a life term.

The cops initially took into custody three friends of the rape victim, booking them for making the extortion bid. Forty-eight hours later, they slapped the same charge against the rape victim.

Fact remains that Uttar Pradesh cops were on an overdrive right from day one to prove the 'extortion' story far more aggressively than the rape charge against the godman, who runs a series of educational institutions in Shahjahanpur, from where he earlier also got elected to the Lok Sabha.

Even as the investigation was on, the girl suddenly turned volte face and withdrew all charges against the Swami. She went to the extent of saying that she had levelled the charges against Swami Chinmayanand under the undue influence of someone else. As a consequence, she was charged with perjury. But, most dramatically, what followed was that Chinmayanand too promptly decided to withdraw his case against the girl and her friends. And that brought the murky case to a happy ending with both sides withdrawing their respective accusations against each other.[20] Is it right to speculate that there was something more than what met the eye? That remains buried and forgotten.

The Hathras Shocker

On 14 September 2020, four upper-caste men gang-raped a 19-year-old Dalit girl and left her with a broken spine and vomiting blood in a nondescript village of the Hathras district barely 180 kilometres from New Delhi. The girl died in Delhi's Safdarjung Hospital 14 days later. What followed defied the tenets of sanatan Hindu dharma, which Chief Minister Yogi Adityanath sought to invoke while launching 'Mission Shakti', the much-hyped programme for women's safety.

The rape victim was rushed to the local hospital from where she was referred by the Uttar Pradesh police to Jawaharlal Nehru Medical College in Aligarh, where she was treated for two weeks. As her condition deteriorated, the Aligarh Medical College doctors referred her to AIIMS, Delhi, but the Uttar Pradesh police preferred to get her admitted at Delhi's Safdarjung Hospital; it was here that the girl breathed her last within the next 24 hours.

The same night, the Uttar Pradesh police took the girl's body to her village, where the cremation was carried out in the dead of the night. The cops also physically prevented any family member of the victim from attending the clandestinely carried out funeral that was bereft of customary Hindu rites and rituals. They even used petrol and sanitizer to ensure that the body burned faster at 2.30 a.m.[21]

According to a report in *Frontline*,[22] the incident of rape took place in the morning when the girl went to cut grass in the fields of the Thakurs in the Bhulgarhi village. Her mother was barely some distance away. When she heard her daughter scream, she rushed to the spot only to find her covered in blood. She called her son, who reached the spot on a motorcycle. Together, they took the victim to the Chandpa police station. An FIR was lodged under section 354 of the IPC (assault on a woman with intent to outrage her modesty) against the main accused, Sandeep.

On 19 September, the girl's statement was recorded at the Aligarh Medical College Hospital. Besides Prashant, she named another accused. After this, section 302 of the IPC was added in the FIR and Sandeep was arrested.[23]

News of her death led to day-long protests by political parties in Delhi in support of the family members, who wanted her body to be handed over to them. But the Uttar Pradesh police furtively took the body from the hospital and reached Hathras, which is 200 kilometres away from Delhi, and burnt it. Vikrant Veer, superintendent of police (SP) of Hathras, denied that the police hurriedly cremated the body. He even went to the extent of claiming that the girl's family members performed the last rites.[24]

The role of the police was under scrutiny for this and other issues. For instance, a week after the incident, the victim is said to have told the police that she was gang-raped and warned against naming the accused. Vikrant Veer said that sexual assault was not confirmed by doctors in either Hathras or Aligarh. He went about emphasizing the strangulation theory, which, according to him, had left the girl paralysed.[25]

The dastardly crime was a blow to the BJP, which came to power in Uttar Pradesh on the promise of making the state safe for women. As mentioned earlier, according to the National Crime Record Bureau data, Uttar Pradesh reported the highest number of cases against women and Scheduled Castes in 2019. With 59,853 cases of crime against women, Uttar Pradesh accounted for 14.7 per cent of such cases in the country. It was also ahead of other states in crimes against girl children under the POCSO Act, with 7,444 cases.[26] The state recorded 11,829 cases against Scheduled Castes in 2019, which is 25 per cent of the total cases in the country.

In response to a PIL moved by some lawyers, the Supreme Court on 27 October 2020 formally ordered a CBI probe into the Hathras gang rape, while directing the Allahabad High Court to monitor the probe. The apex court's order was issued by a bench comprising Chief Justice Sharad A. Bobde, Justice A.S. Bopanna and Justice V. Ramasubramanian, who had earlier on 15 October reserved its verdict on multiple PIL applications moved by different counsels and social activists. Reports from Hathras indicated that this news brought much satisfaction to supporters of the Dalit victim's family who were doubtful about the fairness of the inquiry to be carried out by the CBI.

The court, however, deferred its verdict on the applicants' plea for holding the trial in the case outside Uttar Pradesh. The bench agreed to take a decision on that once the probe by CBI was over.

The CBI chargesheet, indicting the Uttar Pradesh police for shoddy handling of the Hathras gang rape and murder case, was a slap on the face of the state government, which had left no stone unturned to give the case all kinds of twists and turns, so that it could be written off as yet another case of honour killing.

The manner in which the Uttar Pradesh administration in general and the police in particular were moving heaven and earth to deny rape charges had led many to suspect that they would also try to influence the CBI. The chargesheet, however, has shown that the country's premier investigation agency has maintained its independence.

Not only the state police but even Uttar Pradesh Chief Minister Yogi Adityanath initially did seem to dismiss the gang-rape theory as an opposition design, which the latter termed as part of an 'international conspiracy' to defame his government. He even went about floating another theory about a conspiracy to incite caste conflict in the state.

The basis of this allegation was a tapped phone conversation, which was not even authenticated, and an abandoned website. The much-hyped apprehension of caste violence has remained imaginary even to this day. Yet, activists of a select organization as well as a journalist Siddique Kappan from Kerala were arrested on the charge of being part of the alleged conspiracy and were still behind bars in October 2021.[27]

The CBI chargesheet has pointedly blamed the Uttar Pradesh police for the delay in the victim's medical examination, which is believed to have led to loss of evidence. The necessary medical examination meant to establish vaginal penetration was carried out eight days after the gang rape on 22 September. The Uttar Pradesh police found it convenient to go to town with the reports of doctors who had examined her initially in Harthas as well as in Aligarh and had not confirmed rape. However, the 54-page medico-legal examination report prepared by the Jawaharlal Nehru Medical College Hospital clearly spelt out 'complete penetration of the vagina' and 'use of force'. This report was cleverly ignored by the state police. Uttar Pradesh's Additional Director General of Police (law and order) Prashant Kumar cited the 'absence of sperm' in the sample sent to Forensic Science Laboratory as evidence of 'no rape'. He stuck to his claims about 'conspiracy' to stir caste tensions in the region.[28]

The CBI also took note of the fact that for four days the Hathras police did not care to get a woman cop to examine the victim at the local Chandpa police station, where the case was registered in Hathras district.

Top officials of the Uttar Pradesh government later tried to give the case a twist of 'honour killing' perpetrated by the victim's family. According to them, the victim was in a relationship with the key accused Sandeep Singh, of which her family did not approve. The CBI chargesheet, however, described that as a 'half-truth'. Thus, while confirming the 'affair' between the two in the chargesheet, the CBI pointed out that the victim had stopped communicating with the accused since March, even as he was continuing to make phone calls to her. Sure enough, this contradicts the theories that were systematically floated by the state government.

As if holding a brief for the accused, the Uttar Pradesh police had gone about planting stories in defence of the accused. 'At least three of the four accused were not anywhere close to the location of the crime, while one was on duty in a factory', was a theory systematically floated by a top Uttar Pradesh cop. On the contrary, the CBI chargesheet made it loud and clear that none of the accused were able to prove their absence from the location of the crime.

Even as the Uttar Pradesh police stood castigated by the CBI, the Uttar Pradesh police top brass did not hesitate to pat its own back, claiming that the CBI had simply followed the investigation already carried out by them.

Currently, one part of the case is being heard by the Allahabad High Court's Lucknow bench, which 'is considering whether the authorities had the family's consent for the cremation, and if not, what penalties to impose on officials involved'.[29] Proceedings in the main criminal case are on at the Hathras district court in which 16 of the 104 witnesses have testified. The plaintiff has asked for death penalty for the accused.

The accused—Sandeep, 20; his uncle Ravi, 35; and their friends Ramu, 26, and Luv Kush, 23—were booked on charges of murder, gang rape and under the SC/ST Act. In a letter written from jail to the Hathras superintendent of police, they pleaded innocence and went to the extent of alleging that the victim was beaten to death by her own brother and mother because they were opposed to her relationship with one of the accused. Interestingly, this was the theory sought to be systematically spread by the authorities.

Many top officials of the state government as well as the Uttar Pradesh police were desperate to disprove the rape theory. They had also left no stone unturned to run down the 19-year-old-girl, whose character assassination was done by them with impunity.

Significantly, the incident had sparked protests across the country, with opposition parties demanding Chief Minister Yogi Adityanath's resignation.[30]

That is a stark reminder of how facts were twisted in a similar manner way back in 2014 by the then Akhilesh Yadav government to turn the infamous gang rape of two teenaged Dalit sisters in Budaun into a case of suicide. The bodies of the two girls were found hanging from a tree barely half a kilometre from their homes. Just as in the Hathras case the alleged perpetrators of the heinous crime were upper-caste Thakurs—considered close to the ruling dispensation—the alleged rapists in the Budaun case belonged to the then ruling caste of Yadavs.

* * *

Police High-Handedness in Gorakhpur

High-handedness of the police has been rampant in Uttar Pradesh for years. But the extent to which the men in khaki have become insolent and unbridled of late reflects the manifestation of a despotic mindset, sans compassion or humanitarian values.

Some attribute this mindset to Chief Minister Yogi Adityanath's much publicized encounter spree,[31] propelling cops to turn trigger-happy and to start believing that they have the licence to kill. That became amply visible for the first time when a constable on night duty shot down a young man from point blank range simply because he did not halt his car on being signalled by the cop to do so. The bullet pierced through the windscreen of the vehicle and went straight into the chest of the youth who happened to be a manager with the multinational giant Apple. While there have been umpteen cases of police atrocities over the years, what happened on the night of 27 September 2021 in Gorakhpur, the home district and political constituency of Yogi Adityanath, leaves every other act of high-handedness way behind.

A young entrepreneur of barely 36 years was beaten to death by an insolent police inspector, who was allegedly out on his 'extortion' round. A MBA graduate who had earlier worked with a business house in Gurugram, Manish Gupta had shifted to Kanpur and started his business in real estate, and was on a business trip to Gorakhpur. Described as a strong BJP supporter and an ardent Yogi Adityanath fan,[32] he, together with his friends Harbir Singh and Pradeep Chauhan from Gurugram, put up in Krishna Palace Hotel in the Ramgarh Tal area of modern Gorakhpur.

On the night of 27 September, when they had all checked into one large room, they were woken up by loud banging on the door by half a dozen local cops led by Inspector J.N. Singh (SHO), whose name spells terror in the area. On opening the door, the cops barged into the room announcing that they had come for a search though they carried no warrant.

According to one of Manish's friends,[33] the men in khaki, who appeared to be drunk, were very abusive and rough, while frisking through the bags and suitcases of the inmates. When they failed to find anything incriminating with them, Manish simply said, 'So you found nothing', while adding, 'Did you think we are terrorists that you are being so rude with us?' That was enough to infuriate the inspector, who began beating Manish, first with his hands and then with his cane until he fell flat on the floor and turned motionless. Some of the injuries suggest that he was also hit by a rifle butt, say reports.[34]

The cops lifted him and dragged him outside the hotel and took him to a private hospital, which instantly referred him to the Medical College, where he was declared 'brought dead'. That triggered a spate of obviously concocted stories—the foremost one being floated by the police that Manish suffered injuries as

a result of a fall sustained while trying to escape from the room
to avoid the search. But the post-mortem report made it pretty
explicit that the injuries on Manish's body were clearly 'ante-
mortem'.

The 36-year-old trader, who has left behind a four-year old
son, sustained injuries on his forehead, brain, skull, arm, forearm
and left upper eyelid, and according to the post-mortem report,
'Went into coma due to injuries'. The report also suggested that
he died within minutes of sustaining the injuries.

Even the district police chief Vipin Tada left no stone
unturned to dilute the case and shield his police team that
was prima facie guilty of intimidating and killing the youth.[35]
He, along with another official, was caught on video coercing
Manish's wife Meenakshi to not even register a case. Failing in his
effort to do so, he did his bit to dismiss the cold-blooded murder
as an 'accident'. In a press statement issued by him, Manish's
death was attributed to 'falling in a flurry'—something sharply
contradicted by the post-mortem report. However, no sooner
was a decision taken to hand over the case to the CBI, the SSP
backtracked. Significantly, he is the son-in-law of the former
Mumbai police commissioner and currently the ruling party's
Lok Sabha member Satya Pal Singh, who remained Union
minister in the Modi government between 2014 and 2019. The
SSP's superiors also chose to give wishy-wahsy statements.

Akhil Kumar, ADG Gorakhpur Zone, told the media that
arrests would be made on the basis of evidence. 'I would like to
assure that strict action will be taken against the culprits, but
before that we are collecting all the evidence. Court demands
evidence', he said.[36] Even as the probe was entrusted to an SIT
from Kanpur, not a single arrest had been made in the case for
ten days of the incident. Retired top cops were of the view that

prolonged time gaps often led to destruction and distortion of crucial evidence.

Manish's wife, Meenakshi Gupta, has accused the police and hotel employees of destruction of evidence. 'My husband was murdered in that hotel, he was killed by a policeman. There was no blood on the scene even though my husband was beaten badly. Two of his friends said that there was blood everywhere, but the hotel staff cleaned it up', Meenakshi said.[37]

The SHO, who managed to abscond for nearly 12 days, was widely known for his high-handed and extortionist ways and his 'searches' were quite routine, carried out largely to extort money from businessmen visiting Gorakhpur from other cities and states. Rising from being a constable, he had made his way up because of the patronage of bigwigs.[38] The state government did order his suspension together with the other five members of his team, who were described as 'absconding' even after 12 days of the incident.

'The incident has also raised questions on law and order in Uttar Pradesh, but more importantly, the very nature of policing in the state', wrote The Print.

Meanwhile, Manish's family appears to have been somewhat pacified, with Chief Minister Yogi Adityanath assuring Meenakshi Gupta, the victim's wife, of a government job along with an ex gratia payment of Rs 50 lakhs.

Lakhimpur Kheri Violence

It is believed that the administration turned complacent on the Gorakhpur incident largely because the media focus shifted from there to Lakhimpur Kheri, where four protesting farmers were mowed down by a speeding SUV belonging to Union Minister

Ajay (Teni) Mishra's son Ashish Mishra; four others, including a local journalist, were killed in a retaliatory attack and crossfire.

For sometime, it was felt that the agitation of farmers, which has been going on since 9 August 2020, could have some bearing on the voting pattern only in western Uttar Pradesh, where the farmers' movement was strong and relentless. But, the mowing down of four farmers by a speeding vehicle, allegedly occupied by the son of the local MP and Union minister of state for home has clearly re-ignited farmers' agitation against the three new farm laws ushered in by Prime Minister Narendra Modi. And its impact seems to be reverberating not only across Uttar Pradesh and the Uttar Pradesh–Delhi border, where they were camping for more than a year, but also in several other states.

The Union minister's son Ashish Mishra flatly denied his involvement in the incident, while his father moved heaven and earth to ensure that the son got a clean chit. Evidently, that was the reason why the entire opposition has been demanding that Ajay Mishra should be sacked, as his presence in a prime position in the government could negatively influence a fair and objective investigation.

When Ajay Mishra was summoned by Union Home Minister Amit Shah on 6 October 2021, it was widely speculated that he could be asked to step down. But the manner in which Mishra attended his office the same afternoon and was back to his official schedule from the following day was a clear pointer towards how things were turning out in Delhi. According to BJP insiders, it was unlikely that any action would be taken against Mishra, even as the son may be made to face some music only to pacify the rising tempers against him.

Mishra was inducted into the Narendra Modi cabinet during the last expansion in July 2021, essentially because of being a Brahmin. In a caste-ridden Uttar Pradesh, this was believed to be part of the 'Brahmin wooing' exercise undertaken by the BJP to offset Chief Minister Yogi Adityanath's overtly pro-Thakur actions. Not very long ago, the BJP had managed to win over a Brahmin ex-Congressman minister Jatin Prasad, who was ushered into the Yogi Adityanath cabinet last month.

Even though both Mishra and Prasad were not high-profile leaders, it was their Brahmin lineage that served the BJP's purpose of symbolism. 'Now with [the] election just round the corner, Mishra's removal from the Union cabinet could adversely impact BJP's Brahmin wooing', political analyst Govind Pant Raju told the authors.

The state government kept sitting pretty without initiating action in the matter until the Supreme Court, taking suo motu cognizance of the incident, sought an 'action taken report' from them on 7 October 2021. Castigating queries by the apex court bench headed by the Chief Justice of India did stir the government into action; yet, it seemed to continue to shield the key accused Ashish Mishra, who remained at large for nearly a week after the incident. After much reprimand and scathing observations by the apex court, the state police finally got into the act and issued a formal notice to Ashish Mishra to appear before the crime branch of Lakhimpur Kheri district before 11 a.m. on 9 October 2021.[39]

For days, no arrests were made by the state administration, which did not tire of making tall claims of having established 'Ram Rajya' in the country's most populous state. The government's stand was amply displayed in the assertion of the chief minister on 8 October 2021 that 'arrest would be made on the basis of proof and not allegation'.[40] He was speaking at a conclave hosted by a media house in Lucknow. 'Everyone is equal in the eyes of law. Nobody, irrespective of their party affiliation, will be spared', he declared.

Significantly, that came after the Supreme Court bench comprising CJI K.V. Ramanna, Justice Surya Kant and Justice Hima Kohli had already expressed its displeasure with the inaction of the state government. 'Your seriousness is only in words and not in your actions', said the CJI.[41] While questioning the state government's decision to constitute an SIT comprising only local cops, the apex court talked about exploring the possibility of other modes. It went to the extent of pointing out that even a CBI probe may not be any solution as Ajay Mishra was a central minister looking after the home department.

Reacting to the Uttar Pradesh government's plea about issuing a notice to Ashish Mishra to appear before the crime branch on a certain date, the CJI sought to know, 'It is the way you treat the accused in other (murder) cases also: issuing notices to them to appear and not arresting them? When there are serious allegations of murder and gunshot injury . . . what message are you sending? We expect a responsible government and a sensitive police . . .' Justice Hima Kohli told the state, 'There is an old adage which rings true in this situation—the proof of the pudding is in the eating . . .'[42] Justice Surya Kant told the state, 'It is a case of brutal murder of eight persons, law must take its course against all the accused.'[43] Eventually, Ashish Mishra showed up before the crime branch, which then formally arrested him after much dithering and got his judicial custody by a local court.

It was after such reprimand by the highest court of the land that minister Ajay Mishra went on record to assure the media in Lucknow on 8 October 2021, 'My son will appear before the investigating team before 11 am tomorrow.' Interestingly, a copy of the notice was also pasted on the gate of Ajay Mishra's residence a day earlier.[44]

Delayed action against the culprits in any such situation like Lakhimpur naturally arouses suspicion over the sincerity of the authorities in maintaining objectivity. And in case of Lakhimpur, the manner in which opposition leaders were physically prevented for three days from visiting Tikonia village, where the killings took place, further compounds these doubts about the government's intentions. Yogi Adityanath was very critical about the insistence of opposition leaders to visit the fateful village.

Congress General Secretary Priyanka Gandhi, the only opposition leader who managed to hoodwink the police by playing a cat and mouse game and cover some distance on way to Lakhimpur, was eventually intercepted by cops and put under arrest in a police guesthouse in Sitapur. Her refusal to budge finally led the state government to allow her to move on to Lakhimpur after two days. Other opposition leaders including SP chief Akhilesh Yadav followed course a day later when Aam Aadmi Party MP Sanjay Singh and BSP General Secretary Satish Misra also rushed to meet the families of the killed farmers.

It is not clear whether the ruling dispensation can see any writing on the wall: that the issue is not going to die down with the passage of time and it could also have serious repercussions on the Uttar Pradesh state assembly elections, barely a few months ahead.

15

GOVERNANCE

One aspect of Yogi Adityanath that has stood out, besides his strong views on Hindutva, is his personal and financial integrity. There are no whispers in the corridors of Lok Bhawan from where he rules the state, unlike his predecessors who functioned from either the Secretariat Annexe (from Vishwanath Pratap Singh to Akhilesh Yadav) or the old Council House building (from Gobind Ballabh Pant to Banarsi Das).

But all the praise for Yogi was showered much before the onslaught of the second wave of COVID-19. If at all the financial integrity of Yogi has been compromised, people must be too scared to talk about it. This is a refreshing contrast from some of his predecessors who faced numerous charges of misusing their office to accumulate wealth.

After the initial hesitant start and a lot of handholding by the Centre, Yogi took control of governance. Although doubts were cast about the real number of COVID-19 positive cases and fatalities, a word of praise from Prime Minister Narendra

Modi[1] and a certificate from World Health Organization[2] put all doubts to rest. What came as a bigger surprise was Pakistan's leading newspaper *Dawn* also applauding Yogi's effort in managing the first wave of the corona crisis.[3]

After the sudden 'eradication' of Japanese encephalitis under his government, management of COVID-19 was another feather in his cap as the state's health infrastructure was widely known to be quite inadequate to cope with the crisis.

In a presentation made by state health secretaries at the Union Home Ministry on 27 April 2020, Uttar Pradesh, Bihar and Assam had the highest number of districts with grave shortages of isolation beds, ICU beds and ventilators—all necessary requirements for fighting the novel corona virus. Based on data up to 23 April, the presentation showed as many as 53 out of 75 Uttar Pradesh districts to have fewer than 100 isolation beds. And of these 53 districts, 31 had corona virus cases.[4]

About a week later (on 29 April), state Chief Secretary Rajendra Kumar Tiwari said that by end of the following week (first week of May) Uttar Pradesh would have 52,000 isolation beds. That sounded like a really tall order.

Additional Chief Secretary Awanish Kumar Awasthi explained how such an ambitious target would be achieved. 'While 17,000 beds will be arranged by the medical health department, the remaining 35,000 will be arranged by the medical education department', he told mediapersons. It is the medical education department that controls the medical colleges and other medical teaching institutions.[5] Of the total beds, 30,000 were meant for Level 1 hospitals (community health centres), 15,000 in Level 2 hospitals (those with oxygen attached to bed) and 7,000 in Level 3 hospitals which had ventilator facility. Additionally, the government also declared 28 private medical colleges as designated Covid hospitals.

Towards the end of May 2020, there were 56,000 isolation beds, 26,000 quarantine beds and 1,260 ventilator beds in Uttar Pradesh. That the state had ramped up its health infrastructure almost overnight read like the story of 'Jack and the Bean Stalk'.

The Union Health Ministry's reply to a question in the Lok Sabha in November 2019 showed how ramshackle the infrastructure was not very long ago. Against the required strength of 3,621, the state had a shortfall of 2,277 doctors and 'with 942 primary health centres (PHCs) working without electricity, regular water supply and all-weather motorable approach road, Uttar Pradesh's PHCs have the worst patient–doctor ratio and infrastructure in the country'.[6]

The ministry's reply, which was based on Rural Health Statistics, 2018, showed that as against a sanctioned strength of 4,509, and a minimum requirement of 3,621 doctors, Uttar Pradesh had only 1,344 doctors in place. Officials blamed this state of affairs on the unwillingness of doctors to work in government hospitals, largely on account of unattractive remuneration and poor working conditions in the rural areas. Against a requirement of 5,194 PHCs, the state had only 3,621 functioning PHCs, which are the first point of contact for people in villages who are often asked to buy medicines from outside shops.

To make government jobs more attractive for doctors, the Uttar Pradesh government promptly announced a salary hike as per the Seventh Pay Commission recommendations. Apart from 1,300 doctors, the beneficiaries included all senior and junior resident doctors as well as medical college demonstrators. 'The state also has the worst infrastructure PHC-wise with 213 centres not having electricity supply, 270 without regular water supply and 459 without all-weather motorable approach road.'[7]

When it came to priorities in the health sector, the state government and the 15th Finance Commission held different views. While the state's focus was on building new medical colleges, the commission's thrust was on upgrading district-level government hospitals into medical colleges.

The constraints notwithstanding, to everybody's surprise the state was able to magically contain the wider spread of the first wave of COVID-19, keeping active cases low and the death toll at 7,877 as of 4 December 2020. The total cases in Uttar Pradesh were 5,20,637. In that respect, the state fared much better than Maharashtra and Delhi. Nevertheless, it is widely documented that the management of the second wave of the pandemic was shockingly poor.[8]

Some experts did attribute these relatively low numbers to faulty testing and questioned the entire process. They asked whether swabs were being taken from patients dying in hospitals to ascertain the cause of their deaths. According to top officials, it was the chief minister's proactive role that brought about the desired change over a remarkably short period of time. The chief minister constituted a special group of 11 top bureaucrats with whom he would meet every morning to review the state's COVID-19 status. Called Team 11, it was also empowered to coordinate on all COVID-19 related issues with the Centre as well as other states.

Those participating in the meetings confided that the chief minister displayed rare knowledge and experience in handling medical and health-related issues. Perhaps that could be attributed to his keen interest in combating the menace of JE in and around his political turf of Gorakhpur where his

Gorakhnath temple trust has also been running a 300-bed hospital. It is said that Yogi Adityanath personally monitors every aspect of this hospital where treatment is provided at a very nominal price. This hospital, too, is being upgraded into a medical college.

But that was much before the onslaught of the second wave of COVID-19, which created havoc over a short span of 45 days during the months of April and May 2021 (discussed in the next chapter).

Corona and Migrant Workers

Uttar Pradesh was among the first off the block to face the novel coronavirus invasion in March 2020. The sudden imposition of a national lockdown from the midnight of 24 March left lakhs of Uttar Pradesh's migrant workers in different states staring at a stark future. These traumatized men, women and children began marching back to their home states. On the way, policemen waited, as if in ambush, to greet them with lathi blows. Some of them were even put in jail for violating the restrictions. Their woes were compounded by penury, hunger and thirst. What motivated them to brave all adversity was the fervent desire to reach home in far-flung villages, come hail or storm. Sadly, very few states, including Uttar Pradesh, could anticipate the scale and import of the reverse migration when the lockdown was announced. An insensitive bureaucracy did not step in to address the humanitarian crisis with empathy.

The Centre, on the other hand, fumbled with a plan to help the most vulnerable section of our society reach their destinations. First, they were to be ferried by buses, then Shramik Special trains were deployed to transport them. It was left to the states to decide how many trains they required. In the end, Uttar Pradesh settled for trains as a better option.

The brutal treatment meted out to those who undertook a tortuous walk back as well as the lack of arrangements for food and shelter on the way were no deterrents for those desperate to return to their home state. Migrants continued to pour in from all directions on foot, on cycles, in autos and hiding behind raw mangoes and in cement pipes on trucks and trolleys from all directions.

A spate of road accidents followed in which quite a few of these migrant workers were killed. According to a report, Uttar Pradesh saw 51 deaths of migrant workers in road accidents during the lockdown.[9] Just to mention a few, six were run over by a Uttar Pradesh state transport bus on the Muzaffarnagar–Saharanpur Highway on 6 May. A couple set to travel to Chhattisgarh from Lucknow on cycle, died after being hit by a rashly driven vehicle a few kilometers away from their home. There were many more victims of a clueless government, which was jolted out of its slumber when 26 workers tragically died in a crash at Auraiyya near Etawah on 15 May 2020.

Like thousands of others, these unfortunate workers were fleeing hunger and joblessness. In a knee-jerk reaction, on 1 May 2020 the Yogi government ordered seizure of vehicles ferrying migrant workers and stopping those who were walking back. 'No one should enter the State without permission as there is a possibility that they can be coronavirus carriers,' the order said but it did not dissuade the desperate migrants from their homeward journey.

Yogi government's order could not deter the desperate, resource-starved workers, who were willing to be fleeced by the truck and trolley drivers while also exposing themselves to indignities heaped by the police and bureaucracy who seemed totally devoid of empathy. With the flow unabated, the government and district administrations became increasingly less interested in the plight of the trudging migrants.

Though the chief minister's intention might have been good, the manner in which the order was passed, without much thought given to logistics, added to the predicament of the hapless migrants.

This was followed by confusion over payment of fares, which initially the migrant workers were told to pay. After the Congress offered to pay the migrants' fares, the Central government stepped in to clarify that the burden was to be borne by the states and the railways. Initially Uttar Pradesh's Additional Chief Secretary (Home) Awanish Awasthi told this author that migrant workers were to pay their fare for the journey home. It was only following widespread criticism that the government on 14 May decided to pay for tickets of migrant workers returning to the state by trains. 'The Chief Minister has decided that no money will be charged from migrant labourers coming on trains run on the state's request to the railways. For this, advance payment will be given to the railways,' Awasthi said. Ironically, this was decided after 318 trains had already brought 3.84 lakh migrant workers from other states to Uttar Pradesh.[10] According to another report, between 1 March and 30 April, as many as 522 trains brought 6.5 lakh migrants to the state.[11]

The government reportedly deployed 10,000 UPSRTC buses, although it may not have known the exact number of migrants heading towards the state. Though the government said it was providing food and water to the migrants, the arrangements were found to be insufficient at several places. Also, temporary shelters were put up much after the initial waves of returning workers had passed.

In the absence of basic arrangements, contrary to the government's claim that the migrants were being well taken care of, what followed was chaos along Uttar Pradesh's borders with other states. The migrants, stopped at the Delhi, Rajasthan, Madhya Pradesh, Haryana and Bihar's borders with Uttar Pradesh, became restive as there weren't enough buses to send all of them at one go. On 18 May 2020, 40 Haryana Roadways buses from Gurgaon, carrying 1,200 stranded migrant workers, were reportedly asked by the Uttar Pradesh police to turn back. A day earlier, 20 buses from Ambala and 15 from Yamunanagar were sent back from Saharanpur. These buses, incidentally, were coming from the BJP-ruled state of Haryana. Forcing them to return showed that either there was complete lack of coordination between the two states or senior officers sitting in the state capital did not properly brief those in districts about the standard operating procedures. Not only Haryana, Uttar Pradesh police also stopped a thousand buses dispatched from Alwar (Rajasthan) on 17 May 2020, leading to protests, according to the *Times of India* (Lucknow edition), in a box item on its front page dated 19 May 2020.

Migrants could take a sigh of relief with Lockdown 4.0 guidelines issued on 17 May 2020 allowing inter-state bus movement. After probably realizing that the move was ill-planned, Adityanath, on 17 May, 'ordered officials to ready 200 buses in every district to ferry migrants reaching the state,' reported the *Times of India* on 18 May. He also said that in case of shortage of buses the authorities could hire private vehicles. Exposing the hollowness of Uttar Pradesh government's claims of foolproof arrangement for transporting migrants, Mirror Now, in its evening programme on 18 May telecast a scene from Ghaziabad's Ramlila Ground where a few thousand workers waited to register themselves for their onward journey on Shramik Specials. The officials present expected these labourers—many of whom were illiterate and also technology-challenged—to register for the train journey, by filling up a form. Punching holes in Uttar Pradesh government's claims, the report not only showed the officials unable to enforce social distancing but also the migrants airing their anger.[12] Clearly, the government had failed to come to grips with the problem of migrants, whom it intended to treat as its demographic dividend.

At this point, the Congress entered the scene with an offer to provide the Uttar Pradesh government with a thousand buses to facilitate movement of migrants. Yogi Adityanath saw a catch in the offer. Rejecting it outright would have meant the government was unsympathetic towards the stranded labourers. Accepting it would have meant conceding political ground to the Congress. So, the government resorted to guile for a way out, and triggered a political war over the hapless migrants. For two days after receiving Congress Party General Secretary Priyanka Gandhi Vadra's offer on 16 May 2020, the state government remained silent. The Congress leader then tweeted, 'Respected chief minister, I am requesting you this is not the time for politics. Thousands of labourers, migrant brothers and sisters without eating anything, are walking towards their homes. Let us help them, give permission to our buses.'[13]

On 17 May 2020 Priyanka posted a video of buses parked in a row, on Twitter, with the comment, 'Our buses are standing at the border. Thousands of migrants and labourers are walking in the heat. Please give permission chief minister Yogi Adityanath ji, let us help our brothers and sisters.'

Yogi Adityanath was clearly not amused. He retaliated by saying that Congress should be condemned for playing politics during the COVID-19 pandemic. He held the party responsible for the Auraiya accident in which 26 migrants died, claiming that one of the trucks involved in the accident came from Congress-ruled states, Punjab and Rajasthan.

Subsequently, Uttar Pradesh's Additional Chief Secretary (Home) Awanish Awasthi, sent a letter to Priyanka's secretary asking for a list of buses, names of drivers/conductors and registration papers, etc. After the Congress provided the details, Awasthi shot off another letter late on the night of 18 May accepting the offer with the rider that the vehicles must reach Lucknow by 10 a.m. the next day. It was not difficult to see Uttar Pradesh government's ploy, but Congress ignored that and simply asked what purpose would be served by sending empty vehicles to Lucknow. The argument made sense.

That the Uttar Pradesh government had deliberately put a spanner in the works became evident when it came up with an accusation that the list provided by the Congress had registration numbers of autos, two-wheelers and cars. Only 879 of them were buses. The state government could not give any valid reason for not allowing whatever buses were available with the desired documents and authentication. And according to Priyanka, there were no less than 900. Instead, the Uttar Pradesh administration arrested Uttar Pradesh Congress Committee President Ajay Kumar Lallu, while ordering all the buses to be sent back. Lallu remained behind bars for months until he eventually got bail.

Corona and Unemployment

What appears to be a major achievement for the Yogi government in Uttar Pradesh was that the state recorded an unemployment rate of 6.9 per cent, which was three times lower than what it was in March 2017.

Government spokesman and Minister Siddharth Nath Singh said in Lucknow on 3 June 2021:

> The milestone has been achieved by the Yogi government despite numerous challenges, especially in the wake of the ongoing COVID-19 pandemic that brought economic activity across the world to a grinding halt over two years forcing companies either to shut down or layoff jobs. The policies and employment-oriented schemes of the Government have played a big role in this important accomplishment.

He further claimed:

> When the Yogi government took over in 2017, the unemployment rate was 17.5 per cent in UP, three times more than the current rate. However, the government generated job opportunities for the unemployed in the last four years by focusing on increasing industries and businesses and the unemployment rate hit the record low of 4.1 per cent in March this year. Even during the second Covid wave, the government left no stone unturned to provide jobs to a large number of youths. Under Mission Rozgar, different departments, institutions and corporations of the state are offering employment opportunities to the people. The number of jobs given during the Yogi government is much higher than what was provided under SP and BSP governments together.[14]

Picture not all that rosy during first half of 2020

In the early stages of the pandemic and after the influx of migrant labour into the state, the unemployment problem threatened to go out of hand. The Centre for Monitoring Indian Economy (CMIE) in its April 2020 report said that unemployment in Uttar Pradesh had jumped 11.4 per cent points to 21.5 per cent. Subsequent CMIE data till 6 December 2020 showed the number of those without jobs had fallen to 5.2 per cent. A major contributing factor was the government's effort to revive the Micro, Small and Medium Enterprises (MSME) sector by disbursement of loans to units hit by the novel coronavirus—launching the One District, One Product scheme to promote the traditional industrial hubs in each of the 75 districts of the state.

On 4 February 2020, more than a month before the sudden declaration of lockdown in the country, Adityanath government told the state Assembly that the number of educated unemployed youth in India's most populous state had grown by over 12.5 lakh in previous two years to 34 lakh.

Uttar Pradesh Labour Minister Swami Prasad Maurya informed the Assembly in a written reply that 33.93 lakh (over 3 million) jobless persons were registered as on 7 February 2020 with an online portal run by the labour department.

As on 30 June 2018 the number of educated unemployed in the state stood at 21.39 lakh (over 2 million). This means that in two years of Adityanath's government, the number of educated unemployed increased by a whopping 58.43 per cent.

The CMIE report was equally damning about Adityanath government's complete failure in generating employment in the state in his initial period as chief minister. The report said that compared to 2018 the unemployment in Uttar Pradesh almost doubled in 2019. The average unemployment jumped from 5.91 per cent in 2018 to 9.95 during 2019. A 10 per cent unemployment rate meant that 10 in 100 people were without jobs.[15] The national unemployment rate during this period was 7.7 per cent.

Quoting CMIE, a Livemint report dated 1 May 2020 said, 'Uttar Pradesh's unemployment rate increased 11.4 percentage points, rising to 21.5% in Apr 2020.'[16]

That coincided with the arrival of lakhs of migrant workers, who poured in from different corners of the country where they had been earning their livelihood. By the end of May 2020, an estimated 39 lakh (3.9 million) displaced persons had returned to their moorings in the state. With the unemployment rate being 21.5 per cent, the government began unveiling ambitious plans to create jobs for these returnees. A statement issued by the government early in May 2020 said,

> A policy is being framed to provide jobs to around 30 lakh migrant workers through labour reforms in their villages and towns. Directions have been given to officials to prepare data from quarantine centres regarding skills of workers. With jobs, guarantee of a minimum salary of Rs 15,000 and guarantee regarding their work hours and security [will be provided].

The government said that besides new enterprises, workers would also be recruited for existing units. 'Along with the readymade garment industry, a policy for perfumes, incense sticks, agricultural products, food packaging, cow-related rural products, flower-based products and compost and fertilizer business is being formulated by the government,' the statement said.[17]

The government also hoped to create 5 lakh jobs in the MSME sector. Towards end May, the Indian Industries Association (IIA), the Federation of Indian Chambers of Commerce (FICCI) and other industry bodies signed a memorandum of understanding (MoU) with the Uttar Pradesh government to provide employment to 11 lakh migrant workers. Of these, IIA and FICCI were to provide 3 lakh jobs each. Laghu Udyog Bharati and the National Real Estate Development Council promised to provide jobs to 2.5 lakh migrants each.[18]

Some of these efforts bore fruit and got a thumbs up from the Reserve Bank of India (RBI), which in a report placed Uttar Pradesh as the fifth state in the country for creating 2.5 lakh new jobs in the MSME sector and for providing benefits to 4.35 lakh people through the Atma Nirbhar package. It also connected industrial associations with platforms like Amazon and Flipkart to help them reach global markets. The state has about 90 lakh MSME units of which 8.07 lakh registered units employ over 50 lakh workers. Yogi's flagship scheme has been the One District, One Product (ODOP), which is described as a 'game-changer' by triggering job opportunities.[19]

Yogi is in a hurry to ensure that unemployment does not become a key plank in the polls like it did in Bihar. The decisions under Mission Rozgar for creating jobs, have both a social and political purpose. Appointment of 36,950 assistant teachers in December 2020 was part of Mission Rozgar. The government had earlier appointed over 54,000 teachers.

No wonder, there is much emphasis on publicizing what the government has done to generate employment. As on 23

July 2021, the Yogi administration claimed to have created 6,65,339 jobs, while more were in the pipeline. According to a government press release published in several local newspapers including the *Times of India* (Lucknow edition) dated 24 January 2021, since 2017 when BJP came to power in Uttar Pradesh, the state government has directly recruited 3,44,136 people, while 2,73,657 were outsourced and 47,546 were appointed on contract in different government departments.

Elaborating the point, the press release said, 'these appointments included 32,685 jobs through the state's Public Service Commission,18,584 through the Subordinate Services Commission, 1984 through Uttar Pradesh Higher Educational Services Commission, 15,004 by the Uttar Pradesh Secondary Education Services Selection Board, 6,507 by Uttar Pradesh Electricity Services and Promotion Commission,1,43,445 by the Uttar Pradesh Police Recruitment and Commission Board and 1,25,987 by the Basic Education department.'

Development in Corona times

That the state has become a major investment destination under Yogi cannot be denied. With the Centre and Uttar Pradesh being governed by the same party, Uttar Pradesh officials claim that foreign investors inclined to shift base from China, are finding it convenient to establish their units here. As the state government is striving for a trillion-dollar economy, it is happily rolling out the red carpet for major players with tremendous potential to set up or expand base here.

In a major boost to foreign investments in the state, South Korean telecom giant Samsung announced its plan to invest

Rs 4,825 crore in Uttar Pradesh. The company will shift its mobile and IT displays production from China to Noida. It is described as Samsung's first high-tech project to be set up in India and third in the world. The unit will directly employ 510 people. This comes close on the heels of another mobile manufacturing unit of Samsung in Noida that was inaugurated by the Prime Minister in 2018.

Part of the National Capital Region (NCR), Noida has been the hub of investments. With Prime Minister Narendra Modi's strong backing, Yogi Adityanath has been able to increasingly attract foreign investments in the region and some other places in the state. To make the state an attractive destination, the state government will exempt Samsung from paying stamp duty in the transfer of land and provide a financial incentive of Rs 460 crore under the Centre's Scheme for Promotion of Manufacturing Electronic Components.

Yet another foreign company to opt for Uttar Pradesh after moving out of China is Germany's famous footwear brand Von Wellx, which plans to invest Rs 300 crore in three projects in the state. It has already launched a couple of its production units in Agra. Significantly, the investment has the potential to create some 10,000 jobs, claimed the state's Additional Chief Secretary (MSME) Navneet Sehgal, who is credited with several innovative and ambitious industrial development plans across the state.

According to Sehgal, a sizeable investment of Rs 1,02,662 crore was already in the pipeline—as per the MoU during the investors' summit in 2018. This is out of a total MoUs worth 1,88,924 crore signed at the meet and include Pepsico and LULU Group International.

Of special significance, more recently, was the government's decision to set up Rs 5,850 crore leather park in Kanpur. This was a refreshing change from the chief minister's earlier hard line against slaughterhouses. It is also hoped that this change in the policy would bring about the much-needed check on the unbridled vigilantes who seemed to suspect all meat as beef, and find it convenient to vent their ire on anyone they choose to target.

On 22 October 2019, the 15th Finance Commission voiced its concern over 'rising government debt, non-compliance of fiscal responsibility and subdued capital expenditure' in Uttar Pradesh, reported the *Indian Express* (23 October 2019). The commission lauded the state for decline in poverty, increase in forest cover, progress in feeder metering and rural feeder audit, but expressed concern over 24.64 per cent power transmission loss in 2018–19 against the target of 19.36 per cent.

Speaking to reporters in Lucknow, Finance Commission Chairman N.K. Singh said that for Uttar Pradesh to become a trillion-dollar economy a new growth rate will be needed. 'If the goal of PM Modi is to make India a $5 trillion economy, then it's important that Uttar Pradesh becomes a $1 trillion economy. Until and unless the state becomes a $1 trillion economy, India cannot become a $5 trillion economy', Singh emphasized.[20] He added: 'If UP continues to move at this (current) rate, then it will not be able to become a $1 trillion economy.'[21]

In Shekhar Gupta's opinion while Yogi has emerged as the new Hindu Hriday Samrat, Uttar Pradesh has fared abysmally on the economic front. The gross state domestic product (GSDP) rate has consistently fallen under Yogi government. From 8.85 per cent in 2015–16 and the high of 10.87 per cent in 2016–17 under the SP government of Akhilesh Yadav, the GSDP fell substantially to 7.24 per cent in 2017–18, 5.33 per cent in 2018–19 and 4.38 per cent in 2019–20—the first three years of the Yogi government. The GSDP in his pandemic-hit fourth year is unlikely to be any better.[22] Even the appointment of K.V. Raju—an acclaimed economist from Gujarat—as economic advisor to the chief minister in 2018 failed to check the slide.

Apparently alarmed by this trend, the party high command felt the need to send someone to fix the state's economy, which could become a hurdle in realizing the prime minister's vision of turning India into a 5 trillion economy. The sudden para-dropping of high-profile bureaucrat A.K. Sharma, known to be a part of Prime Minister Narendra Modi's inner coterie for nearly two decades, was seen as a step in that direction.

After playing a long innings under Narendra Modi (then Gujarat chief minister) and continuing under him in the PMO, Sharma was holding the office of Secretary (MSME) in the Union Government. With a year and a half still to go for his superannuation, Sharma put in his papers in January 2021 and flew down to Lucknow to file his nomination papers for a berth in the state's upper house of legislature (Legislative Council or Vidhan Parishad). What usually remains a low-key affair, suddenly became a big event, with everyone wondering what the PM had up his sleeve in sending his most-trusted man to don the mantle of just a Member of the Legislative Council (MLC). Surely, this was not simply a post-retirement sinecure for a man who had been calling the shots on his powerful mentor's behalf for 20 years. The corridors of power remained agog with speculation about the purpose of his move to Lucknow. Yogi Adityanath, however, was not amused. He moved heaven and earth to keep Sharma out of his government. All the speculation in both political and media circles fell flat when after a five-month long wait, Sharma was given an insignificant slot in the state BJP unit of which he was named the seventeenth vice president.

With that came yet another milestone in Yogi's rising graph. After all, if the rumour mills were to be believed about the tussle between Modi and Yogi over the issue of A.K. Sharma, then it goes without saying that round one had gone in favour of Yogi. Insiders believe that this was perhaps the first time that the otherwise invincible Modi agreed to concede to Yogi's adamant stand against induction of Sharma in his cabinet.

What followed was even more intriguing—an overdose of praise by PM Modi for the Uttar Pradesh chief minister during his July 2021 visit to his parliamentary constituency Varanasi.

Meeting MLAs and other people's representatives

Achievements aside, one trait of Yogi that did not go down well with party legislators in the early years was his reluctance to meet and hear them out. This came out in the open on 17 December 2019 when over 100 BJP MLAs sat on dharna in the state assembly against their own government.

Angry at being denied from speaking in the House, Nand Kishore Gujjar, the ruling party MLA from Loni in Ghaziabad, led over 100 BJP legislators to sit on dharna in the House on 17 December, causing a huge embarrassment to Chief Minister Yogi Adityanath.[23]

Gujjar later apologized but said, 'If corruption continues in the state machinery, how will the chief minister's zero tolerance policy on corruption be achieved.'[24] Gujjar wanted to speak on harassment by the Ghaziabad district administration but was stopped by the parliamentary affairs minister Suresh Khanna, who asked him to sit down. Later the Speaker Hriday Narain

Dikshit also did not allow him to speak. The notable part of the protest was that there were legislators who could muster courage to rise against Yogi.

With Assembly elections due in 2022, Yogi is putting his best foot forward. 'He meets at least a dozen legislators every day and no one is denied access to the chief minister,' maintains his principal secretary-cum-additional chief secretary, Shashi Prakash Goel, who remains his most trusted aide.

But his anti-minority policies like the anti-conversion law—better understood as 'love jihad'—has taken him two steps backwards. Social harmony is a prerequisite for development. Under Yogi's rule, communal clashes and riots may have been few and far between but the harassment of innocent Muslims in the name of love jihad, anti-CAA protests and cow slaughter do not bode well for the state's future.

More than any other issue, it is love jihad that is proving to be the biggest divisive factor—which would go a long way in fulfilling the ruling party's agenda of religious polarization. The state government may not have been able to corroborate its charge that the new law was necessitated to curb 'rising number of forced religious conversions'. The fact remains that the state government went all out to blow the issue far beyond proportion. The state law commission's report advocating the enactment of some anti-conversion law came in handy to push the love-jihad law. The commission's report submitted to the chief minister by its chairman, Justice A.N. Mittal, included a draft legislation providing for punishment in cases of forcible, coerced, alluring religious conversions. It also sought to give power to the civil court to declare a marriage null and void if it was solemnized for religious conversion as its primary purpose.

With the draft legislation in hand, Yogi Adityanath ushered in an ordinance exactly on the lines recommended by the law commission. And that was also hastily passed by Governor Anandiben Patel.

The manner in which the Uttar Pradesh police went on an overdrive to book people under the new law naturally invited much criticism. A group of 104 retired top civil servants got together to shoot off an open letter to Chief Minister Yogi Adityanath urging him to annul the law, which they felt, was against the spirit of the Indian Constitution. Precisely six days later, a group of 224 senior citizens issued a statement backing the Uttar Pradesh chief minister. This group included retired IAS and IPS officers, besides retired judges as well as officers from other central and defence services. Not only did they lambast those who signed the earlier letter to the Uttar Pradesh chief minister, but they even went to the extent of accusing their rivals of 'stoking communal fire' simply because they had termed the law as 'anti-Muslim'.

As if there was a race for enacting the love-jihad law, close on the heels of the Uttar Pradesh ordinance came a similar one in Madhya Pradesh followed by another in Uttarakhand. Evidently, in the game of upmanship, Yogi Adityanath had beaten his counterparts from both these states—Shivraj Singh Chauhan of MP and Trivendra Nath Singh of Uttarakhand.

Yet another controversy that arose towards the end of his fourth year in office was a three-page write-up singing paeans for Yogi in *Time* magazine. Initially, most readers took it for a rich tribute by the world's leading journal for the Uttar Pradesh chief minister. But even a cursory reading unravelled the mystery— that it was an advertorial (paid news).

The three-page *Time* ad mentioned how Adityanath's 'excellent and efficient' Covid management model had allegedly seen the Covid death rate fall to 1.3 per cent in India's most populous state. 'Being positive in a negative situation is not naïve, it is leadership,' it declared. 'No other leader exemplifies this than the Uttar Pradesh chief minister Yogi Adityanath.'[25]

The projection of himself as a development man who is also a strong Hindutva votary makes Adityanath a contender for the role of prime minister in the future. And the brand of aggressive Hindutva politics which he has been able to build through his controversial actions has led several chief ministers of BJP-ruled states to envy and emulate him. This postulation has also been put forth by D.K. Singh, political editor of The Print.[26]

> Remember the ONIDA TV tagline of the 1980s? 'Neighbour's envy, owner's pride.' But it is not envy that is prompting BJP CMs to emulate Adityanath. For them, he is a role model who knows how to become the owner's pride. His counterparts can't ignore the accolades the UP CM keeps getting from the PM.

Nine days after the love-jihad law was passed by the Yogi government, Madhya Pradesh Assembly protem speaker Rameshwar Sharma was sent to Lucknow to study the law, which was hastily copied by the MP Chief Minister Shivraj Singh Chauhan. The manner in which Yogi Adityanath had ushered in the new law through an ordinance in early November 2020 apparently led his MP counterpart to feel left behind in the race for upmanship.

Haryana Chief Minister Manohar Lal Khattar was also quick to follow course. He formed a three-member committee to study the Uttar Pradesh law, and shortly thereafter enacted the law for his own state on similar lines.

Vijay Rupani, the chief minister of Gujarat, and B.S. Yediyurappa of Karnataka, too, rushed to copy two other laws promulgated by the Yogi government. Rupani seemed keen on picking up the U.P. Recovery of Damage to Public and Private Property Ordinance, 2020 to recover damages from anti-CAA protestors, while Yediyurappa's focus was on taking a leaf out of Yogi Adityanath's anti-cow slaughter law.

With these party veterans donning the chief minister's mantle for a much longer period than Yogi Adityanath, racing to play catch-up, the Uttar Pradesh chief minister seems poised for a bigger role in national politics. Some surveys already project him as a future prime minister.

16

FUTURE PRIME MINISTER?

No sooner than Yogi Adityanath's name was pushed as chief minister of Uttar Pradesh, his ardent followers began to visualize him as a potential successor to Narendra Modi. Slogans describing him as 'future PM' rent the air in his hometown Gorakhpur as well as in Lucknow.

Comparisons have been drawn between Prime Minister Narendra Modi and Yogi based on their pro-Hindutva image. After the 2002 pogrom in Gujarat, Modi became a Hindutva mascot. Yogi, in the meanwhile, was pondering over ways to reinvent himself after his cow-protection idea through the Gau Raksha Manch failed to make Hindus come flocking to him.

One may call it sheer coincidence that while Modi emerged as a strong Hindutva leader, drawing criticism from around the world, Yogi Adityanath was busy giving shape to his private muscular outfit—the HYV.

Post the Gujarat riots, Modi, as it was overtly visible, became a polarizing figure, but he also built a reputation for his organizational skills and governance. With every 'Vibrant

Gujarat' event, Modi's stock as a development-oriented chief minister kept rising. Investors were ready to put their money on Gujarat despite Modi's starkly communal image. The Gujarat massacre propelled Modi as someone who could lead the Hindu resurgence and give the community a sense of pride. He was unambiguous about his stand on minority appeasement—his refusal to wear a skull cap was a strong symbolic message which set him apart from most other Indian politicians.

Like Adityanath, Modi, too, was inexperienced in administration when he was handpicked by Lal Krishna Advani to don the mantle of Gujarat chief minister for the first time in 2001. Perhaps Modi was not only sharper than Adityanath, but also a swift learner. So, he did not take long to pick up the ropes of governance.

Ironically, what actually took Modi to a different level was his negative image cast in the backdrop of the infamous Gujarat riots of 2002. All the disadvantage that came on account of his alleged role in the riots was skillfully turned by Modi into an advantage, and it gave him two more successive terms as chief minister. Eventually, he was able to build his image of a development icon, which helped him sweep both the 2014 and 2019 Lok Sabha elections.

Yogi Adityanath's stock, on the other hand, rose for exactly the opposite reasons. With religious bigotry as his forte, Yogi and his HYV became a polarizing force in eastern UP.

He may be very particular about singing paens to Narendra Modi, but it is believed—rightly or wrongly—that he has his eyes on the ultimate throne in Delhi. He also makes it a point to repeatedly emphasize Modi's oft-repeated 'sabka saath, sabka vikas' slogan. However, when it came to constituting his 47-member council of ministers, he handpicked one Muslim

by way of tokenism in the absence of any elected Muslim
legislator. That was Mohsin Raza, a Shia—better known as a
cricketer having played for Uttar Pradesh in first-class Ranji
Trophy rather than as a Muslim with any kind of a political
background. Perhaps Raza's distant relationship with senior BJP
leader Najma Heptullah came in handy in getting the job.

Having played the dual role of head priest of Gorakhnath
temple and Gorakhpur's MP, Adityanath may be credited with
helping out many in distress irrespective of their caste or religion,
but nobody ever associated development with Yogi Adityanath.

This raises the question: was Adityanath appointed with
Narendra Modi and Amit Shah's concurrence or did RSS trump
them to have a man of its choice in Uttar Pradesh? Yogi himself
has said that the Shah–Modi combine was behind his political
anointment. An RSS ideologue insisted that it was the Sangh
which handpicked Adityanath, and not Modi.

Adityanath's appointment was significant as he was different
from the leaders picked as chief ministers in states like Maharashtra
and Haryana, where the incumbents were political lightweights.
While Devendra Fadnavis did not have any strong political base
in Maharashtra, Manohar Lal Khattar was a political novice in
Haryana. Neither can ill afford to defy the RSS, their mentor.

Adityanath is from a different mould and has carved his own
identity without the help of the RSS, wrote columnist Sushil Aaron
in the *Hindustan Times*.[1] He also sought to ask if Yogi Adityanath
was a candidate to succeed Narendra Modi in the future?

Aaron wrote:

Adityanath's appointment flies in the face of BJP's claim to
privilege development as a governance priority. His career
has been marked by anti-Muslim messaging and this account

of a riot in 2007 by Prof. Apoorvanand should clear any
misunderstanding of the UP CM's politics.

He added,

A measure of development-related spending and activity is,
in any case, inevitable, especially when the state and central
governments are aligned but there's little doubt that the Yogi's
tenure will be marked by dramatic changes in social equations
in UP. Simply put, Adityanath's ascent to power will see a
drive towards complete subjugation of Muslims in UP, which
has become a sort of a Hindutva sport. Pratap Bhanu Mehta
has written about Adityanath that "the already accomplished
political fact of the marginalisation of minorities in UP and
elsewhere will now be translated into a programme of their
cultural, social and symbolic subordination.

According to Aaron,

The BJP could have achieved the same outcome, quietly, with
any other CM, but only Adityanath can turn that subordination
into a spectacle that affords the satisfaction to those who say
that if Muslims have to live in India, they have to live on terms
the Sangh spells out. Whatever succour Muslim communities
had in previous regimes by way of attentive politicians, officials
and police officers is now threatened or gone.

He went on to add,

Far from the daily indignities of the marginalised, the
dynamics between Yogi and Narendra Modi will be

interesting to watch. The Yogi's appointment may have already slightly dented Modi's standing among sections of middle class that back the Prime Minister. This section, which fervently believes that Modi knows what is good for India, will wonder if Adityanath is indeed the vehicle of progress that the country needs.[2]

Precedent shows that Modi prefers only low-profile leaders to occupy the post of chief minister in different states. It was, therefore, unusual for him to put his seal of approval on Yogi Adityanath, who happens to be a mass leader, a polarizing figure, a rabble-rouser and a Hindu mascot, all qualities usually associated with Modi himself. And that further reinforces the common perception about Yogi being the first choice of the RSS to head India's politically most crucial state of Uttar Pradesh.

Given his age, integrity and commitment towards Hindutva, perhaps the Sangh sees Adityanath as potential prime minister.

Modi clearly had smooth sailing in the 2019 national election and it is unlikely that the same pattern will follow in 2024. Questions could be raised within the party over his continuation in 2024 when Modi will be 74 years of age. On the other hand, Adityanath would be only 51, and with Modi having himself fixed a retirement age of 75 for BJP leaders, the monk could easily be considered among the frontrunners for the top job. Other prime ministerial hopefuls like Rajnath Singh will turn 73.

The only person who could upstage Yogi at the goalpost is Union Home Minister Amit Shah as he is only 53 at present. Union Transport Minister Nitin Gadkari and Madhya Pradesh Chief Minister Shivraj Singh Chouhan could form the second rung of aspirants for the PM's post.

As of now, there is a yawning gap in the popularity of Modi and Yogi Adityanath among the poor and middle-class Hindus with the Prime Minister way ahead of the latter.

Yogi does, however, share some similarities with Modi. While the Prime Minister was charged with presiding over the Godhra carnage as chief minister of Gujarat, Adityanath was charged with instigating riots in Gorakhpur in 2007. Modi has been absolved of all the charges, while Yogi has closed all the pending criminal cases against himself.

Both Modi and Adityanath are described by their fans as karmayogis and selfless workers. Modi has his mother and brothers, and a wife whom he deserted decades ago. After losing his father in April 2020, Yogi's family includes his mother and siblings, but he is unmarried and a celibate. Modi does visit his mother occasionally. Yogi chose to even keep away from his father's funeral. However, as far as the remaining kin are concerned, both Modi and Yogi have maintained a detached attachment with their respective brothers and sisters. Neither Adityanath's father nor mother was invited for his swearing in as chief minister. No family member of either of the two leaders has been seen flaunting their VIP kin's name to gain recognition in society and move out of their humble moorings.

Modi, it is said, is incorruptible and has no pecuniary ambitions. Yogi enjoys the same reputation, more so because as the head priest of Gorakhnath temple he sits over funds and assets running into hundreds of crores. He leads a spartan lifestyle, if one does not take into consideration his official Mercedes Benz SUV and other luxury vehicles in tow as a matter of routine; or for that matter the air-conditioned comforts of his official residence which he initially claimed to have shunned.

His personal wealth, as per the affidavit filed before the Election Commission, runs into just a few lakh rupees.

His supporters jokingly point out that unlike his predecessors, Yogi does not have pockets in his kurtas—to assert that the chief minister does not intend to misuse his office to accumulate wealth illegally. Other than development, another big difference between the two leaders is that while Yogi's integrity has been above reproach so far, Modi has faced controversy over his expensive custom-made suit and allegations of crony capitalism.

The similarities between Modi and Adityanath extend to their style of work. Both practice yoga, the perceived secret of their energy, are frugal eaters and vegetarian. According to Yogi's brother Mahendra, 'Adityanath's day begins early, around 4.00 a.m. . . . Modi too is an early riser, he is stated to be starting his day around 5.'

After Modi, it is Yogi who is seen as a defender of the faith and one who, like Modi, does not believe in symbolism, like wearing a skull cap—although Gorakhnath temple employs Muslims and extends its facilities to the community's members.

Other BJP leaders from the state, including Kalyan Singh, who the saffron ranks credited with the demolition of the Babri Mosque, did not acquire the stature of a Hindutva icon that Yogi achieved in a relatively much shorter time. Despite their grounding in RSS ideology, they never spoke of Hindu Rashtra with the same fervour and passion as Yogi. They were more into caste politics than religion or Hindutva.

The similarities end here because when Modi became the Prime Minister, he had 15 years' experience of running Gujarat as chief minister, which Yogi totally lacked. The only experience he had was that of running his private fiefdom of the Gorakhnath temple trust, besides having been an MP.

Modi's popularity, despite those who are lined up against him, has gone transnational. Yogi's name, on the other hand, has just begun to filter beyond the country but primarily for his saffron robe.

Yogi seems to have learnt a lot by observing Modi. He believes in doing his homework before departmental presentations to keep—like Modi—the bureaucracy on its toes.

Yet, despite some of his 'Modi-like qualities', Adityanath does not immediately qualify to be the Prime Minister's successor. Nor does he overtly look at himself as future prime minister. For the record, he has stated that he neither coveted the post of chief minister nor did he expect to be appointed as one. However, it would be naive to believe that having come this far, he would not aspire to be prime minister one day.

As if to buttress his assertion, in almost every sentence that he speaks, Yogi makes it a point to praise the prime minister, whom he describes as 'the nishkaam [selfless] sanyasi', whose ideas he is here to implement. In politics, these words cannot be taken at face value, but even Yogi knows that Modi continues to be the tallest of the BJP leaders at the moment and will continue to enjoy that stature.

While Narendra Modi has passed many tests, Yogi has just begun his innings in the complex state which he heads. The parliamentary elections in 2019 was a test that Yogi passed, even as BJP's tally came down to 62 from 71 in 2014. That was despite Yogi's oft-repeated proclamation, 'we will win all of 80 Lok Sabha seats in the state'.

That Yogi's stock is fairly high in the party was clear from the way he was sent to campaign in Kerala, Gujarat, Himachal

Pradesh, Karnataka and Bihar. In Gujarat, he failed to get the desired response as video clips showed him drawing very thin crowds during a road show. In any case, in Gujarat, no leader other than Modi is relevant. The real test of Yogi's brand of Hindutva was in Kerala where he was high on rhetoric, as he spoke of love jihad as a 'dangerous trend' and 'a reality'.

The template which Adityanath used in Kerala was the same as one followed in Uttar Pradesh during the 2014 Lok Sabha poll and Assembly bye-elections. The progenitor of the idea were the RSS mouthpieces *Panchjanya* and *Organiser* which ran a cover story on love jihad.[3]

The Hadiya case came in handy for Yogi's emotional outreach as the BJP began to sow seeds of discord with the aim of drawing political mileage in terms of seats and vote percentage in the Communist Party of India (Marxist)'s (CPM) virtually impregnable bastion. This was a case in which the Kerala High Court ordered a 24-year-old Hindu medical student to move out of her Muslim husband's house and return to her Hindu parents' home. The girl, originally named Akhila Asokan, a resident of Kerala, had converted to Islam before marrying Shafeen Jahan. The girl's plea that she was a major and had adopted Islam to marry a Muslim entirely on her own, fell flat before the High Court.[4]

Yogi lapped up the controversy, terming it as a glaring case of love jihad. However, his balloon got punctured when the Supreme Court restored Hadiya's marriage.[5] His political stock would have risen overnight if he had succeeded in capitalizing on the Hadiya case and had managed to make any difference in the southern state where Christians and Muslims far outnumber the Hindus.

Now that he is close to completing his five-year term in office, Yogi has certainly managed to elevate his stature as a

Hindutva icon. On the other hand, Modi began to observe restraint and systematically refrained from any kind of overt assertion of Hindutva politics.

Conclusions began to be drawn after Yogi Adityanath was appointed chief minister. From day one, he has been viewed as a possible successor to Modi. Some have gone to the extent of saying that Modi has created his nemesis by appointing Adityanath as chief minister. Now if Modi were to nominate Yogi as his successor, would it probably mean an Advani moment for Modi. About two decades ago, when Advani pitched for Modi as chief minister of Gujarat, he could not have imagined that a time would come when he would himself get sidelined, and his own protege would overtake him. One wonders if history could repeat itself.

Sushil Aaron pointed out, 'There is no guarantee that an ideologically charged figure will necessarily cap his ambition on becoming a chief minister. He may not pitch to be Prime Minister yet but also would not be entirely comfortable with his subordinate status for long.'[6]

A hard taskmaster, Adityanath is particular about maintaining a clean image of his government. He, therefore, plugged many loopholes in the system, thereby making pilferage of money difficult. Many MLAs and even some ministers holding key portfolios were known to be at loggerheads with the chief minister because of his penchant for transparency in the system.

Now this was clearly unacceptable to many who went complaining to the party bigwigs in Delhi that they were not being allowed to function. It was in the wake of such complaints that barely four months after Yogi was installed as chief minister, BJP chief Amit Shah flew down to Lucknow on 29 July 2017 and spent three days there to sort out differences between the chief minister and his own cabinet colleagues as well as those between him and the RSS ranks, who were averse to Yogi's HYV.

RSS senior functionaries held three coordination meetings with Adiyanath during the first three months of Yogi raj. Meanwhile, BJP workers went on alleging that government officers in various districts were not paying heed to their complaints and blamed the state government for not taking strict action against such officers. Cabinet minister Om Prakash Rajbhar went to the extent of declaring that he would stage a dharna in Ghazipur, demanding the transfer of the DM. He, however, called off the protest after the chief minister pacified him. Rajbhar's Suheldeo Bharatiya Samaj Party (SBSP) was a BJP ally, differences with which led to a formal parting in 2019.

Shah was accompanied by BJP National Vice President and State In-Charge Om Prakash Mathur, and National General Secretary Arun Singh. Shah also met office-bearers of the Kashi, Gorakhpur, Avadh and Kanpur regions, amid reports that the organization was feeling 'let down' by the state government.

In fact, no sooner than Yogi assumed the reins of governance, it evoked unprecedented euphoria among BJP supporters, who like everyone else, had never imagined in their wildest dreams that a saffron-clad sadhu would one day be installed as chief minister in Lucknow.

Besides conceiving it as the first step towards fulfillment of their long-cherished dream of establishing a Hindu Rashtra, somewhere deep down it also gave birth to this desire of reaping a harvest of material benefits associated with power. Many of them began to imagine themselves in the shoes of their SP counterparts who until sometime back, were conveniently extracting their pounds of flesh.

Little could they fathom that their expectations would remain short-lived and would be belied, compelling them to look up to the party bigwigs in Delhi to literally jostle that very leader on whom they had pinned all their hopes. That was why some of them had earlier gone all the way to Delhi and conveyed their grievances to both Prime Minister Modi and party chief Amit Shah.

Some in-house complainants were understood to have gone to the extent of telling Modi that unless 'corrective' steps were taken, they would find it difficult to mobilize support for the 2019 Lok Sabha election.

Evidently, the dissatisfaction was largely with Yogi—his priorities and his style of governance. No wonder Shah made it a point to give every party functionary a fair chance to freely speak his mind. The common concern was about how the party would mobilize funds for the next election as Yogi's style of working had made things 'difficult' for most ministers.

Even though Yogi Adityanath remained glued to Amit Shah throughout his stay, some partymen including a few legislators and district presidents did not hesitate to vent their grievance against him. Most of them seemed to be irked because 'the chief minister was not conceding' their 'petty requests'. A senior party functionary from eastern Uttar Pradesh confessed to the authors about telling the party bosses, 'If we are not able to oblige those who have supported us in the last Lok Sabha and state Assembly election, then with what face can we go before them for support in 2019.'

It was not as if complaints were made only by those who had a personal axe to grind. A large number of party leaders expressed deep concern over the state's deteriorating law and order, which seemed to be continuing the way it was under an ineffective Akhilesh Yadav regime. Some wondered why the chief minister, who was seen as a 'no nonsense' man, had failed to make any difference to the law and order situation that was largely responsible for the devastating debacle that Akhilesh faced.

It is said that issues were also raised about the 'bureaucratic' ways of the Yogi government. Some party leaders went to the extent of complaining to Shah how they were finding themselves as ineffective as they used to feel under other political dispensations. 'Our electorate has certain expectations from us because we are now in power and if we are not able to fulfill at least some of their expectations, then where do we go?' was the common refrain of many important ruling party leaders

Some complained that the bureaucracy refused to listen to public representatives because the chief minister had himself been telling them not to entertain his partymen. When Amit Shah looked towards Yogi, he was swift to clarify that all he had done was to tell officers not to get pressurized by anyone to do anything in violation of rules and regulations.

All the misgivings—that came as a surprise for Yogi— largely arose out of the high expectations of partymen, who were hoping to make hay while the sun shone, as their party was in power after a long time.

Yogi's only asset—personal financial integrity—was coming sharply in the way of his working. In the bargain, he had created more critics from within than from outside. Striking a balance between maintaining his clean image and keeping the party cadres in good humour became a tough call for him.

What made matters worse were some of his own cabinet colleagues who pointedly blamed him for being 'uncooperative'. Be it the lucrative mining contracts or road building and other construction or supply contracts, Yogi was busy emphasizing on 'transparency'—that would not allow many from his own stock to have their way.

Perhaps, there would have been no grudges if the rule had been followed without discrimination. But the fact remains that some exceptions were made. Thus, recommendations made by party organization secretary Sunil Bansal were carried out without any 'ifs' or 'buts'. Naturally, that did irk many, whose requests went unheeded.

Bansal, who was para-dropped from Rajasthan by none other than Shah himself to run the party war-room during the 2014 Lok Sabha and 2017 state Assembly elections, had become the most significant parallel power centre. It was said that what you could not get in Yogi Adityanath's court, could be managed in the Bansal durbar—though for a price.

Even as partymen discuss Bansal in hushed tones, none could dare to complain against him in front of Shah. After all, Bansal's close proximity to Shah, and that his power flows from Shah, is an open secret.

Constraints notwithstanding, Yogi made it a point to convey the impression that he had no shackles and that he functioned independently. The aggression with which he sought to defend every act of omission or commission of his government reflects that there was very little room for admitting faults or shortcomings. Perhaps old habits die hard. As a spiritual head of a temple trust that enjoys a blind following of millions of people, it is perhaps quite natural for him to feel offended when anyone raises a question. In a spiritual order, the head has the last word and there is no way that anyone questions him. His word is law for all those who pay obeisance to him and his temple.

In his new role, he was confronted with the ground reality, which was often in sharp contrast to the picture conceived in his mind. Thus, whenever he found himself cornered, he chose to conveniently blame everything either on the Opposition or on the media.

Notwithstanding his oft-repeated proclamations about 'sabka saath, sabka vikas' as also his assertions about putting the state on the development path, Yogi Adityanath can apparently not look beyond Hindutva, which he sees as the only route for achieving higher goals.

Ever since he muscled his way to the chief minister's chair, Yogi has been devising subtle ways of keeping the Hindutva flame alive.

Having built the hype around volatile issues like love jihad, ghar wapsi, beef and cow slaughter, with which he skillfully served his objective of Hindu polarization, Yogi has found yet newer ways to play up Hindutva when the state headed into civic elections.

Initially, when he sought to give various things a saffron hue, it was considered as an obsession of a monk, but as time went by, it has become increasingly evident that even that was aimed as a reminder of an aggressive Hindutva. Among the key cards played by him in the initial months was the creation of teerth sthals (pilgrimage centres) through declaration of two small towns in Mathura district as teerth sthals.

Vrindavan and Barsana towns in Mathura district were declared as official teerth sthals—something unheard of in many decades. According to official records, such a special status was given to no city other than Haridwar during the days of an undivided Uttar Pradesh before Uttarakhand was carved out. Even far bigger religious destinations such as Ayodhya, Varanasi,

Prayagraj (Allahabad) have not enjoyed the special status of teerth sthals so far. Of course Mathura was formally declared a 'teerth sthal' only as late as on 10 September 2021. With Vrindaban and Barsana already bearing the designation, now a 10 sq km area is a 'teerth sthal', with all the new restrictions in place.

Declaration as teerth sthal entailed ban on liquor and meat shops, besides special emphasis on promotion of religious and cultural tourism. A formal declaration for Vrindaban and Barsana was made on 27 October 2017 by the then Religious Affairs and Culture Minister Laxmi Narayan Chaudhary during his visit to Agra. He said, with the status of 'teerth sthals', both these places would be free of liquor and all non-vegetarian food. 'After this declaration, sale of meat and liquor would be banned within the municipal limits of the towns and they would be further developed for religious tourism.'[7]

Could this be another way of taking people's attention away from his failure to deliver the promises he made—'gaddha mukta' (pothole free) roads, or making Uttar Pradesh corruption-free and crime-free? Or was it part of a smart strategy to also play up 'Hindutva'?

And to add colour to his obvious Hindutva mission, came his fad for saffron. While wearing saffron robes was a part of the tradition of most Hindu monks, giving a saffron hue to various things reflects the expression of an aggressive 'Hindutva'. As if it was part of that agenda, the Uttar Pradesh Secretariat Annexe—that is better known as the chief minister's main office building—was painted in Yogi's favourite ochre.

The five-storied building, erected during the regime of the then Chief Minister Vishwanath Pratap Singh in 1982 remained cream for many years until the arrival of BSP supremo Mayawati who in her last stint as chief minister (2007–12) decided to make it spotless white. In fact, she even got the older Council House stone facade painted white. Her successor, Akhilesh Yadav of SP, chose to maintain the elegant white.

No sooner than Yogi Adityanath rode on to the high office situated on the building's well-known power centre, 'pancham tal' (fifth floor), the scenario began to change. As long as Yogi's chair was draped in saffron—it was understandable. After all, as Mahant and head of the Gorakhnath temple, anyone in Yogi's place was bound to prefer sitting on a saffron chair. But turning the entire building saffron could not be perceived as anything without a deeper design, especially when the incumbent, widely recognized as a hardcore Hindutva icon, was so adept in the politics of polarization.

Yogi went ahead with his saffronization spree in a spirit of some kind of obsessive compulsion. After draping each of his chairs in saffron—in different offices as well as his official residence—the next thing on his agenda was conversion of all bags given to children in government schools into the saffron colour. Begun during the Akhilesh Yadav regime, the school bags carried portraits of both Akhilesh and his father Mulayam Singh Yadav. Removal of those pictures was quite obvious for any new government, but Yogi Adityanath ensured that the new colour was saffron and no other.

The next thing to be painted saffron were some buses of the state road transport corporation. The exercise began with a batch of 50 buses launched under what was christened Sankalp Bus Sewa that was intended to establish transport linkage between villages across the state. The launch ceremony was carried out from a pandal that was also carefully made in saffron.

Interestingly, when the New Zealand cricket team arrived in Kanpur for the one-day international in October 2017, the team members were welcomed on behalf of the Yogi government with saffron-coloured scarves.

There can be no denying that the politics of colour was pursued in their respective ways by Adityanath's predecessors Mulayam Singh Yadav, Mayawati as well as Akhilesh. While the SP kept it limited to the tokenism of donning red caps or red and green flags, banners and bunting, Mayawati took it to another level. She not only got the colour of road dividers and railings changed from the international yellow and black to blue and white, but even forced traffic cops to switch from khakhi and white to blue and white. Clearly, Yogi Adityanath had beaten all his political rivals hollow in the colour war.

Perhaps with a view to taking his mission—self-promotion—forward, Yogi Adityanath decided to take a plunge to lead his party's campaign in the crucial civic polls that followed precisely eight months after his rise to power. Though chief ministers were not known to be indulging themselves in these local elections, Adityanath sought to make this an opportunity to establish his leadership in the state. After all, the mantle of chief minister was given to him by Prime Minister Narendra Modi on a platter. There was precious little that Yogi had contributed to the massive state Assembly win in March 2017, when it was propelled to power with a record number of 324 seats in a 403-member house. Surely, that was clearly the result of Modi magic.

Yogi did earn several feathers in his cap when BJP swept the mayoral seats—14 of the 16 seats of mayors in tier-one cities, went to the BJP. And even in tier-two towns, the party rode well ahead of the key opposition parties—SP, BSP and the Congress.

Notwithstanding BJP's sweep on the mayoral seats, its vote percentage was on a slide. As such, BJP got 42 per cent votes in the 2014 Lok Sabha, and 39 per cent votes in the 2017 Vidhan Sabha elections, while it rolled down to 30 per cent in the November 2017 civic poll.

What followed was the ruling party's defeat in the bye-elections to the three parliamentary constituencies of Gorakhpur, Phulpur and Kairana, besides one assembly constituency of Noorpur. The party shockingly lost all the four elections, suffering the worst humiliation in Gorakhpur, the seat held for five consecutive terms by Yogi Adityanath himself. The defeat in Phulpur was equally devastating as the seat was held by Deputy Chief Minister Keshav Prasad Maurya.

The loss in Kairana was no less significant. The seat was a bastion of party veteran Hukum Singh, whose demise led the party to field his daughter Mriganka Singh in the hope that she would fetch the sympathy vote. But the party's hopes were dashed. Kairana had gained prominence because the BJP made the alleged exodus of Hindus from the town a big communal issue to polarize voters in 2014.

These results which came as a shattering blow to Yogi, were the outcome of realignment of political forces against the ruling party. Sworn political enemies—SP and BSP—decided to sink their differences to fight their common foe. The Congress and Rashtriya Lok Dal (RLD) also pitched in. The birth of a united Opposition, following the changed chemistry between SP and BSP, did rattle the BJP, which started reworking its poll strategy.

And full marks to Yogi for moving heaven and earth in the succeeding years to establish himself and write his own success story. Even though he could not retain BJP's 2014 Lok Sabha tally of 71 out of 80 seats in 2019, when it dipped to 62, Yogi found reason to boast that he could ensure the party's victory in each of three Lok Sabha seats which BJP had lost in the 2017 bye-election.

He also made it a point to blow his own trumpet for retaining six of the seven Assembly seats that went to bye-poll in November 2020. However, he could not snatch the seventh seat from SP.

That Yogi is trying to build his own image is no secret. Some of his recent decisions have already fetched him the sobriquet of a Hindutva icon. And what he was particularly aiming to push aggressively were his uncompromising ideas on Hindutva.

Since Ayodhya has outlived its political potential after the vexed issue has been settled by a verdict of the highest court of the land, and the cow had failed to give the desired political dividends, Yogi reverted to love jihad.

The exercise began with Uttar Pradesh chief minister once again raising the pitch on love jihad to an extent that his cabinet on 24 November 2020 finally gave the go-ahead for legislating a stringent law to deal with it. And the manner in which the ordinance has been worded is quite discreet as it avoids using the term love jihad.[8]

No one could fathom what was the tearing hurry to bring an ordinance. After all, it could have been done routinely through a bill that could have been introduced before the state legislature once it was in session. That would have kept the doors open for debate and discussion that are essential in a democratic process. But dissent is not Yogi's cup of tea.

However, the fact remains that undeterred by criticism about his obsession for the much-hyped love jihad issue, it topped the agenda for Yogi's cabinet meeting followed by an equally quick approval by Uttar Pradesh Governor Anandiben Patel.

Under this new law, all inter-religion marriages and religious conversions would require the DM's prior permission, which would have to be sought at least two months in advance. Anyone entering into a wedlock through deception and through misrepresentation of religious identity would be liable to imprisonment up to 10 years, according to the Uttar Pradesh Prohibition of Unlawful Conversion of Religion Ordinance 2020.

According to the ordinance,

> No persons shall convert or attempt to convert, either directly or otherwise, any other person from one religion to another by use or practice of misrepresentation, force, undue influence, coercion, allurement or by any fraudulent means or by marriage, nor shall any person abet, convince or conspire such conversion.[9]

However, the law carefully exempts persons who choose to reconvert to their immediate previous religion. Not only the aggrieved persons, but also parents, brother, sister or any relative have been authorized to lodge an FIR about such conversion. The DM is empowered to get an inquiry conducted by the police into the 'intention, purpose and cause of the proposed conversion'.

Any marriage for the sole purpose of conversion or conversion for the sole purpose of marriage would be rendered void. Apparently, this was done in the light of a prior order of single-judge bench of the Allahabad High Court. Interestingly, however, that order was promptly overruled and declared 'bad in law', by a division bench of the same court on the very day that the ordinance was brought before the cabinet.

Even as the ordinance refrains from mentioning the term love jihad in as many words, it may be pertinent to point out that love jihad, as seen by the BJP and its right-wing allies, is about Muslim men enticing Hindu women into marriage by concealing their actual religious identity, with the sole objective of converting them.

Studies carried out in the country on interfaith marriages, however, suggest a completely different story. The Central government–run Mumbai-based International Institute for Population Sciences presented a paper on interfaith marriages in India in 2013 by analysing data from the 'India Human Development Survey (IHDS) data, 2005'.

The study discovered that only 2.21 per cent of all married women in the age group 15–49 had married outside their religion.[10] Surely this does not go with the picture that was being painted by BJP leaders like Yogi Adityanath and others who were keen to extract political mileage by building a false notion that the practice was rampant.

In reality there are few cases to support the government's propaganda on conversions through enticement or allurement. Yet, the government is gung-ho about the law, which, it is feared, is meant to harass genuine couples.

Many of the cases reported to the police by parents of girls have turned out to be false. This was amply demonstrated in Kanpur, which was officially described as a love-jihad hotspot. Kanpur zonal Inspector General (IG) of Police Mohit Agarwal had gone to the extent of constituting a special investigation team (SIT) to go into all cases of inter-religion marriages over the past two years in the city.

The police eventually discovered that there was very little truth in the complaints. IG Mohit Agarwal himself announced that there was no evidence of Muslim youth being funded from abroad to carry out 'love lihad' missions.[11]

However, the SIT's findings should be an eye-opener for the government and others who choose to paint a larger-than-life narrative of love jihad. The police could not identify more than 14 such cases over the laid down span of two years. And at the end of the probe, they discovered that only three of those could be made to fit into the definition of love jihad. No deception was discovered in the remaining 11 cases. Four of the cases involved minors, while four others were about men enticing young girls into a love affair and then abandoning them after enjoying physical intimacy with them. Concealment of religious identity did not figure in any of these eight cases. As for the remaining three cases, the Hindu girls stuck to their guns and maintained that they had married Muslim men entirely of their own accord. The complaints in each of the cases were made by parents of the girls to save themselves from the social stigma attached to interfaith marriages.

Significantly, IG Police Agarwal's own statement contradicts the much-hyped love jihad charge of the ruling dispensation and Hindu hardliner groups like the VHP under whose pressure the SIT was set up. 'SIT has not got any concrete evidence about "love jihad" being done in any organized manner,' Agarwal pointedly told mediapersons. He also categorically ruled out 'funding of "love jihad" from overseas' that was one of the key accusations made by a local VHP leader.

Ironically, the SIT report became public around the same time that the Uttar Pradesh cabinet passed the new law.

That gave rise to the obvious question: why was the state government so desperate to build an impression that the menace was widespread and warranted a special legislation? It is also intriguing that taking a cue from Uttar Pradesh, a few other BJP-ruled states like Madhya Pradesh, Haryana, Karnataka and Assam also declared their intention to follow course.

It may not be too far-fetched to assume that this artificially-hyped love-jihad theory could be the right-wing stratagem to push the agenda of religious polarization.

Nothing could demonstrate that better than a diktat issued by Yogi's government to recover the financial penalties levied on those who dared to join protests and demonstrations against the Citizens Amendment Act (CAA). In March 2019, the Lucknow police had initiated proceedings against 57 such protestors, bulk of whom happened to be Muslims. However, the government's order for attachment of their properties to recover the penalty was stayed by the High Court.

The Yogi administration had set 25 June 2020 as deadline for depositing the fine of Rs 64 lakh imposed on the protestors for allegedly causing damage to government property during the demonstrations in December 2019 and January 2020. What was shown as damage to government property included damage to police motorcycles, vehicle windscreens, helmets as well as window glasses of buses. Damages for burning of an OB van belonging to a TV channel was also slapped on the protestors. Their property would be attached and auctioned if the protestors failed to deposit the fine in the government treasury before that deadline, said an official statement. Senior officials could not recall the last time when such recovery was sought to be made from people staging protest demonstrations against any government.

The recovery order further emphasized that the administration would be free to even put the protestors behind bars, in case they failed to shell out the penalty. The administration's persistence was proved when the protestors continued to be hounded all through the COVID-19 phase. One such protestor was hauled up by cops and sent to jail 11 months after the demonstrations had taken place, simply because he had failed to deposit the fine. A daily wage earner, the 21-year-old boy did not have the means to muster up the penalty that was levied on him.

It took 9 months for 25-year-old Tauseef to get bail from the Allahabad High Court after he was booked for his alleged participation in the anti-CAA protests. His family has accumulated a debt of nearly Rs 2 lakh which was required in the entire judicial process. The rented room in which his parents and two sisters live is now without electricity as they did not even have money to pay their bills. His sisters are on the verge of being thrown out of school because of the default in payment of monthly fees. Emphasizing that he was not even present during the protest demonstration, he told The Wire,

> I am an auto driver and earn about 250–300 rupees a day, which came in handy to run the house as my father also earned the same amount. But with one income gone for nine months you can imagine our plight specially since so much money had to be borrowed to get me out of jail.[12]

Earlier, the chief minister also made it a point to shame the protestors by putting up their names, pictures and addresses on hoardings in public places—an exercise that had not been undertaken even against rapists and other hardened criminals. Much later, Yogi Adityanath announced that posters of molesters would also be put up in public places.

Even BJP insiders believe that none other than Yogi could have been so consistent in such a ruthless stand against protestors.

And that is what makes him stand out in the eyes of the RSS. His tirade against love jihad or his vindictive stand against anti-CAA protestors, most of whom were booked under deterrent laws like the Gangsters Act, was enough to demonstrate his intolerance to any kind of disagreement or dissent.

What seems to have boosted Yogi's confidence and increased his belligerence was the virtual decimation of the entire Opposition. BSP supremo Mayawati already appears to have gone into submission before the BJP, while SP's Akhilesh Yadav has reduced himself to a paper tiger, whose politics remained limited for a long time to issuing press releases and tweets. Albeit late in the day, realization appeared to have dawned on Akhilesh that it was time to get into the act. SP's resounding success—largely by default—in the initial phase of panchayat election when the party-supported nominees stood well ahead of rival BJP's, clearly woke up Akhilesh from his slumber. And that is what seems to make the BJP jittery. To add to BJP's discomfiture, Congress general secretary Priyanka Gandhi has also taken a plunge into the centre stage of Uttar Pradesh's politics.

If the Opposition had continued to remain complacent, Yogi Adityanath could have definitely had a free run in 2022, when the state goes to polls.

In fact, the 2022 Assembly election next year will be the litmus test of Yogi's political prowess. The election will reveal whether he is still dependent on the Modi magic or is now capable of steering the party to victory on his own steam. That is what could enable him to seek a place ahead of other contenders to Modi's throne.

NOTES

CHAPTER 1: THE KILLER PANDEMIC

1   Rajeev Dikshit, 'PM Narendra Modi Lauds Yogi Adityanath for Managing Covid, Overall Development of Uttar Pradesh', https://timesofindia.indiatimes.com/city/varanasi/pm-narendra-modi-lauds-yogi-adityanath-for-managing-covid-overall-development-of-uttar-pradesh/articleshow/84436236.chief ministers (accessed on 9 September 2021).

2   Ayush Tiwari and Muhammad Tahir Shabbir, 'Adityanath's Press Release Is an Ad in Time, but a "Report" in Indian Media', https://www.newslaundry.com/2021/01/06/adityanaths-press-release-is-an-ad-in-time-but-a-report-in-indian-media (accessed on 9 September 2021).

3   Ibid.

4   PTI, 'WHO Praises Uttar Pradesh Government's "Exemplary" Efforts for Covid Management', https://www.ndtv.com/india-news/who-praises-uttar-pradesh-governments-exemplary-efforts-for-covid-19-management-2326399 (accessed on 9 September 2021).

5   Nidhi Jacob, 'Fact-check: Did WHO Really Praise Uttar Pradesh Govt For COVID Testing?', https://www.factchecker.in/fact-

check/fact-check-did-world-health-organisation-really-praise-up-govt-for-covid-19-testing-748853 (accessed on 9 September 2021).

6   PTI, 'Another BJP Leader Criticises COVID-19 Handling in Uttar Pradesh', https://www.thehindu.com/news/national/other-states/another-bjp-leader-criticises-covid-19-handling-in-uttar-pradesh/article35001786.ece (accessed on 9 September 2021).

7   *India Today*, 'Will Face Sedition Charges If I Speak Too Much: BJP MLA on Uttar Pradesh Govt's Handling of Covid', https://www.indiatoday.in/india/uttar-pradesh/story/bjp-mla-uttar-pradesh-covid-sedition-rakesh-rathore-charges-speak-too-much-1803872-2021-05-18 (accessed on 9 September 2021).

8   PTI, 'BJP MLA In Uttar Pradesh Says Covid-Positive Wife Not Getting Proper Treatment', https://www.ndtv.com/agra-news/bjp-mla-ramgopal-lodhi-in-up-says-covid-positive-wife-not-given-proper-treatment-2439129 (accessed on 9 September 2021).

9   Shailvee Sharda, 'Uttar Pradesh: Record 9,695 new Covid cases take April tally to 47k', https://timesofindia.indiatimes.com/city/lucknow/uttar-pradesh-record-9695-new-covid-cases-take-april-tally-to-47k/articleshow/81998774.chief ministers (accessed on 9 September 2021).

10 Subhash Mishra, '"Inefficient": Uttar Pradesh Minister's Scathing Letter to Health Officials Amid Covid Crisis', https://timesofindia.indiatimes.com/india/up-law-minister-writes-scathing-letter-to-lucknow-health-officials-over-covid/articleshow/82053825.chief ministers (accessed on 9 September 2021).

11 TNN, 'Uttar Pradesh Law Min Donates Rs 1cr for Enhancing Health Facilities', https://timesofindia.indiatimes.com/city/lucknow/up-law-min-donates-rs-1cr-for-enhancing-health-facilities/articleshow/82092862.chief ministers (accessed on 9 September 2021).

12 The state health department issued a press release everyday with the day's Covid data. All copies are available with the authors.

13 Asad Rehman, 'Grappling with Oxygen Shortage, Two Uttar Pradesh Hospitals Ask Kin to Shift Patients', https://indianexpress.

com/article/india/up-lucknow-covid-hospital-oxygen-7283832/ (accessed on 9 September 2021).

14 Jyoti Yadav and Prashant Srivastava, 'In Uttar Pradesh, Oxygen Is Now Exclusive for Hospitals. Patients in Home Isolation Not Getting Any', https://theprint.in/health/in-up-oxygen-is-now-exclusive-for-hospitals-patients-in-home-isolation-not-getting-any/644793/ (accessed on 9 September 2021).

15 Ismat Ara, 'Uttar Pradesh Police Lodge FIR Against Lucknow Hospital Which Put Up "Oxygen Shortage" Notice', https://thewire.in/government/up-police-lodge-fir-against-lucknow-hospital-which-put-up-oxygen-shortage-notice (accessed on 9 September 2021).

16 Omar Rashid, 'Oxygen Shortage—Seize Property of Those Spreading Rumours: Yogi Adityanath', https://www.thehindu.com/news/national/other-states/seize-property-of-those-spreading-rumours-up-chief minister/article34404518.ece (accessed on 9 September 2021).

17 https://navbharattimes.indiatimes.com/metro/lucknow/politics/uttar-pradesh-medical-minister-suresh-khanna-told-no-one-died-due-to-lack-of-oxygen-in-lucknow/articleshow/82217268.chief ministers (accessed on 9 September 2021)

18 https://thelogicalindian.com/trending/yogi-adityanth-oxygen-supply-rumour-seize-property-27943 (accessed on 9 September 2021)

19 Anchal Rana, 'Seize Property of Those Spreading Rumours of Shortages in Oxygen Supplies: Yogi Adityanath', https://www.indiatoday.in/india/story/man-sends-sos-oxygen-for-grandfather-up-police-books-for-rumours-1795832-2021-04-28 (accessed on 9 September 2021).

20 Shruti Vibhavari, 'Lucknow Girl Challenges Adityanath to Arrest Her for Complaining of Oxygen Shortage', https://www.siasat.com/lucknow-girl-challenges-adityanath-to-arrest-her-for-complaining-of-oxygen-shortage-2130866/ (accessed on 9 September 2021).

21 Scroll.in, 'Coronavirus: SC Tells States Not to Shut Down Social Media Voices, Warns of Contempt Action', https://scroll.in/

latest/993728/coronavirus-sc-tells-states-not-to-shut-down-social-media-voices-warns-of-contempt-action (accessed on 9 September 2021).

22 *Indian Express*, 'Action against Private Hospitals if They Lie about Oxygen Shortage, Warns Chief Minister Yogi Adityanath', https://indianexpress.com/article/cities/lucknow/action-against-private-hospitals-if-they-lie-about-oxygen-shortage-warns-chief minister-yogi-adityanath-7289165/ (accessed on 9 September 2021).

23 Areeb Uddin Ahmed, '"System Would Collapse": Allahabad High Court Steps In, Orders Near Total Lockdown in Five Cities of Uttar Pradesh till April 26', https://www.barandbench.com/news/litigation/allahabad-high-court-imposes-near-total-lockdown-in-five-cities-of-uttar-pradesh-april-26 (accessed on 9 September 2021).

24 LiveLaw, 'Supreme Court Stays Allahabad High Court Order which Imposed Lockdown in 5 Uttar Pradesh Cities', https://www.livelaw.in/top-stories/supreme-court-stays-allahabad-high-court-judgment-which-imposed-lockdown-in-5-up-cities-172834?infinitescroll=1 (accessed on 9 September 2021).

25 Areeb Uddin Ahmed, '"System Would Collapse": Allahabad High Court Steps In, Orders Near Total Lockdown in Five Cities of Uttar Pradesh till April 26', https://www.barandbench.com/news/litigation/allahabad-high-court-imposes-near-total-lockdown-in-five-cities-of-uttar-pradesh-april-26 (accessed on 9 September 2021).

CHAPTER 2: THE DRAMA BEFORE YOGI'S RISE TO THE HOT SEAT

1 https://www.dailymotion.com/video/x5nim0k (accessed on 9 June 2021).

2 https://www.youtube.com/watch?v=hLPeFv-qmpk. Also, https://fb.watch/609IDDCRMy/ (accessed on 9 June 2021).

3 Anant Zanane, 'In Yogi's Gorakhpur, Ghosts of "Hindu Vahini" Past Haunt the Uttar Pradesh CM', https://www.thequint.com/

news/india/yogi-adityanath-gorakhpur-uttar-pradesh-hindu-vahini-rebellion-elections-2019 (accessed on 16 June 2021). Also, Danish Raza, 'Adityanath's Army: Hindu Yuva Vahini Gets Set for Hindutva Agenda in Uttar Pradesh, https://www. hindustantimes.com/india-news/here-comes-adityanath-s-army-hindu-yuva-vahini-gets-set-for-hindutva-agenda/story-BODyr5GWuIaZ8Jzz069euN.html (accessed on 16 June 2021).

4   Akhilesh Sharma, 'Yogi Adityanath Is Amit Shah's Choice: Here's Why', https://www.ndtv.com/blog/yogi-adityanath-is-amit-shahs-choice-heres-why-1671408 (accessed on 16 June 2021).

5   Rohini Mohan, "Yogi Adityanath—BJP MP cum Hindutva Don in Uttar Pradesh', *Tehelka Magazine*, Vol. 6, Issue 6, 14 February 2009.

6   Ibid.

7   Ashutosh, 'Why Yogi Adityanath Is in No Imminent Danger of Having to Renounce His Position?', https://www.freepressjournal. in/analysis/why-yogi-adityanath-is-in-no-imminent-danger-of-having-to-renounce-his-position-ashutosh-explains (accessed on 16 June 2021).

8   PTI, 'Yogi Adityanath: A Hindutva Mascot and Controversy's Favourite Child', https://www.livemint.com/Politics/ zEhArfbwGyyFfJ0fBxKSUL/The-rise-of-Yogi-Adityanath-as-a-Hindutva-mascot.html (accessed on 16 June 2021).

9   Newsclick Report, 'Yogi on a Name Changing Spree', https:// www.newsclick.in/yogi-name-changing-spree (accessed on 11 August 2021).

10 PTI, 'Ghar Vapasi to Continue till Conversions Are Banned: BJP MP Yogi Adityanath', https://economictimes.indiatimes. com/news/politics-and-nation/ghar-vapasi-to-continue-till-conversions-are-banned-bjp-mp-yogi-adityanath/ articleshow/46354415.cms?from=mdr (accessed on 11 August 2021).

11 Ibid.

12 Rohan Venkataramakrishnan, 'How Does Adityanath Withdrawing Criminal Case against Himself Not Count as "Jungle Raj?"', https://scroll.in/article/862892/how-does-adityanath-

withdrawing-criminal-case-against-himself-not-count-as-jungle-raj (accessed on 16 June 2021).

13 TNN, 'Gorakhpur on the Boil, BJP MP Arrested', https://timesofindia.indiatimes.com/india/gorakhpur-on-the-boil-bjp-mp-arrested/articleshow/1525851.cms (accessed on 16 June 2021).

14 Sudha Pai and Sajjan Kumar, 'How Yogi Adityanath Made it to Where He Is', https://thewire.in/politics/yogi-adityanath-uttar-pradesh-bjp (accessed on 11 August 2021).

15 Yogi Adityanath, 'Hindu Rashtra Nepal: Past and Present', 2006, p. 41, available at http://www.yogiadityanath.in/pdf/Hindu_Rashtra_Nepal.pdf (accessed 13 September 2021).

16 'Antar-raashtreey sazishon ke jaal me phansta Himalayee Rashtra Nepal', available at http://www.yogiadityanath.in/pdf/Hindu_Rashta_Nepal.pdf Page (accessed 13 September 2021).

17 'Sanatan dharma' could be best described as 'orthodox Hinduism with primacy of idol worship'.

18 Personal interview, 17 October 2017.

19 Ibid.

20 Ibid.

CHAPTER 3: EARLY LIFE, FAMILY AND EDUCATION

1 https://myneta.info/upmlc/candidate.php?candidate_id=182 (accessed on 11 August 2021).

2 Christophe Jaffrelot, 'The Other Saffron', https://indianexpress.com/article/opinion/columns/the-other-saffron/ (accessed on 11 August 2021).

3 Pravin Kumar, *Yogi Adityanath: The Rise of A Saffron Socialist* (Times Books, 2017), pp. 46–47.

4 Pratul Sharma, 'Boy Who Became Yogi', https://www.theweek.in/theweek/cover/uttar-pradesh-cm-yogi-adityanaths-story.html (accessed on 11 August 2021).

5 Ibid.

6 ABP News, 'Meet the Sister of CM Yogi Adityanath Who Sells Flowers and Lives Simple Life', https://www.youtube.com/watch?v=XbphQ5QGkM8 (accessed on 11 August 2021).

7   Ibid.

8   Nikhil Pandhi, 'As Yogi Adityanath's Village Celebrates His Rise, Advice From His Father', https://www.ndtv.com/india-news/ yogi-adityanaths-village-celebrates-advice-from-chief-ministers-father-1671266 (accessed on 11 August 2021).

9   Pratul Sharma, 'Blood Relatives', http://www.theweek.in/ theweek/cover/yogi-adityanath-mahant-avaidyanath.html (accessed on 11 August 2021).

10   FE Online, 'Clerics in Uttar Pradesh Hope New State Government under Yogi Adityanath Will Dispel Fear', https:// www.financialexpress.com/india-news/clerics-in-uttar-pradesh-hope-new-state-government-under-yogi-adityanath-will-dispel-fear/594872/ (accessed on 11 August 2021).

11   Ilma Hasan, 'Ground Report on Yogi Adityanath: What Aligarh Muslim University Campus Thinks about UP Chief Minister', https://www.indiatoday.in/india/story/yogi-adityanath-what-aligarh-muslim-university-campus-thinks-about-up-chief-minister-967737-2017-03-26 (accessed on 11 August 2021).

12   Shantanu Gupta, *The Monk Who Became Chief Minister* (Bloomsbury, 2017).

13

14   Ibid. p. 100.

15   As told to the authors.

CHAPTER 4: THE SEER WHO BECAME CHIEF MINISTER

1   As noted by the authors while they were covering the event.

2   inKhabar, 'Prime Minister Narendra Modi Addresses Dussehra Rally in Lucknow', https://www.youtube.com/watch?v=Luz9_pnmp9E (accessed on 13 August 2021).

3   *Indian Express*, 'PM Modi's Graveyard Remark in Fatehpur Is Unfortunate', https://indianexpress.com/article/opinion/ editorials/narendra-modi-diwali-ramzan-up-assembly-elections-2017-4535245/.

4   Oneindia Staff Writer, '*Gujarat ke gadhe*? No, Donkeys on Sale in Uttar Pradesh', https://www.oneindia.com/india/gujarat-ke-gadhe-no-donkeys-on-sale-uttar-pradesh-2381244.html (accessed on 28 June 2021).

5   Rajesh Ahuja and Manish Chandra Pandey, 'Kanpur Train Accident Was a Conspiracy from across the Border: PM Modi in UP', https://www.hindustantimes.com/india-news/kanpur-train-accident-was-a-conspiracy-from-across-the-border-pm-modi-in-up/story-hm5LX6lLekisS5YRUXQcVL.html (accessed on 28 June 2021).

6   Factchecker Team, 'Home Minister Is Correct; PM Did Not Mention ISI In Gonda Speech', https://www.factchecker.in/home-minister-is-correct-pm-did-not-mention-isi-in-gonda-speech/ (accessed on 13 August 2021).

7   Ramendra Singh, Avishek G. Dastidar, Deeptiman Tiwary, 'UP Elections 2017: PM Modi Says Cross-Border Plot in Kanpur Train Accident, Probe Unclear', https://indianexpress.com/elections/uttar-pradesh-assembly-elections-2017/up-polls-2017-pm-modi-says-cross-border-plot-in-kanpur-train-accident-probe-unclear-4542592/ (accessed 14 September 2021).

8   PTI, 'UP Elections 2017: After 'SCAM', BJP Coins 'KASAB' Acronym for Congress, SP and BSP', available at https://economictimes.indiatimes.com/news/politics-and-nation/up-elections-2017-after-scam-bjp-coins-kasab-acronym-for-congress-sp-and-bsp/articleshow/57296718.cms?from=mdr (accessed on 13 September 2021).

9   Sudha Pai and Sajjan Kumar, 'How Yogi Adityanath Made It to Where He Is', https://thewire.in/politics/yogi-adityanath-uttarpradesh-bjp (accessed on 13 August 2021).

10   On 5 January 2012, Yogi Adityanath held a press conference in New Delhi to raise his objection against the move.

11   India TV, 'BJP MP Adityanath Opposes Induction of Kushwaha', https://www.indiatvnews.com/news/india/bjp-mp-adityanathopposes-induction-of-kushwaha-13395.html (accessed on 13 September 2021).

12   Ibid.

13 *India Today*, 'A Bizarre Analysis of Riots, by Yogi Adityanath', https://www.indiatoday.in/india/story/yogi-adityanath-muslims-bjp-kashmir-love-jihad-206498-2014-08-31 (accessed on 13 September 2021).

14 *India Today*, 'Love Jihad Row: Yogi Adityanath's Hate Speech Caught on Camera, https://www.indiatoday.in/india/video/love-jihad-row-yogi-adityanath-speech-caught-on-camera-454534-2014-08-28 (accessed on 13 August 2021).

15 https://timesofindia.indiatimes.com/city/dehradun/dad-to-aditya-nath-women-in-burqa-too-voted-for-you/articleshow/57763049.cms (accessed on 1 August 2021).

16 Swapan Dasgupta, 'Yogi Adityanath Has Cross-Caste Support, Judge Him on Performance', https://www.hindustantimes.com/analysis/yogi-adityanath-has-cross-caste-support-judge-him-on-performance-not-his-past/story-KpIJuxZ3R6Xv6Eu2iMlL6J.html (accessed on 13 August 2021).

17 Tarun Vijay, 'Why Adityanath Will Be a Good CM', https://www.rediff.com/news/column/why-adityanath-will-be-a-good-cm/20170320.htm (accessed on 13 August 2021).

18 Syed Firdaus Ashraf, 'Secularists, Muslims Need to Accept Yogi', https://www.rediff.com/news/column/secularists-muslims-need-to-accept-yogi/20170320.htm (accessed on 13 August 2021).

19 *The New York Times*, 'Firebrand Hindu Cleric Yogi Adityanath Picked as Uttar Pradesh Minister', https://www.nytimes.com/2017/03/18/world/asia/firebrand-hindu-cleric-yogi-adityanath-picked-as-uttar-pradesh-minister.html (accessed on 13 August 2021).

20 The Editorial Board, 'Mr. Modi's Perilous Embrace of Hindu Extremists', https://www.nytimes.com/2017/03/23/opinion/mr-modis-perilous-embrace-of-hindu-extremists.html (accessed on 13 August 2021).

21 PTI, 'India Questions NYT's Wisdom to Criticise Yogi Adityanath Becoming CM', https://economictimes.indiatimes.com/news/politics-and-nation/india-questions-nyts-wisdom-

to-criticise-aditya-nath-becoming-cm/articleshow/57814175. cms.

22 Al Jazeera, 'Modi BJP Picks Firebrand to Head India's Uttar Pradesh', https://www.aljazeera.com/news/2017/3/18/modi-bjp-picks-firebrand-to-head-indias-uttar-pradesh (accessed on 13 August 2021).

23 BBC, 'Yogi Adityanath: Uttar Pradesh Chief Minister Choice Criticised', https://www.bbc.com/news/world-asia-india-39316597(accessed on 13 August 2021).

24 Douglas Busvine, 'Hardline Priest Yogi Adityanath's Elevation a Sign Modi Is Moving toward Hindu India', https://www.livemint.com/Politics/3kYURcGVNJEGWje3Ts64NM/Hardline-priest-Yogi-Adityanaths-elevation-a-sign-Modi-is-m.html (accessed on 13 August 2021).

25 *The Economist*, 'Reward: Uttar Pradesh's New Leader', https://espresso.economist.com/178b0113689dce8a7e48360c3886dc99 (accessed on 13 August 2021).

26 David Frawley, 'PM Modi Has Given Yogi Adityanath a Chance for a Dharmic Purpose', https://www.dailyo.in/politics/yogi-adityanath-hindu-india-up-cm-modi-bjp/story/1/16270.html (accessed on 13 August 2021).

27 Pratap Bhanu Mehta, 'In the Moment of His Political Triumph, Modi Has Chosen to Defeat India', http://indianexpress.com/article/opinion/columns/yogic-madness-yogi-adityanath-uttar-pradesh-bjp-narendra-modi-4576588/ (accessed on 13 August 2021).

28 Chaitanya Kalbag, 'Yogi Adityanath—Will This Tiger Change Its Saffron Stripes?', https://economictimes.indiatimes.com/news/politics-and-nation/view-yogi-adityanath-will-this-tiger-change-its-saffron-stripes/articleshow/57787479.cms (accessed on 13 August 2021).

29 R. Jagannathan, 'Yogi Adityanath May Be a Risky Choice for UP, But He Ticks Many of the Right Boxes for BJP', https://swarajyamag.com/politics/yogi-adityanath-may-be-a-risky-choice-for-up-but-he-ticks-many-of-the-right-boxes-for-bjp (accessed on 13 August 2021).

30 Shobhit Kalra, 'Who Said What on Yogi Adityanath as New UP Chief Minister!', https://english.newstrack.com/political-news/opposition-leaders-attack-bjp-yogi-adityanath-chief-minister-56247.html (accessed on 13 August 2021).

31 PTI, 'Congress Slams BJP's Choice of Yogi Adityanath as Uttar Pradesh Chief Minister', https://indianexpress.com/article/india/congress-slams-bjps-choice-of-yogi-adityanath-as-up-chief-minister-4575341/ (accessed on 13 August 2021).

32 Shobhit Kalra, 'Who Said What on Yogi Adityanath as New UP Chief Minister!', https://english.newstrack.com/political-news/opposition-leaders-attack-bjp-yogi-adityanath-chief-minister-56247.html (accessed on 13 August 2021)..

33 Sabir Hussain, 'Assault on Secularism: How Parties Reacted to Adityanath's Elevation to UP CM', https://www.hindustantimes.com/assembly-elections/assault-on-secularism-how-oppn-reacted-to-yogi-adityanath-s-elevation-to-up-cm/story-J2DUptEuAmD2CFv9ehCQYP.html (accessed on 13 August 2021).

34 *Hindustan Times*, 'Assault on Secularism: How Parties Reacted to Adityanath's Elevation to UP CM', https://www.hindustantimes.com/assembly-elections/assault-on-secularism-how-oppn-reacted-to-yogi-adityanath-s-elevation-to-up-cm/story-J2DUptEuAmD2CFv9ehCQYP.html (accessed on 13 August 2021).

35 ANI, 'Steer Clear of Controversial Remarks: Shiv Sena's Advice to Yogi Adityanath', https://www.asianage.com/india/politics/190317/steer-clear-of-controversial-remarks-shiv-sena-to-up-cm-designate-yogi-adityanath.html (accessed on 13 August 2021).

36 Swarajya Staff, 'Subramaniam Swamy Hails PM Modi's Selection of Yogi Adityanath As UP CM', https://swarajyamag.com/insta/subramanian-swamy-hails-pm-modis-selection-of-yogi-adityanath-as-up-cm (accessed on 13 August 2021).

37 PTI, 'My Govt Will Work for All, Says UP CM Adityanath in Lok Sabha', business-standard.com/article/pti-stories/my-govt-will-work-for-all-says-up-cm-adityanath-in-lok-sabha-117032101069_1.html (accessed on 13 August 2021).

CHAPTER 5: HINDU YUVA VAHINI

1   The Citizen Editorial (16 May 2017), https://www.thecitizen.in/index.php/en/NewsDetail/index/2/10697/RSS-and-Hindu-Yuva-Vahini-Fight-For-The-Same-Turf (accessed on 16 August 2021); DH News Service, 'Yogi's Hindu Vahini Worries Saffron Party', https://www.deccanherald.com/content/611451/yogis-hindu-vahini-worries-saffron.html (accessed on 16 August 2021); Sumit Pande, 'Yuva Vahini Is Growing, and BJP Is Not Very Happy', https://www.news18.com/news/politics/yogi-adityanaths-hindu-yuva-vahini-is-growing-and-bjp-is-not-very-happy-1400265.html (accessed on 16 August 2021).

2   Lalmani Verma, 'RSS Red-Flags Growing Hindu Yuva Vahini Clout to Yogi' Adityanath', https://indianexpress.com/article/india/rss-red-flags-growing-hindu-yuva-vahini-clout-to-yogi-adityanath-4657557/ (accessed on 16 August 2021).

3   Dhirendra K. Jha, 'Is Adityanath's Hindu Yuva Vahini Being Dismantled Quietly to Appease the RSS?', https://scroll.in/article/870112/is-adityanaths-hindu-yuva-vahini-being-dismantled-quietly-to-appease-the-rss (last accessed 15 September 2021).

4   FE Online, 'Yogi Adityanath Warns Hindu Yuva Vahini to Maintain "Decent Behaviour", Says Reputation of BJP at Stake', https://www.financialexpress.com/india-news/yogi-adityanath-warns-hindu-yuva-vahini-to-maintain-decent-behaviour-says-reputation-of-bjp-at-stake/648711/ (last accessed 15 September 2021).

5   Lalmani Verma, 'Latest BJP Rival in UP is Yogi Adityanath's Outfit', https://indianexpress.com/elections/uttar-pradesh-assembly-elections-2017/up-polls-latest-bjp-rival-in-up-is-its-own-stars-outfit-yogi-adityanath-4495205/ (last accessed 15 September 2021).

6   PTI, 'Yogi Adityanath's Outfit Emerges as BJP Rival in UP Polls', https://www.rediff.com/news/report/yogi-adityanaths-outfit-emerges-as-bjp-rival-in-up-polls/20170128.htm (last accessed 15 September 2021).

7   Lalmani Verma, 'Yogi's Vahini in demand: Over 5,000 Membership Requests a Day', https://indianexpress.com/article/india/yogis-vahini-in-demand-over-5000-membership-requests-a-day-4597020/ (last accessed 15 September 2021).

8   DNA, 'Following Violent Attacks, Yogi Adityanath's Hindu Yuva Vahini Freezes Membership for 6 Months', https://www.dnaindia.com/india/report-following-violent-attacks-yogi-adityanath-s-hindu-yuva-vahini-freezes-membership-for-6-months-2427041 (last accessed 15 September 2021).

9   ET Bureau, 'Bulandshahr murder: Police claim role of Hindu Yuva Vahini members' https://economictimes.indiatimes.com/news/politics-and-nation/bulandshahr-murder-police-claim-role-of-hindu-yuva-vahini-members/articleshow/58499486.cms (last accessed 15 September 2021).

10   Janta ka Reporter, 'Lynching of Muslim Man: CM Yogi Adityanath's Desperate Defence of Hindu Yuva Vahini', https://www.jantakareporter.com/india/hindu-yuva-vahini-2/121288/ (last accessed 15 September 2021).

11   PTI, 'No Remedy If Someone Makes Up Mind to Blame an Outfit: Uttar Pradesh CM Yogi Adityanath', https://economictimes.indiatimes.com/news/politics-and-nation/no-remedy-if-someone-makes-up-mind-to-blame-an-outfit-uttar-pradesh-cm-yogi-adityanath/articleshow/58534580.cms?from=mdr (last accessed 15 September 2021).

12   Naveen Lal Suri, 'Yogi's Hindu Yuva Vahini Will Play a New Role in Uttar Pradesh', https://hindi.news18.com/news/uttar-pradesh/lucknow-hindu-yuva-vahini-will-play-the-new-role-in-uttar-pradesh-upns-2314573.html (last accessed 15 September 2021).

13   Dhirendra K. Jha, *Yogi Adityanath and the Hindu Yuva Vahini* (Juggernaut, 2017)

14   Ibid.

15   Amrita Basu, *Violent Conjunctures in Democratic India* (New Delhi: Cambridge University Press, 2015), p. 223.

16   Jha, *Yogi Adityanath.*

17   Ibid.

18 See https://hinduyuvavahini.co.in/join-hyv.

19 See http://www.hinduyuvavahini.in/samvidhan_1.aspx. For the
    sanitized website see https://hinduyuvavahini.co.in/join-hyv (last
    accessed 15 September 2021).

20 Basu, *Violent Conjunctures,* p. 223.

21 Express Web Desk, 'What Is the Yogi Adityanath Hate Speech
    Case of 2007?' indianexpress.com/article/what-is/what-is-the-
    yogi-adityanath-hate-speech-case-of-2007/ (last accessed 15
    September 2021).

22 Jha, *Yogi Adityanath.*

23 Pratik Sinha, 'Yogi Adityanath: Agar ek Hindu ka khoon bahega,
    kam se kam 10 aise logon ki hatya karvayenge . . .', https://www.
    altnews.in/yogi-adityanath-agar-ek-hindu-ka-khoon-bahega-
    kam-se-kam-10-aise-logon-ki-hatya-karvayenge/ (last accessed 15
    September 2021).

24 Rohini Mohan, 'Yogi Adityanath – BJP MP cum Hindutva Don
    in 6UP', *Tehelka Magazine,* Vol 6, Issue 6, 14 February 2009 in
    https://communalism.blogspot.com/2009/02/yogi-adityanath-
    bjp-mp-cum-hindutva-don.html (last accessed 15 September
    2021).

25 *India Today,* 'Hindu Yuva Vahini members barge into home and
    harass couple: Man booked, but Vahini let loose' https://www.
    indiatoday.in/india/video/yuva-vahini-love-jihad-in-meerut-
    nagendra-singh-tomar-849256-2017-04-12 (last accessed 15
    September 2021).

26 *Economic Times,* 'Why Yogi Adityantah Needs to Keep Hindu
    Yuva Vahini in Check', https://economictimes.indiatimes.
    com/news/politics-and-nation/why-yogi-adityanath-needs-
    to-keep-hindu-yuva-vahini-in-check/articleshow/59717854.
    cms?from=mdr (last accessed 15 September 2021).

27 PTI, 'Yogi Adityanath's outfit emerges as BJP rival in UP polls',
    https://www.rediff.com/news/report/yogi-adityanaths-outfit-
    emerges-as-bjp-rival-in-up-polls/20170128.htm (last accessed 15
    September 2021).

28 Manoj Singh, 'Before the Rise of Hindutva, Gorakhnath Nurtured
    Muslim Yogis', https://thewire.in/culture/before-the-rise-of-

hindutva-gorakhnath-nurtured-muslim-yogis (last accessed 15 September 2021).

29 Altervista, 'Before the Rise of Hindutva, Gorakhnath Nurtured Muslim Yogis', https://bakshi786islam.altervista.org/gorakhnath-promosse-gli-yogi-musulmani/ (last accessed 15 September 2021).

CHAPTER 6: POLITICO-RELIGIOUS TRANSFORMATION OF AN EGALITARIAN ORDER

1   Manoj Singh, 'Before the Rise of Hindutva, Gorakhnath Nurtured Muslim Yogis', https://thewire.in/culture/before-the-rise-of-hindutva-gorakhnath-nurtured-muslim-yogis (accessed on 17 August 2021).

2   'Osho on Gorakhnath', https://spiritualsatya.com/osho-on-gorakhnath/ (accessed on 17 August 2021).

3   http://ignca.gov.in/Asi_data/7348.pdf, Chapter 1, pp. 1–6 (accessed on 17 August 2021).

4   Manoj Singh, 'Before the Rise of Hindutva', https://thewire.in/culture/before-the-rise-of-hindutva-gorakhnath-nurtured-muslim-yogis (accessed on 17 August 2021).

5   Mohan Singh, 'Gorakhnath and Mediaeval Hindu Mysticism', https://archive.org/details/in.ernet.dli.2015.147272/page/n15/mode/2up (accessed on 17 August 2021).

6   Gyan Manthan, 'Raja Bhartrihari ki Sampoorna Kahani', https://www.youtube.com/watch?v=Tq7-SUvLEFI (accessed on 17 August 2021).

7   Interviewed in the village on 5 November 2020.

8   Aakar Patel, 'Akshaya Mukul's First-Rate Analysis of the Gita Press Reveals How Putrid Some Aspects of Hindu Nationalism Are (Book Review of *Gita Press and the Making of Hindu India*)', https://www.indiatoday.in/magazine/books/story/20150824-gita-press-making-of-hindu-india-akshaya-mukul-820266-2015-08-13 (accessed on 17 August 2021).

9   *The Statesman*, 13 June 1950.

10   C. Marrewa-Karwoski, 'Far from Hindutva, Yogi Adityanath's Sect Comes from a Tradition That Was Neither Hindu Nor Muslim', https://scroll.in/article/833710/far-from-hindutva-yogi-adityanath-comes-from-a-tradition-that-was-neither-hindu-nor-muslim (accessed on 15 September 2021).

CHAPTER 7: THE LEGACY OF GORAKHNATH TEMPLE

1   George Weston Briggs, *Gorakhnath and the Kanphata Yogis*, first Indian edition in 1938, New Delhi: Motilal Banarsidas Publishers, 2016, pp. 6–9.
2   India.com News Desk, 'Yogi Adityanath Has Movable Assets Worth Rs 95.98 Lakh, Owns Firearms and 10 Gram Gold Earring', https://www.india.com/news/india/yogi-adityanath-has-movable-assets-worth-rs-95-98-lakh-owns-firearms-and-10-gram-gold-earring-2452030/ (accessed on 18 August 2021).
3   Briggs, *Gorakhnath and the Kanphata Yogis*, p. 87.
4   Krishna Jha and Dhirendra K. Jha, *Ayodhya: The Dark Night: The Secret History of Rama's Appearance in Babri Masjid*, Harper Collins, 2012, p. 28.
5   Zee News, 'Will Install Gauri-Ganesh in Every Mosque, Says Yogi Adityanath', https://zeenews.india.com/news/india/will-install-gauri-ganesh-in-every-mosque-says-yogi-adityanath_1543681.html (accessed on 15 September 2021).

CHAPTER 8: AYODHYA BECKONS

1   Rajesh Kumar Singh, 'Tracing the Role of Yogi Adityanath and Gorakhnath Math in Ram Temple Movement', https://www.hindustantimes.com/india-news/tracing-the-role-of-yogi-adityanath-and-gorakhnath-math-in-ram-temple-movement/story-0zaFhkWuRY62qic8FSuWsI.html (accessed on 23 August 2021).
2   The Hindu Net Desk, 'Full Text of Ayodhya Verdict', https://www.thehindu.com/news/resources/full-text-of-ayodhya-verdict/article29929786.ece (accessed on 23 August 2021).

3   India Today Web Desk, 'Ayodhya Ram Mandir Case Judgment: Supreme Court Rules in Favour of Ram Lalla, 10 Highlights', https://www.indiatoday.in/india/story/ayodhya-ram-mandir-case-supreme-court-judgment-top-10-highlights-1617304-2019-11-09 (accessed on 23 August 2021).

4   Dhirendra K. Jha, 'These Are the Communal Achievements of the Guru Modi Wants Commemorate with a Stamp', https://scroll.in/article/758817/these-are-the-communal-achievements-of-the-guru-modi-wants-to-commemorate-with-a-stamp (accessed on 23 August 2021).

5   Liberhan Commission Report, https://archive.org/stream/LiberhanCommissionReport/Liberhan%20Commission%20Report_djvu.txt (accessed on 23 August 2021).

6   http://elegalix.allahabadhighcourt.in/elegalix/ayodhyafiles/honsukj.pdf (accessed on 25 August 2021).

7   PTI, 'Ravi Shankar Prasad Favours Consensus on Ram Temple Issue', https://economictimes.indiatimes.com/news/politics-and-nation/ravi-shankar-prasad-favours-consensus-on-ram-temple-issue/articleshow/50521953.cms?utm_source=contentofinterest&utm_medium=text&utm_campaign=cppst (accessed on 23 August 2021).

8   News18, 'Ayodhya Dispute: Sunni Board Sees "Political Motive" in Shia Affidavit', https://www.news18.com/news/india/ayodhya-dispute-sunni-board-sees-political-motive-in-shia-affidavit-1487367.html (accessed on 20 September 2021).

9   *The Hindu*, 21 March 2021.

CHAPTER 9: FLIRTING WITH CONTROVERSIES

1   Scroll Staff, 'Hindutva unmasked: Yogi Adityanath, BJP's most strident face, will be its chief minister in UP' https://scroll.in/article/832168/hindutva-unmasked-yogi-adityanath-bjps-most-strident-face-will-be-its-chief-minister-in-up (accessed 25 August 2021).

2   https://www.news18.com/news/politics/from-varanasi-to-prayagraj-ayodhya-bjps-kalash-yatra-roadmap-to-immerse-kalyan-singhs-ashes-4124786.html (accessed 25 August 2021).

3 *Deccan Chronicle*, 'Hindutva and Development Complementary to Each Other: Yogi Adityanath', https://www.deccanchronicle. com/nation/current-affairs/151117/hindutva-and-development-complementary-to-each-other-yogi-adityanath.html (accessed 25 August 2021).

4 PTI, 'Twitter Takes Down Yogi Adityanath's Controversial Tweets on EC's Directive', https://economictimes.indiatimes. com/news/elections/lok-sabha/uttar-pradesh/twitter-takes-down-yogi-adityanaths-controversial-tweets-on-ecs-directive/ articleshow/68925371.cms?from=mdr (accessed 25 August 2021).

5 Ibid.

6 Peter Popham, 'Why Can't Hindus and Muslims Get Along Together? It's a Long Story', https://www.independent.co.uk/ voices/why-cant-hindus-and-muslims-get-along-together-its-a-long-story-1162319.html (accessed on 25 August 2021).

7 PTI, 'Will Follow "Sabka Saath, Sabka Vikas" but There Won't Be Any Appeasement: Yogi Adityanath in Gorakhpur', https://economictimes.indiatimes.com/news/politics-and-nation/will-follow-sabka-saath-sabka-vikas-but-there-wont-be-any-appeasement-yogi-adityanath-in-gorakhpur/ articleshow/57828450.cms (accessed on 25 August 2021).

8 https://www.youtube.com/watch?v=jjoQYxHUibI (accessed on 25 August 2021).

9 Shamsur Rahman Faruqi, 'Agony of the Marginalized', *The Indian Express*, 5 April 2018.

10 Zee News, 'Will Install Gauri–Ganesh in Every Mosque, Says Yogi Adityanath', https://zeenews.india.com/news/india/will-install-gauri-ganesh-in-every-mosque-says-yogi-adityanath_1543681. html (accessed on 25 August 2021); Amit Verma, 'Given a Chance, Will Put Ganesh Idols in All Mosques: Yogi Adityanath', https://www.deccanchronicle.com/150210/nation-current-affairs/article/given-chance-will-put-ganesh-idols-all-mosques-yogi-adityanath (accessed on 25 August 2021).

11 The interview took place on 30 July 2020. Subsequently, Colonel Fasih Uddin Ahmed expressed similar views even more explicitly

in an article he wrote for India Ahead on 25 August 2021. See https://indiaaheadnews.com/opinion/the-frustration-of-being-a-muslim-voter-in-up-a-retired-army-colonel-writes-46036/.

12 https://www.youtube.com/watch?v=jjoQYxHUibI (accessed on 25 August 2021).

13 FP staff, 'Yogi Adityanath Believes Taj Mahal "Has No Connection with India's Culture or Heritage"', https://www.firstpost.com/india/yogi-adityanath-believes-taj-mahal-has-no-connection-with-indias-culture-or-heritage-3704485.html (accessed on 25 August 2021).

14 Audrey Truschke, 'Taj and Bigotry', https://indianexpress.com/article/opinion/columns/taj-mahal-controversy-sangeet-som-blot-remark-bjp-yogi-adityanath-mughal-empire-4903344/ (accessed on 25 August 2021).

15 *TOI*, 'Taj Pride of India, Made by Sweat and Blood of Artisans: Yogi Adityanath', https://timesofindia.indiatimes.com/city/lucknow/taj-pride-of-india-made-by-sweat-and-blood-of-artisans-yogi-adityanath/articleshow/61127244.cms (accessed on 25 August 2021).

16 PTI, 'Swachh Bharat and More as Yogi Visits Taj, Calls It a Gem', https://www.thehindubusinessline.com/news/national/swachh-bharat-and-more-as-yogi-visits-taj-calls-it-a-gem/article9925349.ece (accessed on 25 August 2021).

17 http://www.yogiadityanath.in/lekh/lekh_9730_22021405364822022014.pdf (accessed on 25 August 2021).

18 'Savdhan! Yeh Islami Aatankvad Hai', p. 1, http://www.yogiadityanath.in/lekh/lekh_9730_22021405364822022014.pdf.

19 http://www.yogiadityanath.in/lekh/lekh_0214_22021405445922022014.pdf (accessed on 25 August 2021).)

20 'Islam Aur Atankvad', p. 3, http://www.yogiadityanath.in/lekh/lekh_0214_22021405445922022014.pdf.

21 Tufail Ahmed, 'India Will Be Home to World's Largest Muslim Population by 2050, but Is the Country Ready for the Change?', https://www.firstpost.com/india/india-will-be-home-to-worlds-largest-muslim-population-by-2050-but-is-

the-country-ready-for-the-change-3313660.html (accessed on 25 August 2021).

22 http://www.yogiadityanath.in/lekh/lekh_7263_22021405485622022014.pdf (accessed on 25 August 2021).

23 Ibid.

24 Ibid.

25 https://censusindia.gov.in/DigitalLibrary/data/Census_1951/Publication/India/23685-1951-REP.pdf (accessed on 25 August 2021).

26 Rukmini S. and Vijaita Singh, 'Muslim Population Growth Slows', https://www.thehindu.com/news/national/Muslim-population-growth-slows/article10336665.ece (accessed on 25 August 2021).

27 Hindu New Desk, 'Produce More Children, RSS Tells Hindu Couples', https://www.thehindu.com/news/national/other-states/Produce-more-children-RSS-tells-Hindu-couples/article14582028.ece (accessed on 25 August 2021).

28 Sandeep Joshi, 'Hindu Women Should Have 10 Children: Shankaracharya', https://www.thehindu.com/news/national/other-states/hindu-women-should-have-10-kids-shankaracharya/article6800004.ece (accessed on 25 August 2021).

29 Conrad Hackett, 'By 2050, India to Have World's Largest Populations of Hindus and Muslims', https://www.pewresearch.org/fact-tank/2015/04/21/by-2050-india-to-have-worlds-largest-populations-of-hindus-and-muslims/ (accessed on 25 August 2021).

30 Tufail Ahmad, 'India Will Be Home to World's Largest Muslim Population', https://www.firstpost.com/india/india-will-be-home-to-worlds-largest-muslim-population-by-2050-but-is-the-country-ready-for-the-change-3313660.html (accessed on 25 August 2021).

31 Ibid.

32 Ibid.

33 Aarefa Johar, 'BJP Leader Asks Hindu Women to Have Five Babies, but Hindutva Fears of Being Outnumbered Are Unfounded', https://scroll.in/article/700251/bjp-leader-asks-

hindu-women-to-have-five-babies-but-hindutva-fears-of-being-outnumbered-are-unfounded (accessed on 25 August 2021).

34 See https://www.youtube.com/watch?v=W3NGRiTBl-0 (accessed on 25 August 2021).

35 Samuel P. Huntington, *The Clash of Civilizations and the Remaking of World Order* (Penguin Random House India, 2016), p. 266.

36 Ibid.

37 Ibid., p. 34.

38 Eram Agha and Suhas Munshi, 'Hukum Singh Now Says Never Raised Kairana Exodus Issue', https://www.news18.com/news/politics/hukum-singh-now-says-never-raised-kairana-exodus-issue-1347927.html (accessed on 25 August 2021).

39 PTI, 'Kairana Exodus: BJP MP Hukum Singh Takes a U-turn, Now Says It's Not a Communal Issue', https://indianexpress.com/article/india/india-news-india/kairana-exodus-bjp-does-a-u-turn-now-says-its-not-a-communal-issue-2852665/ (accessed on 25 August 2021).

40 PTI, 'Those Opposing "Surya Namaskar" Should Drown in Sea: Yogi Adityanath', https://economictimes.indiatimes.com/news/politics-and-nation/those-opposing-surya-namaskar-should-drown-in-sea-yogi-aditynath/articleshow/47598430.cms?from=mdr (accessed on 25 August 2021).

41 ANI News, 'Adityanath Compares Shahrukh to Hafiz Saeed', https://www.youtube.com/watch?v=OhselMEhmnM (accessed on 25 August 2021).

42 *Hindustan Times*, 'Venom against SRK for Intolerance Comment Spills Over: Who Said What', https://www.hindustantimes.com/india/who-said-what-on-shah-rukh-s-extreme-intolerance-comment/story-UcLFTSrpQ7sd1odscoeocM.html (accessed on 25 August 2021).

43 Manmohan Rai, 'BJP MP Yogi Adityanath Accuses Mother Teresa of Religious Conversion', https://economictimes.indiatimes.com/news/politics-and-nation/bjp-mp-yogi-adityanath-accuses-mother-teresa-of-religious-conversion/articleshow/52842431.cms (accessed on 25 August 2021).

44 PTI, 'Kairana "Exodus", Love Jihad Key Issues for BJP: Yogi Adityanath', https://economictimes.indiatimes.com/news/politics-and-nation/kairana-exodus-love-jihad-key-issues-for-bjp-yogi-adityanath/articleshow/56970202.cms?from=mdr (accessed on 25 August 2021).

45 Christophe Jaffrelot, 'The Other Saffron', http://indianexpress.com/article/opinion/columns/the-other-saffron (accessed on 25 August 2021).

46 *TOI*, 'Uttar Pradesh Civic Polls: BJP Fields 25 Muslims in First Phase', http://timesofindia.indiatimes.com/articleshow/61515147.cms?utm_source=contentofinterest&utm_medium=text&utm_campaign=cppst (accessed 25 August 2021).

CHAPTER 10: YOGI: THE PEOPLE'S REPRESENTATIVE

1 PTI, 'Double Lawmakers' Salaries, Recommends Parliament Panel', https://www.ndtv.com/india-news/100-per-cent-hike-in-parliamentarians-salary-recommends-panel-777596 (accessed on 26 August 2021).

2 www.prsindia.org/mptrack/yogiadityanath (accessed on 26 August 2021).

3 Alison Saldanha, 'In 8 Years of Parliament, Yogi Adityanath's Recurring Debate Topic: Hindu Affairs', https://www.hindustantimes.com/india-news/in-8-years-of-parliament-yogi-adityanath-s-most-recurring-debate-topic-hindu-affairs/story-7ZBjXFwV2vFx3wCmkgdg0I.html (accessed on 26 August 2021).

4 Ibid.

5 Alison Saldanha (FactChecker.in), 'In Eight Years as MP, Yogi Adityanath's Most Favoured Debate Topic Was "Hindu Affairs"', https://thewire.in/politics/yogi-adityanath-lok-sabha (accessed on 26 August 2021).

6 Bill No. 38 of 2014 the Ban on Cow Slaughter Bill, 2014.

7 https://cjp.org.in/wp-content/uploads/2017/12/UTTAR-PRADESH-PREVENTION-OF-COW-SLAUGHTER-ACT-1955.pdf (accessed on 26 August 2021).

8   Bill No. 121 of 2014, the Constitution (Amendment) Bill, 2014.

9   The Constitution (Amendment) Bill, 2015 (Insertion of new article 25A) by Shri Yogi Adityanath, M.P.

10   https://www.prsindia.org/mptrack/15loksabha/yogiadityanath (accessed on 26 August 2021).

11   India.com News Desk, 'Rahul Gandhi Meets Families of Children Who Died in Gorakhpur BRD Medical College', https://www. india.com/news/india/rahul-gandhi-meets-families-of-children-who-died-in-gorakhpur-brd-medical-college-2412716/ (accessed on 26 August 2021).

12   Vikas Pathak, 'Adityanath Adds to BJP Woes on Women's Bill', http://www.hindustantimes.com/delhi-news/adityanath-adds-to-bjp-woes-on-women-s-bill/story-yCKaEissuZr8PX6f1kZxHP. htm (accessed on 26 August 2021).

13   https://www.youtube.com/watch?v=kNuJRmMHYTg (accessed on 26 August 2021).

14   https://www.youtube.com/watch?v=kNuJRmMHYTg (accessed on 26 August 2021).

15   Yogi's speech in Lok Sabha, https://www.youtube.com/ watch?v=kNuJRmMHYTg (accessed on 26 August 2021).

16   Ibid.

17   https://www.youtube.com/watch?v=kNuJRmMHYTg (Yogi's speech in Lok Sabha).

18   https://www.youtube.com/watch?v=kNuJRmMHYTg (accessed on 26 August 2021).

19   Ibid.

20   https://www.artic.edu/swami-vivekananda-and-his-1893-speech (accessed on 26 August 2021).

21   https://www.youtube.com/watch?v=kNuJRmMHYTg (accessed on 26 August 2021).

22   Ibid.

23   Ibid

24   Ibid.

25   Ibid.

26   Ibid.

27   Ibid.

28 http://zeenews.india.com/news/videos/top-stories/watch-yogi-adityanaths-farewell-speech-in-lok-sabha_1988724.html (accessed on 26 August 2021).

29 'A Review of Japanese Encephalitis in Uttar Pradesh, India', *WHO South- East Asia Journal of Public Health,* 2012 1(4): 374–95.

30 http://elegalix.allahabadhighcourt.in/elegalix/WebShowJudgment.do (accessed on 6 August 2021).

31 Nelanshu Shukla, 'UP Successfully Controlled Spread of Encephalitis: Yogi Adityanath', https://www.indiatoday.in/india/story/up-successfully-controlled-spread-of-encephalitis-yogi-adityanath-1554329-2019-06-22 (accessed on 6 August 2021).

32 Scroll Staff, 'Encephalitis Outbreak: SC Asks Centre, Bihar And UP to List Steps Taken to Stop Spread of Disease', https://scroll.in/latest/928161/encephalitis-outbreak-sc-asks-centre-bihar-and-up-to-list-steps-taken-to-stop-spread-of-disease (accessed on 6 August 2021).

33 Aman Sharma, 'Encephalitis Deaths Drop by 66% in East UP in 2018', https://economictimes.indiatimes.com/news/politics-and-nation/encephalitis-deaths-drop-by-66-in-east-up-in-2018/articleshow/68051563.cms?from=mdr (accessed on 6 August 2021).

CHAPTER 11: THE NEPAL CONNECTION

1 Raj, 'Two Yogis, Two Countries', http://kathmandupost.ekantipur.com.np/news/2017-07-04/two-yogis-two-countries.html (accessed on 27 August 2021).

2 C. Marrewa-Karwoski, 'Far from Hindutva, Yogi Adityanath's Sect Comes from a Tradition That Was Neither Hindu nor Muslim', https://scroll.in/article/833710/far-from-hindutva-yogi-adityanath-comes-from-a-tradition-that-was-neither-hindu-nor-muslim (accessed on 27 August 2021).

3 Yubaraj Ghimire, 'Yogi Adityanath's Mutt, Hardline Hindutva's Hub', https://indianexpress.com/article/explained/yogi-adityanath-uttar-pradesh-chief-minister-bjp-yogis-mutt-hardline-hindutvas-hub-4578072/ (accessed on 27 August 2021).

4 http://ayo-gorkhali.believecreative.com/en/timeline/mythic-beginnings/guru-gorakhnath (accessed on 27 August 2021).

5 Raj, 'Two Yogis, Two Countries', http://kathmandupost.ekantipur.com.np/news/2017-07-04/two-yogis-two-countries.html (accessed on 27 August 2021).

6 Veronique Bouillier, 'The King and His Yogi: Prithvi Narayan Shah, Bhagavantanath and the Unification of Nepal in the Eighteenth Century', https://www.academia.edu/10704119/The_King_and_his_Yogi_Prithvi_Narayan_Shah_Bhagavantanath_and_the_Unification_of_Nepal_in_the_Eighteenth_Century, pp. 3–4 (accessed on 27 August 2021).

7 Raj, 'Two Yogis, Two Countries', http://kathmandupost.ekantipur.com.np/news/2017-07-04/two-yogis-two-countries.html (accessed on 27 August 2021).

8 http://www.yogiadityanath.in/pdf/Hindu_Rashta_Nepal.pdf (accessed on 27 August 2021).

9 Ibid., p. 40.

10 Dipanjan Roy Chaudhury, 'Yogi Adityanath's Royal Connection: Former Royal Family of Nepal Trace Their Origin to Guru Gorakshanath', https://economictimes.indiatimes.com/news/politics-and-nation/yogi-adityanaths-royal-connection-former-royal-family-of-nepal-trace-their-origin-to-guru-gorakshanath/articleshow/57722870.cms (accessed on 27 August 2021).

11 http://www.yogiadityanath.in/pdf/Hindu_Rashta_Nepal.pdf, p. 48 (accessed on 27 August 2021).

12 http://www.yogiadityanath.in/pdf/Hindu_Rashta_Nepal.pdf (accessed on 27 August 2021).

13 Ibid., p. 44.

14 Faizan Mustafa, 'The Defender Of Faith', https://indianexpress.com/article/opinion/columns/yogi-adityanath-secularism-the-defender-of-faith-4955993/ (accessed on 27 August 2021).

15 Ibid.

16 Sanjeev Sabhlok, 'Who's Pseudo-Secular Now', https://epaper.timesgroup.com/Olive/ODN/TimesOfIndia/shared/ShowArticle.aspx?doc=TOIM%2F2017%2F11%2F27&entity=Ar01401&sk=D68FB4D6&mode=text# (accessed on 27 August 2021).

17   Ibid.

18   http://www.yogiadityanath.in/pdf/Hindu_Rashta_Nepal.pdf
('Antar-rashtreey saazishon ke jaal me phansta Himalayee Rashtra
Nepal'), p. 40 (accessed on 27 August 2021).

19   Uli Schmetzer, 'Pope Concludes Visit To India With Call For
Crusade In Asia' https://www.chicagotribune.com/news/ct-xpm-
1999-11-08-9911080178-story.html.

20   Yubaraj Ghimire, 'Next Door Nepal: Yogi's Kathmandu
Connect', https://indianexpress.com/article/opinion/columns/
yogi-adityanaths-kathmandu-connect-nepal-maoists-gorakhnath-
peeth-4586892/.

21   Ibid.

22   https://www.hinduismtoday.com/blogs-news/hindu-press-
international/world-hindu-conference-concludes-in-nepal/6491.
html (accessed on 27 August 2021).

23   Prashant Jha, *Battles of the New Republic: A Contemporary History
of Nepal* (Aleph, 2014), p. 109.

24   Ibid.

25   Ibid., p. 110.

26   http://www.yogiadityanath.in/lekh/lekh_9900_
22021405314922022014.pdf ('Khatre Mein Hindu') (accessed
on 27 August 2021).

27   Jha, *Battles of the New Republic*, p. 112.

28   Ibid., p. 113.

CHAPTER 12: WHEN ADITYANATH BROKE DOWN

1   https://www.youtube.com/watch?v=czyLaDsIkw0 (accessed on
31 August 2021).

2   Ibid.

3   Book excerpts from Dhirendra K. Jha's *How Yogi Adityanath's
Arrest Changed Him*, https://www.ndtv.com/book-excerpts/how-
yogi-adityanaths-arrest-changed-him-1671469 (accessed on 31
August 2021).

4   Ibid.

5   https://www.youtube.com/watch?v=Q5KiCVghJB0 (accessed on
31 August 2021).

6   Ibid.
7   Alok Pandey, 'High Court Upholds Quashing of Order Against Yogi Adityanath in 2007 Case', https://www.ndtv.com/india-news/high-court-upholds-quashing-of-order-against-yogi-adityanath-in-2007-case-1807488 (accessed on 31 August 2021).
8   Sara Hafeez, '2007 Riots in Gorakhpur: Allahabad HC Upholds Relief to Yogi Adityanath', https://indianexpress.com/article/india/2007-riots-in-gorakhpur-allahabad-hc-upholds-relief-to-yogi-adityanath-5048525/ (accessed on 31 August 2021).
9   Ibid.
10 https://indiankanoon.org/doc/129115615/ (accessed on 31 August 2021).
11 Ibid.
12 https://indiankanoon.org/doc/129115615/ (accessed on 31 August 2021).
13 Ibid.
14 'The UP Government's Colossal Cover-Up Attempt to Protect Adityanath', https://thewire.in/communalism/adityanath-anti-muslim-cover-up (accessed on 31 August 2021).
15 https://indiankanoon.org/doc/129115615/ (accessed on 31 August 2021)..
16 'The UP Government's Colossal Cover-Up Attempt to Protect Adityanath', https://thewire.in/communalism/adityanath-anti-muslim-cover-up (accessed on 31 August 2021).
17 Ajit Sahi, 'The UP Government's Colossal Cover-Up Attempt to Protect Adityanath' https://thewire.in/communalism/adityanath-anti-muslim-cover-up (accessed on 31 August 2021).
18 https://indiankanoon.org/doc/129115615/ (accessed on 31 August 2021).
19 Ibid.
20 Debayan Roy, 'Gorakhpur Riots: Allahabad HC Dismisses Plea Seeking CBI Probe Against Yogi Adityanath', https://www.news18.com/news/india/gorakhpur-riots-allahabad-hc-dismisses-plea-seeking-cbi-probe-against-yogi-adityanath-1668301.html (accessed on 31 August 2021).
21 https://indiankanoon.org/doc/129115615/ (accessed on 31 August 2021).

22 Scroll Staff, 'UP Claims Video of Alleged Yogi Adityanath Hate Speech Was Doctored—Though He Admitted to It on TV', https://video.scroll.in/837348/up-claims- video-of-alleged-yogi-adityanath-hate- speech-was- doctored-though- he-admitted-to-it-on tv (accessed on 31 August 2021).

23 Indo-Asian News Service, '20-Year-Old Murder Case against Yogi Adityanath Dismissed', https://www.indiatoday.in/india/story/20-year-old-murder-case-against-yogi-adityanath-dismissed-1570308-2019-07-17 (accessed on 31 August 2021).

24 Jitendra Sarin, 'Plea Challenging Dismissal of 1999 Case against Yogi Turned Down', https://www.hindustantimes.com/lucknow/plea-challenging-dismissal-of-1999-case-against-yogi-turned-down/story-mnp4hNx7RLIgG4gITbru4H.html (accessed on 31 August 2021).

CHAPTER 13: ACTIONS, RESTRAINTS, OBSESSIONS AND FAILURES

1 https://myneta.info/ls2014/candidate.php?candidate_id=9254 (accessed 15 September 2021).

2 Asianet Newsable, '7 Controversies and Cases against Yogi Adityanath You Must Know', https://newsable.asianetnews.com/india/7-controversies-and-cases-against-yogi-adityanath-you-must-know (accessed 15 September 2021).

3 TNN, 'Uttar Pradesh Government Sacks Hathras ADM Over Facebook Post against Yogi Adityanath', https://timesofindia.indiatimes.com/city/lucknow/govt-sacks-hathras-adm-over-fb-post-against-yogi/articleshow/72192174.cms (accessed on 31 August 2020).

4 PTI, 'UP Must Grow at Full Capacity to Make India USD 5 Trillion Economy: Finance Commission', https://economictimes.indiatimes.com/news/economy/finance/up-must-grow-at-full-capacity-to-make-india-usd-5-trillion-economy-finance-commission/articleshow/71709018.cms?from=mdr (accessed on 31 August 2020).

5   Aman Sharma, 'Uttar Pradesh Drops Kisan Rahat Bond Plans to Fund Rs 36,000 Crore Farm Waiver', https://economictimes. indiatimes.com/news/politics-and-nation/uttar-pradesh-drops-kisan-rahat-bond-plans-to-fund-rs-36000-crore-farm-waiver/ articleshow/59762949.cms?from=mdr (accessed on 31 August 2020).

6   Quint, 'Kanpur "Love Jihad" SIT Finds No Funding or Organised Conspiracy', https://www.thequint.com/news/india/ kanpur-sit-love-jihad-report-no-funding-organised-conspiracy-seen (accessed 15 September 2021).

7   TNN, 'MoUs Worth Rs 4,000cr in Production Phase', https:// timesofindia.indiatimes.com/city/lucknow/mous-worth-rs-4000cr-in-production-phase/articleshow/77987511.cms (accessed on 31 August 2020).

8   ANI, 'Moradabad: 14 Cops Suspended, Inquiry Initiated for Failure to Prevent Animal Slaughter', https://www. aninews.in/news/national/general-news/moradabad-14-cops-suspended-inquiry-initiated-for-failure-to-prevent-animal-slaughter20191125215730/ (accessed on 15 September 2021).

9   New18.Com, '"It Was an Accident": CM Yogi Adityanath Finally Speaks on Cop's Murder in Bulandshahr', https://www.news18. com/news/india/it-was-an-accident-cm-yogi-adityanath-finally-speaks-on-cops-murder-in-bulandshahr-1963693.html (accessed on 31 August 2020).

10   Atul Chandra, 'UP Govt's Bovine Bonanza: Upkeep of Cattle to Be Part of CSR Now', http://www.catchnews.com/india-news/ up-govt-s-bovine-bonanza-upkeep-of-cattle-to-be-part-of-csr-now-83781.html (accessed on 15 September 2021).

11   Ministry of Agriculture Department of Animal Husbandry, Dairying and Fisheries, *19th Livestock Census-2012 All India Report*, http://dahd.nic.in/sites/default/filess/Livestock%20%20 5_0.pdf (accessed on 31 August 2020), p. 117.

12   Biswajit Banerjee, 'In Yogi's UP, Stray Cattle Turn into Farmers' Foes', https://www.nationalheraldindia.com/india/in-yogis-up-stray-cattle-turn-into-farmers-foes.

13 https://www.pressreader.com/india/the-times-of-india-new-delhi-edition/20170220/281921657809562 (accessed on 31 August 2020).

14 Harish Damodaran, 'Uttar Pradesh's Animal Farm: The Cow Count', https://indianexpress.com/article/india/uttar-pradeshs-animal-farm-the-cow-count-yogi-adityanath-beef-ban-slaughterhouse-ban-5524944/ (accessed on 31 August 2020).

15 Brijendra Prashar, 'Cattle Population again Down in UP but Decline Rate Far Lower Than 2012's', https://www.hindustantimes.com/cities/cattle-population-again-down-in-up-but-decline-rate-far-lower-than-2012-s/story-8oqaScv19Y98IFODK8DloL.html (accessed on 31 August 2020).

16 Yusra Husain, 'UP: Two Years after BRD College Tragedy, Govt Probe Absolves Kafeel Khan', https://timesofindia.indiatimes.com/city/lucknow/2-years-after-brd-tragedy-govt-probe-absolves-kafeel/articleshow/71320327.cms (accessed on 15 September 2021).

17 *TOI Edit*, 'Stop NSA Misuse: There Needs to Be Greater Check on the Application of a Law Originally Meant to Protect National Security', https://timesofindia.indiatimes.com/blogs/toi-editorials/stop-nsa-misuse-there-needs-to-be-greater-check-on-the-application-of-a-law-originally-meant-to-protect-national-security/ (accessed on 31 August 2020).

18 India TV, 'Gorakhpur Tragedy: Guilty Will Not Be Spared, Assures CM Yogi Adityanath after Visit to Hospital', https://www.indiatvnews.com/politics/national-gorakhpur-tragedy-guilty-will-not-be-spared-assures-cm-yogi-after-visit-to-brd-medical-college-396230 (accessed on 31 August 2020); Abdul Jadid, 'Gorakhpur Tragedy: 60 Children Die in Baba Raghav Das Medical College in a Week Amid Oxygen Supply Disruption', https://www.hindustantimes.com/india-news/up-30-dead-in-48-hours-due-to-disruption-of-oxygen-supply-in-gorakhpur-hospital/story-TwMrMJxhAZzIkn3pXcZEMN.html (accessed on 31 August 2020).

19 Ajit Kumar Singh, 'Priorities of Uttar Pradesh Budget: As Infrastructure Expenditure Rises, Health and Education Face

Neglect', https://www.epw.in/engage/article/uttar-pradesh-budget-neglects-social-sector (accessed on 31 August 2020).

20 Devika Bhattacharya, 'Explosive Recovered from UP Assembly, Yogi Adityanath Claims "Terror Conspiracy"', https://timesofindia.indiatimes.com/india/explosive-recovered-from-up-assembly-yogi-adityanath-claims-terror-conspiracy/articleshow/59590886.cms (accessed on 15 September 2021).

21 *India Today*, 'Yogi Adityanath Seeks NIA Probe after PETN Explosive Found Inside UP Assembly', https://www.indiatoday.in/india/story/yogi-adityanath-uttar-pradesh-assembly-bomb-petn-security-meet-1024238-2017-07-14 (accessed on 15 September 2021).

CHAPTER 14: SAFETY OF WOMEN? UNBRIDLED POLICE

1 *Financial Express*, 'Uttar Pradesh: Yogi Adityanath Launches Mission Shakti for Security of Women in the State', available at https://www.financialexpress.com/india-news/uttar-pradesh-yogi-adityanath-launches-mission-shakti-for-security-of-women-in-the-state/2107931/ (accessed on 12 October 2021).

2 Ibid.

3 'Yogi Govt Asks Police to Put Up "Name and Shame" Posters of Harassers to Check Crimes Against Women', available at https://www.news18.com/news/india/yogi-govt-asks-police-to-put-up-name-and-shame-posters-of-harassers-to-check-crimes-against-women-2904639.html (accessed on 12 October 2021).

4 Scroll.in, 'UP Had Most Cases of Violence Against Women in 2019; Across India, 87 Rapes Reported per Day: NCRB', available at https://scroll.in/latest/974499/up-had-most-cases-of-violence-against-women-in-2019-across-india-87-rapes-reported-per-day-ncrb (accessed on 12 October 2021).

5 'The 2017 Unnao Rape Case—A Case Study', available at https://blog.ipleaders.in/the-2017-unnao-rape-case-a-case-study/ (accessed on 12 October 2021).

6 Bloomberg Quint, 'Unnao Rape: MLA Kuldeep Singh Sengar Transferred to Sitapur Jail', available at https://www.

bloombergquint.com/politics/unnao-rape-case-live-updates
(accessed on 12 October 2021).

7   *Hindustan Times*, 'Kuldeep Sengar, MLA Accused of Raping Unnao
Girl, Expelled from BJP', available at https://www.hindustantimes.
com/india-news/kuldeep-sengar-mla-accused-of-raping-unnao-
girl-expelled-from-bjp/story-Yf1bnQPlJkYj58NohGlm4N.htm
(accessed on 12 October 2021).

8   *Indian Express*, 'Unnao Rape Case: Court Seeks Report on Security
of Witnesses, Arrangements for Family's Stay in Delhi', available
at   https://www.newindianexpress.com/nation/2019/aug/07/
unnao-rape-case-court-seeks-report-on-security-of-witnesses-
arrangements-for-familys-stay-in-delhi-2015123.html   (accessed
on 12 October 2021).

9   *TOI*, 'Lucknow: UP DGP Addresses Rape Accused BJP MLA
as 'Mananiya', available at https://timesofindia.indiatimes.com/
city/lucknow/lucknow-up-dgp-addresses-rape-accused-bjp-mla-
as-mananiya/articleshow/63733537.cms (accessed on 12 October
2021).

10   *TOI*, 'Unnao Rape Case: Allahabad High Court Tears into UP
State Machinery', available at https://timesofindia.indiatimes.
com/city/allahabad/file-unnao-report-by-may-2-hc-to-cbi/
articleshow/63755515.cms (accessed on 12 October 2021).

11   Case, Criminal Writ-Public Interest Litigation No. 1 of 2018,
available   at   https://elegalix.allahabadhighcourt.in/elegalix/
WebShowJudgment.do (accessed on 12 October 2021).

12   Ibid.

13   India Legal, 'Unnao Rape Case: Allahabad High Court CJ Tears
into State Advocate General for Avoiding Arrest of MLA Sengar',
available at https://www.indialegallive.com/top-news-of-the-day/
news/unnao-rape-case-allahabad-high-court-cj-tears-into-state-
advocate-general-for-avoiding-arrest-of-mla-sengar/ (accessed on
12 October 2021).

14   *India Today*, 'Tamil Nadu: Chain-Snatcher Who Fired in
Air after Attacking Woman Shot Dead in Police Encounter',
available at https://www.indiatoday.in/india/story/tamil-nadu-
chain-snatcher-fired-in-air-attack-woman-shot-dead-police-

encounter-1863613-2021-10-11 (accessed on 12 October 2021).

15 *Economic Times*, 'Chinmayanand Case: Body Cam, Sleaze, Counter-Sting, but "Slow" Police Action', available at https://economictimes.indiatimes.com/news/politics-and-nation/chinmayanand-case-body-cam-sleaze-counter-sting-but-slow-police-action/articleshow/71321780.cms (accessed on 12 October 2021).

16 *Outlook*, 'UP Student, Who Accused Chinmayanand of Rape, Sent To Jail in Extortion Case', available at https://www.outlookindia.com/website/story/india-news-up-student-who-accused-chinmayanand-of-rape-arrested-in-extortion-case/339368 (accessed on 12 October 2021).

17 *Economic Times*, 'Chinmayanand Case: "Rape Victime" Arrested', available at https://economictimes.indiatimes.com/news/politics-and-nation/chinmayanand-case-rape-victim-arrested/articleshow/71300726.cms?utm_source=contentofinterest&utm_medium=text&utm_campaign=cppst (accessed on 12 October 2021).

18 *Hindustan Times*, '"Am Ashamed of My Deeds", Chinmayanand Told UP Cops in Law Student Case', available at https://www.hindustantimes.com/india-news/swami-chinmayanand-accepts-taking-massage-from-the-woman-who-accused-him-of-rape-up-sit/story-OcKuRJmkdbEXMTLn2KTLxO.html (accessed on 12 October 2021).

19 *India Today*, 'SIT arrests Chinmayanand but No Rape Charge, Victim Also Booked in Extortion Case', available at https://www.indiatoday.in/india/story/sit-arrests-chinmayanand-but-no-rape-charge-victim-also-booked-in-extortion-case-1601542-2019-09-21 (accessed on 12 October 2021).

20 NDTV, 'Former BJP Leader Swami Chinmayanand Acquitted In Rape Case: Lawyer', available at https://www.ndtv.com/india-news/former-bjp-leader-swami-chinmayanand-acquitted-in-rape-case-lawyer-2399970 (accessed on 12 October 2021).

21 *Frontline*, 'Hasty Cremation of Hathras Gang-Rape Victim Raises Doubts About Administration's Role', available at https://

frontline.thehindu.com/social-issues/hasty-cremation-of-hathras-gang-rape-victim-raises-doubts-about-administrations-role/article32751174.ece (accessed on 12 October 2021).

22 Ibid.

23 The Wire, 'Hathras Gang-Rape and Murder Case: A Timeline', available at https://thewire.in/women/hathras-gang-rape-and-murder-case-a-timeline (accessed on 12 October 2021).

24 *Indian Express*, 'UP Police Out in Full Force to Cremate Hathras Woman, Away from Family', available at https://indianexpress.com/article/india/hathras-rape-victim-cremation-up-police-6638470/ (accessed on 12 October 2021).

25 *The Tribune*, 'Gang-raped and Left Paralysed, Hathras Woman Dies in Delhi Hospital a Fortnight Later', available at https://www.tribuneindia.com/news/nation/gang-raped-and-left-paralysed-hathras-woman-dies-in-delhi-hospital-a-fortnight-later-148329 (accessed on 12 October 2021).

26 Scroll.in, 'UP Had Most Cases of Violence Against Women in 2019; Across India, 87 Rapes Reported per Day: NCRB', available at https://scroll.in/latest/974499/up-had-most-cases-of-violence-against-women-in-2019-across-india-87-rapes-reported-per-day-ncrb (accessed on 12 October 2021).

27 Omar Rashid, 'Journalist and Three Others, Arrested on Their Way to Hathras, Booked for Sedition in U.P.', available at https://www.thehindu.com/news/national/other-states/malayalam-journalist-3-others-arrested-near-hathras-booked-under-sedition-law/article32791003.ece (accessed on 12 October 2021).

28 The Wire, 'Hathras Gang-Rape and Murder Case: A Timeline', available at https://thewire.in/women/hathras-gang-rape-andmurder-case-a-timeline (accessed on 12 October 2021).

29 BBC, 'Hathras Rape Case: Prisoners in Their Own Home, Lives On Hold, a Village Divided', available at https://www.bbc.com/news/world-asia-india-58706861 (accessed on 12 October 2021).

30 *The Hindu*, 'Hathras Gang-rape: Opposition Parties Demand Resignation of U.P. Chief Minister Yogi Adityanath', available at https://www.thehindu.com/news/national/hathras-gang-rape-opposition-parties-demand-resignation-of-up-chief-minister-

yogi-adityanath/article32734523.ece (accessed on 12 October 2021).

31 Firstpost, 'Uttar Pradesh Police's Encounter Spree Raises Uncomfortable Questions Over Bypassing Legal Procedures', available at https://www.firstpost.com/india/uttar-pradesh-polices-encounter-spree-raises-uncomfortable-questions-over-bypassing-legal-procedures-4207241.html (accessed on 12 October 2021).

32 *The Telegraph*, 'Adityanath Fan "Beaten to Death" by Uttar Pradesh Police', available at https://www.telegraphindia.com/india/adityanath-fan-beaten-to-death-by-uttar-pradesh-police/cid/1832810 (accessed on 12 October 2021).

33 The Print, 'This Is What Transpired at Room no. 512 of Gorakhpur Hotel Where Cops 'Killed' UP Businessman', available at https://theprint.in/india/this-is-what-transpired-at-room-no-512-of-gorakhpur-hotel-where-cops-killed-up-businessman/744200/ (accessed on 12 October 2021).

34 Report Wire, 'Manish Gupta Murder: Serious Accidents on Head, Face, Gorakhpur Police Surrounded by Postmortem Report... Full Story of Manish Gupta Case', available at https://www.reportwire.in/manish-gupta-murder-serious-injuries-on-head-face-gorakhpur-police-surrounded-by-postmortem-report-full-story-of-manish-gupta-case/ (accessed on 12 October 2021).

35 Times Now, 'Gorakhpur Realtor Murder Case: Mobile Video of DM, SP Goes Viral; Authenticity Being Verified', available at https://www.timesnownews.com/mirror-now/in-focus/article/details-gorakhpur-realtor-murder-case-mobile-video-of-dm-sp-goes-viral-authenticity-being-verified/818519 (accessed on 12 October 2021).

36 The Print, 'This Is What Transpired at Room no. 512 of Gorakhpur Hotel Where Cops 'Killed' UP Businessman', available at https://theprint.in/india/this-is-what-transpired-at-room-no-512-of-gorakhpur-hotel-where-cops-killed-up-businessman/744200/ (accessed on 12 October 2021).

37 *India Today*, 'Kanpur Businessman Killed During Police Raid Had Joined BJP 4 Months Ago, Says Brother', available at https://

www.indiatoday.in/india/story/kanpur-businessman-was-bank-manager-at-private-bank-had-joined-bjp-4-months-ago-says-brother-1859065-2021-09-30 (accessed on 12 October 2021).

38 Quint Hindi, 'Gorakhpur Murder Case: History Sheet of Inspector JN Singh, Allegations of Murder Already', available at https://hindi.thequint.com/news/india/gorakhpur-manish-gupta-murder-case-accused-inspector-jn-singh-fir-police-encounter-extortion#read-more (accessed on 12 October 2021).

39 GaonConnection, 'Accused Ashish Mishra Arrested in Lakhimpur Kheri Violence Case', available at https://en.gaonconnection.com/ashish-mishra-arrest-lakhimpur-kheri-violence-ajay-mishra-uttar-pradesh-farmers-bjp-yogi-adityanath/ (accessed on 12 October 2021).

40 *TOI*, 'Lakhimpur Kheri Violence: Won't Act under Pressure, Arrest on Basis of Proof, Says UP CM Yogi Adityanath', available at https://m.timesofindia.com/india/wont-act-under-pressure-arrest-on-basis-of-proof-yogi-adityanath/articleshow/86879140.cms (accessed on 12 October 2021).

41 *The Hindu*, 'Lakhimpur Kheri Violence: Supreme Court Dissatisfied with U.P. Government's Status Report', available at https://www.thehindu.com/news/national/lakhimpur-kheri-violence-supreme-court-dissatisfied-with-up-governments-status-report/article36893201.ece (accessed on 12 October 2021).

42 Ibid.

43 Ibid.

44 *Hindustan Times*, 'Lakhimpur Kheri Highlights: UP Police Paste Notice Outside Union Minister Ajay Mishra's Residence', available at https://www.hindustantimes.com/india-news/lakhimpur-kheri-live-updates-uttar-pradesh-thursday-7th-october-2021-101633563459272.html (accessed on 12 October 2021).

CHAPTER 15: GOVERNANCE

1 Biplob Ghosal, 'PM Narendra Modi Praises Yogi Adityanath Govt's Handling of COVID-19 Crisis, Says It Saved 85,000

Lives', https://www.timesnownews.com/india/article/narendra-modi-praises-yogi-adityanath-govt-s-handling-of-covid-19-crisis-says-it-saved-85000-lives/612298 (accessed on 6 September 2021).

2 PTI, 'WHO Praises UP Govt for COVID-19 Management', https://indianexpress.com/article/india/who-praises-up-govt-for-covid-19-management/ (accessed on 6 September 2021).

3 Pervez Siddiqui, 'Pakistan's 'Dawn' Editor Praises UP's Handling of Covid-19 Crisis', https://timesofindia.indiatimes.com/city/lucknow/dawn-editor-praises-ups-handling-of-covid-19-crisis/articleshow/76252840.cms (accessed on 6 September 2021).

4 Liz Mathew and Maulshree Sethi, 'UP Govt Ramps Up Health Infra, to Add 52,000 More Hospital Beds', https://indianexpress.com/article/india/govt-ramps-up-health-infra-to-add-52000-more-hospital-beds-6385935/ (accessed on 6 September 2021).

5 'CM Ordered for Making Arrangements of 52,000 Beds in L1, L2, L3 COVID-19 Hospitals: Awanish K Awasthi', https://www.indiatvnews.com/video/news/cm-ordered-for-making-arrangements-of-52-000-beds-in-l1-l2-l3-covid-19-hospitals-awanish-k-awasthi-612529 (accessed on 6 September 2021).

6 Bindu Shajan Perappadan, 'Uttar Pradesh Primary Health Centres Ailing, Says Centre in Lok Sabha', https://www.thehindu.com/news/national/uttar-pradesh-primary-health-centres-ailing-says-centre-in-lok-sabha/article30069899.ece (accessed on 6 September 2021).

7 Ibid.

8 Omar Rashid, 'Oxygen Shortage—Seize Property of Those Spreading Rumours: Yogi Adityanath', https://www.thehindu.com/news/national/other-states/seize-property-of-those-spreading-rumours-up-cm/article34404518.ece (accessed on 28 July 2021).

9 Shailvee Sharda, '37% Road Crash Casualties During Lockdown Were Migrant Workers', https://auto.economictimes.indiatimes.com/news/industry/37-road-crash-casualties-during-lockdown-were-migrant-workers/75817391 (accessed on 6 September 2021).

10 Indo-Asian News Service, 'No Train Fares for Migrants Coming to UP Now', https://www.hindustantimes.com/lucknow/no-train-fares-for-migrants-coming-to-up-now/story-9nJgXmxubqLSDtaag70XIP.html (accessed on 6 September 2021).

11 TNN, '200 Buses in Every District to Ferry Migrants: Uttar Pradesh CM Yogi Adityanath', *The Times of India,* Lucknow, 18 May 2020.

12 Mirror Now, 'Ghaziabad: Thousands Violate Social Distancing Norms—The Big Story', https://www.facebook.com/watch/?v=1666032866870844 (accessed on 6 September 2021).

13 https://www.youtube.com/watch?v=l8h5La6u2jo (accessed on 6 September 2021).

14 PNS, 'UP's Unemployment Rate Lowest in Recent Times', https://www.dailypioneer.com/2021/state-editions/up---s-unemployment-rate-lowest-in-recent-times.html (accessed on 6 September 2021).

15 BusinessToday.in, 'Unemployment: Number of Jobless in UP Rises by 58% to 34 Lakh in Two Years', https://www.businesstoday.in/jobs/story/unemployment-number-of-jobless-in-up-rises-by-60-to-34-lakh-in-two-years-250173-2020-02-15 (accessed on 6 September 2021).

16 Mint Analytics, 'Unemployment in Uttar Pradesh Increased 11.4 pct points, Rose to 21.5% in Apr 2020: CMIE Survey', https://www.livemint.com/news/india/unemployment-in-uttar-pradesh-increased-11-4-pct-points-rose-to-21-5-in-apr-2020-cmie-survey-11588316047392.html (accessed on 6 September 2021).

17 Asad Rehman, 'UP Readies Plan to Provide Jobs to 20 Lakh Returning Migrants', https://indianexpress.com/article/india/up-readies-plan-to-provide-jobs-to-20-lakh-returning-migrants-6402474/ (accessed on 6 September 2021).

18 PTI, 'Uttar Pradesh Govt Inks MOUs with Industry Bodies for 11 Lakh Jobs to Migrant Workers', https://economictimes.indiatimes.com/news/economy/policy/uttar-pradesh-govt-inks-mous-with-industry-bodies-for-11-lakh-jobs-to-migrant-workers/articleshow/76089247.cms?from=mdr (accessed on 6 September 2021).

19 Express News Service, 'UP Fifth in Generating Jobs in MSMEs, Says Govt Citing RBI Report', https://indianexpress.com/article/cities/lucknow/up-fifth-in-generating-jobs-in-msmes-says-govt-citing-rbi-report-6932914/ (accessed on 6 September 2021).

20 India.com Business Desk, '"Uttar Pradesh Needs to Become $1 Trillion Economy," Says 15th Finance Commission Chairman', https://www.india.com/business/uttar-pradesh-needs-to-become-1-trillion-economy-says-15th-finance-commission-chairman-3815921/ (accessed on 6 September 2021).

21 PTI, 'UP Must Grow at Full Capacity to Make India $5-tn Economy: Finance Commission', https://www.livemint.com/news/india/up-must-grow-at-full-capacity-to-make-india-5-tn-economy-finance-commission-11571763913559.html (accessed on 6 September 2021).

22 Shekhar Gupta, 'As UP Sinks, Yogi Adityanath Soars—Enough to Compete for Limelight with Modi', https://theprint.in/national-interest/as-up-sinks-yogi-adityanath-soars-enough-to-compete-for-limelight-with-modi/595067/ (accessed on 6 September 2021).

23 Nelanshu Shukla, 'BJP MLAs Sit on Dharna Inside UP Assembly against Their Own Government', https://www.indiatoday.in/india/story/bjp-mlas-sit-on-dharna-inside-up-assembly-against-their-own-government-1629173-2019-12-17 (accessed on 6 September 2021).

24 Express News Service, 'Day After Protest Over Not Being Allowed to Raise Issue, Loni MLA Expresses Regret', https://indianexpress.com/article/india/day-after-protest-over-not-being-allowed-to-raise-issue-loni-mla-expresses-regret-6174109/ (accessed on 6 September 2021).

25 Ayush Tiwari and Muhammad Tahir Shabbir, 'Adityanath's Press Release Is an Ad in Time, but a "Report" in Indian Media', https://www.newslaundry.com/2021/01/06/adityanaths-press-release-is-an-ad-in-time-but-a-report-in-indian-media (accessed on 6 September 2021).

26 D.K. Singh, 'Dear Modi Critics, Like It or Not, Yogi Is BJP CMs' Role Model. Now Fight with Me, with Facts', https://theprint.

in/opinion/dear-modi-critics-like-it-or-not-yogi-is-bjp-cms-role-model-now-fight-with-me-with-facts/568358/ (accessed on 6 September 2021).

CHAPTER 16: FUTURE PRIME MINISTER?

1   Sushil Aaron, 'Is Yogi Adityanath a Candidate to Succeed Narendra Modi in the Future?', https://www.hindustantimes.com/opinion/is-yogi-adityanath-a-candidate-to-succeed-narendra-modi-in-the-future/story-6Xpql9APk4977Wml5O64KK.html (accessed on 6 September 2021).

2   Ibid.

3   Christophe Jaffrelot, 'On "Love Jihad", BJP Picks Up Baton from Vigilante Groups. Police, Judicial Apparatus Have Aided This Move', https://indianexpress.com/article/opinion/columns/love-jihad-law-india-bjp-7067013/; 'Love Jihad Is a Demographic Invasion—Alok Kumar', https://vskbharat.com/love-jihad-is-a-demographic-invasion-alok-kumar/?lang=en (accessed on 6 September 2021).

4   https://en.wikipedia.org/wiki/Hadiya_case (accessed on 6 September 2021).

5   https://indiankanoon.org/doc/18303067/ (accessed on 6 September 2021).

6   'Is Yogi Adityanath a Candidate to Succeed Narendra Modi in the Future?', https://www.hindustantimes.com/opinion/is-yogi-adityanath-a-candidate-to-succeed-narendra-modi-in-the-future/story-6Xpql9APk4977Wml5O64KK.html (accessed on 6 September 2021).

7   Anuja Jaiswal, 'UP Gets First Officially Designated "Teerth Sthals" in Vrindavan and Barsana', http://timesofindia.indiatimes.com/articleshow/61277272.cms?utm_source=contentofinterest&utm_medium=text&utm_campaign=cppst (accessed on 15 September 2021).

8   Warisha Farasat, 'Why the UP Ordinance on "Love Jihad" Doesn't Deserve Legal Scrutiny', https://lifestyle.livemint.com/news/opinion/why-the-up-ordinance-on-love-jihad-doesn-t-

deserve-legal-scrutiny-111607344366893.html (accessed on 6 September 2021).

9 https://en.wikipedia.org/wiki/Prohibition_of_Unlawful_ Religious_Conversion_Ordinance,_2020#:~:text=The%20 Uttar%20Pradesh%20Prohibition%20of,Government%20 of%20Uttar%20Pradesh%2C%20India (accessed on 6 September 2021).

10 https://aspirantworld.in/interfaith-marriages-in-india/ (accessed on 6 September 2021).

11 Quint, 'Kanpur "Love Jihad" SIT Finds No Funding Or Organised Conspiracy', https://www.thequint.com/news/india/ kanpur-sit-love-jihad-report-no-funding-organised-conspiracy-seen#read-more (accessed on 15 September 2021); Manish Sahu, 'A Case Just Fell Flat, but VHP Push Makes UP Police Probe "Love Jihad"', https://indianexpress.com/article/cities/lucknow/ a-case-just-fell-flat-but-vhp-push-makes-up-police-probe-love-jihad-6595005/ (accessed on 15 September 2021).

12 Asad Rizvi, 'Burden of Debt Piles Up on Family of Imprisoned Anti-CAA Protester' https://thewire.in/rights/lucknow-anti-caa-protester-released-from-jail (accessed on 15 September 2021).